Ecological Economics and Sustainable Development

In association with:

L.C. Braat
A.J. Gilbert
R. Janssen
P. Nijkamp
J.B. Opschoor

Ecological Economics and Sustainable Development

Theory, Methods and Applications

Jeroen C.J.M. van den Bergh

Department of Spatial Economics
Vrije Universiteit
Amsterdam, Netherlands

Edward Elgar
Cheltenham, UK • Brookfield, US

Published by
Edward Elgar Publishing Limited
8 Lansdown Place
Cheltenham
Glos GL50 2HU
UK

Edward Elgar Publishing Company
Old Post Road
Brookfield
Vermont 05036
US

British Library Cataloguing in Publication Data
Bergh, Jeroen C. J. M. Van Den
   Ecological Economics and Sustainable
   Development: Theory, Methods and
   Applications
   I. Title
   333.7

Library of Congress Cataloguing in Publication Data
Bergh, Jeroen C. J. M. van den, 1965–
   Ecological economics and sustainable development: theory,
methods and applications / Jeroen C.J.M. van den Bergh.
   Includes bibliographical references and index.
   1. Environmental economics. 2. Sustainable development.
HC79.E5B457 1996
333.7—dc20   95–34566
                                                               CIP

ISBN 1 85898 316 9

Printed and bound in Great Britain by
Hartnolls Limited, Bodmin, Cornwall

Contents

v

Acknowledgements

This project could not have been realised without the support of a number of individuals and organisations. The Vrije Universiteit (Free University) has provided substantial support for the fundamental research component through its USF grant program. Both the Department of Spatial Economics (Faculty of Economics and Econometrics) and the Institute for Environmental Studies have supported the research via projects for government agencies and international organisations. The principal author received support via a grant (project 450-230-007) by the (former) Foundation for Advancement of Economic Research, resorting under the Dutch Organisation for Scientific Research (N.W.O.). In addition, financial and material support was given by the Faculty of Economics and Econometrics of the Free University and the Tinbergen Institute.

I would like to express my indebtedness to the supervisors of the SPIDER project, professors Peter Nijkamp and Hans Opschoor, for their support and advice at various stages during the preparation of this book. For inspiration I owe a special thanks to Peter, whose energy, efficiency and reliability are unequalled. Largely due to the interdisciplinary nature of the project there have been many time-consuming interactions in the past between myself and the ex-SPIDER team members Leon Braat, Alison Gilbert, Ger Klaassen and Frits Soeteman. These and other colleagues, notably Vassilios Despotakis, Jan Feenstra and Marjan van Herwijnen, have indirectly contributed to the contents of the book, via collaboration with some of us, as is noted at relevant places in the book. Wim Hafkamp and David James kindly supported the project in an initial stage. Finally, I would like to note that detailed comments on editorial style and consistency by a proofreader of Edward Elgar are much appreciated.

Preface

In 1987 the Department of Spatial Economics and the Institute for Environmental Studies, both at the Vrije Universiteit in Amsterdam, developed a multidisciplinary research program SPIDER, to investigate the use of various methods for the analysis of ecologically sustainable economic development. SPIDER, an acronym for 'Sustainability Planning for Integrated Development of Economies and Resources' aimed at a collaboration between economists and ecologists, and combined fundamental scientific research with applied and policy-oriented research.

The present book brings together insights obtained about theory and frameworks for integrated economic – ecological analysis, an overview of the use of methods and techniques for operational analysis, and applications of the concepts and methods in various case studies. The result is an effort to combine economics and ecology in a systematic and methodologically consistent way, suitable for future elaboration and extensions.

Although much of the research reported here has been a collaborative effort, putting together the pieces, as well as revising and adding material in parts One and Two, has been my responsibility. In addition, it should be noted that Chapters 7, 8 and 10 were written by A.J. Gilbert, L.C. Braat, and R. Janssen, respectively. These chapters were only slightly adapted and edited to meet the style of the book.

In spite of the unavoidable personal biases at certain places, this book will without any doubt offer several viewpoints and approaches that link individual experiences and preferences. Hopefully the result is something that will stimulate economists, ecologists and others to continue the refinement and application of frameworks and methods necessary for innovative and effective economic – ecological research.

Jeroen van den Bergh   Amsterdam, August 1995

PART ONE

Concepts, Theories and Frameworks

1. Methods and Policy for Sustainable Development

1.1. MOTIVATION AND PURPOSE

It is well understood nowadays that integrated economic–environmental and economic–ecological analysis can play an important role in generating information for the design of environmental management and policy. Such integrated analysis may not only involve the combining of multidisciplinary information, concepts and theories, but also the synthesis of methods and models. The formulation and implementation of environmental management and policy requires information that originates from different sciences. Integration of the different pieces of information often has lacked a systematic character. However, the number of method-oriented studies seems to be increasing quickly, especially since a wide interest has arisen for 'ecological economics' (see Costanza, 1991; Jansson *et al.*, 1994; Barbier *et al.*, 1994).

This book aims to give an account of the variety of available methods for integrated economic–ecological research, and to show how they can be applied and combined to deal with specific management and policy issues involving economic–environmental conflicts. Economic–ecological analysis is used here to refer to the description and analysis of systems of interactive economic and ecological processes, as well as the evaluation of management and policy options applicable to such systems. This type of approach is especially relevant in cases where long-term processes are involved, since assumptions of fixed environmental circumstances are excessively restrictive then.

The context of the present study is related to the perspective of ecological sustainability and sustainable development. As a consequence, the orientation chosen here shares with the broader field of 'ecological economics' the adoption of a wide perspective on relevant causes and effects in time, space, and parts of economic–environmental systems (see Costanza *et al.*, 1991, p. 3). In such a setting, it seems almost impossible to indicate the impacts, relevance and ranking of development and policy options without the support of accurate methods for analysing complex evaluation and decision problems. This book gives an overview of suitable methods and techniques, and presents some illustrative applications in the context of environmental—economic interactions, systems and conflicts. For each method dealt with, several theoretical and technical details are discussed, and an overview is given of relevant studies. The use and integration of different methods and techniques is also embedded in a historical, theoretical and integrative context. For this reason attention is given to four other important issues. First, historical economic approaches to economic—environmental issues are discussed. Second, a classification is given of alternative theories that reflect some interaction between economics, environmental science, ecology and thermodynamics. Third, some attention is devoted to different concepts and frameworks underlying specific approaches to the integration of theories, models or information otherwise coming from separate scientific disciplines, in particular economics and ecology. Finally, there is a discussion of how to combine analytical methods in order to generate information suitable for guiding management and policy decisions towards sustainable development.

1.2. POLICY FOR SUSTAINABLE DEVELOPMENT

In modern environmental and ecological economics, as well as in environmental policy analysis, 'sustainable development' has become a key concept. Despite its misuse in both scientific and policy documents, it may, when adequately specified, add new elements and criteria to the formulation and evaluation of environmental policy. This holds especially true for issues related to indirect uses and non-use values of (complex) ecosystems, ethical positions regarding man and nature, long-term development, and the global environment. To clarify this point, one may note that sustainable development was originally proposed as a starting point in exploring solutions for the potential conflict that may arise between striving for several sub-goals, or between interest groups supporting them:

(i) increasing or maximising human welfare for the present generation;
(ii) maintaining sufficient opportunities for, or not of hampering the welfare realisation of future generations;
(iii) conservation or improvement of environmental quality and (renewable) natural resource availability; and
(iv) preservation of biotic and genetic diversity, and specific instances of natural systems and species.

From the political formulation of sustainable development, as most clearly reflected in the formulation in the publication 'Our Common Future' of the 'Brundtland Commission' (WCED, 1987), it is evident that questions of sustainable development cover a much broader ground than those of environmental protection, as is sometimes fallaciously thought. Instead, a trade-off is to be strived for in terms of multiple use, multisectoral, spatial and temporal dimensions. This involves simultaneously solving problems of scale, allocation, equity and adjustment via investment and technological advance (i.e. change or development). It is important to realise that sustainable development calls for potentially drastic changes in our current modes of production, consumption and decision-making. It means that sustainable development is not a fixed state but a balanced, adaptive process of change in a multi-dimensional complex integrated system. This relates immediately to the approach proposed in this book, namely to deal with long-run environment—economy conflicts from a multidimensional complex systems perspective, allowing for dynamic interactions between economic and environmental processes, and multi-criteria type of evaluation of policies, strategies and development scenarios.

Although a large body of literature has evolved around the concept of sustainable development many contributions deal with it only in a general and descriptive manner and forego theoretical and operational analysis. One reason for this may be that elaborating the concept requires a rather complicated and interdisciplinary approach. In the Bergen Conference on 'Sustainable Development, Science and Policy' (NAVF, 1990) it was concluded that our scientific apparatus is far from adequate to perform such elaboration. Consequently, that conference has stressed the need for science to assist in achieving sustainable development. Thus there is a clear need for a re-orientation of our analytical thinking.

The roots of the notion of ecologically sustainable economic development can be traced back to Physiocrat and Classical thinking in economics (see also Section 2.1). However, the goal of sustainable development as a guideline for economic and environmental policy-making, and as a research topic in environmental and ecological economics, is very recent. In the Brundtland Report the notion of sustainable development plays a central role as a political orientation towards a change to a situation in which the exploitation of resources, the direction of investments, the orientation of technological development and institutional changes are made consistent with future as well as present needs. This broad interpretation of sustainable development goes far beyond the traditional concept of environmental protection, as sustainable development − in the global policy-oriented context of the

Brundtland Report – presupposes a radical change of priority setting and agenda formation within the socio–economic and environmental policy institutions. It also requires a new adjusted planning structure for sectoral and intersectoral development, as well as an international alignment of policy, given the global impacts of regional environmental issues.

Sustainable development calls also for a more general – instead of a partial – and a more long-term – instead of a short-term – oriented policy perspective. But more important, there should be worldwide political support for attaining the pace towards sustainable development. One cannot expect this to exist in a world of poverty, and consequently sustainable development presupposes a policy oriented towards equity not only between, but also within generations, in other words, both in space and time. An adequate use of such broad international political will requires also a greater extent of democracy in international decision-making.

The Brundtland Report is clearly a political document meant to influence governments, industrialists, and scientists. Without describing doomsday scenarios, the Report has argued – with quite some impact, considering the attention it did receive – that the world economy is totally interlocked with the earth's ecology, whereas our institutions have remained independent; i.e. institutions governing the economy are almost completely separated from those managing our environment. Environmental policy towards sustainable development will necessarily be based on the use of economic instruments and policies.

The present situation poses an enormous challenge to predominant policies, e.g., regarding growth, as well as to current ways of policy-making with respect to distribution, welfare and the environment. A change in economic, financial, agricultural and industrial decision-making will be required. This means that sustainable development is not exclusively a task of environmental institutions, but to the same extent of economic and industrial institutions. Therefore, environment and economics are to be 'merged' on all levels of decision-making.

The impact of the Brundtland Report has been far reaching. Various governments (e.g., Norway, Denmark, the Netherlands, Canada) have officially adopted a sustainable development policy, which means that new policy initiatives will be judged on their contribution to achieving sustainable development. Furthermore, also at the international level various new developments have taken place. For instance, the World Bank has increasingly adopted the idea of sustainable development by including sustainability criteria in project evaluation (see van Pelt *et al.*, 1990). But also international bodies such as FAO and UNIDO are reviewing their programs and ideas from the perspective of sustainable development. And – last but not least – various international policy initiatives on global sustainability have emerged, such as in the area of climate change, ozone depletion, global environmental security. In addition, concrete actions have been taken in many countries, like discouraging the use of tropical timber, favouring urban district heating, discouraging the use of persistent micro-pollutants (e.g., pesticides) in agriculture, and favouring the development of mass transit systems. Finally, besides global measures also many local and regional policy interventions are taking place in various countries. It is clear that these may be as important for the long-run sustainability of development as international environmental agreements and policy coordination.

The conference of the UN on environment and development (UNCED) in Rio de Janeiro in June 1992 – the largest conference ever held – was meant to take a giant step forward in the international agreement about global goals and cooperation towards global policies. For this purpose a list was set up of principles for development and management of the planet in the next century ('Earth Charter') and an agenda was made ('Agenda 21') specifying global targets, actions, costs, financial resources and required agencies. Important issues at the conference were a review of negotiations on global warming, deforestation and biodiversity. Furthermore, its purposes included to come up with financial commitments for policies and compensationary measures, as well as close to implementable plans on integration and adaptation of institutions such as the World Bank, UN organisations and Organisations of Developing Countries. As could be expected, only minor results were reached, not in the least because of the wait-and-see policies of most Western countries.[1] Still, it may well have been the start of a more international concern for global environment, which is required to come to agreement and cooperation.

Thus, politically the concept of sustainable development seems to have become a promising and successful formula. However, whether this re-orientation in political decision-making is keeping pace with the increasing urgency of environmental and development questions is still an open question, which will be decided upon by political willingness on the one hand and progress in scientific research on the other hand. An illustrative example of the latter is the question whether economic growth

---

[1] Both powerful blocks (EU and US) were not willing to commit themselves so as to give major impetuses to negotiations. The US even showed an attitude of unwillingness and opportunism. Furthermore, the GATT was kept outside of the UNCED, so that not all opportunities for international negotiation – including trade policies adapted to development and environmental issues – could seriously be addressed.

is a *sine qua non* for effective environmental policy. In OECD-circles, for instance, it has often been stated that zero (or negative) economic growth is detrimental to environmental quality, as in such a situation financial resources − and consequently the policy space − are lacking to develop expensive environmental programs. At the same time other scientists claim that economic growth will destroy the necessary environmental conditions for life on earth. The solution to such questions is essentially an empirical one, requiring a great deal of analysis, with a particular view on the long-run development of economies and their environmental conditions.[2] Furthermore, this would also require a clear distinction into local, regional or global policies for sustainable development. Thus an intensified research effort on sustainable development conditions would be a necessary complement to the above mentioned political concept of sustainability. Some basic questions to be solved are linked to the identification of (see James *et al.*, 1989):

- crucial ecological processes, ecosystems and resource regenerative systems;
- long-term and long-range driving forces which impact on both the economy and the environment;
- conditions under which perturbations (shocks, discontinuities, etc.) may emerge;
- irreversible developmental processes (e.g., land use transformations);
- long-term feasible boundaries or safety margins within which economic and environmental developments can take place.

In the light of these observations, there is a clear need for improved assessment methods (with particular emphasis on long-term developments), for new resource accounting methods (e.g., for judging renewable resource productivity), and for adjusted integral policy evaluation methods (e.g., by using multi-criteria analysis, geographic information systems modelling, simulation and decision support systems, etc.). The ambition of the present book is to offer operational contributions and research tools which may be helpful in coming to grips with the important notion of sustainable development.

---

[2] One important factor explaining the different perspectives on the relationship or conflict between growth and environment is the time horizon. It seems that, although implicitly, different choices are made here. For instance, thermodynamic limits are − in any case − clearly significant in the very long run, say a million years from now, whereas economists generally interpret already one hundred years as an extreme time horizon (van den Bergh and de Mooij, 1995). See further Sections 2.2, 2.3.1, 2.3.2 and 3.2.2.

1.3. ORGANISATION OF THE BOOK

The present work's aim is to show that there is both much need and scope for operational analysis for sustainable development based on a set of formal research methods and techniques. In Chapter 2 this is elaborated, by considering traditional and alternative perspectives, focusing on economic, ecological and integrated theories, with specific attention for thermodynamics. A basic dynamic analysis of economic−ecological interactions is presented, as well as a typology of direct interactions between economic and ecological systems. This chapter also offers a detailed discussion of different methodological frameworks for integrated economic−ecological analysis, with special attention for input−output and systems approaches. Systems or modelling characteristics will also be linked to the categorisation of theoretical perspectives.

The policy context, as stated in the previous section, derives from the notions of sustainable development and sustainable management, i.e. a focus on system-wide implications of activities and policies, and incorporation of long-term horizons in analysis and evaluation. Therefore, one needs to consider the relationships between economy, development, resources, ecosystems and natural environment. In Chapter 3, the perspective determined by principles such as care for nature and future generations is adopted. This includes discussions of ethics, social evaluation and discounting in the context of multi-generational periods. Important issues dealt with are environmental functions and processes, sustainable and multiple resource use, regional or spatial sustainability and barriers to sustainable development. Various definitions of sustainable development have been offered in the literature. Rather than trying to survey these, here the classification of theoretical perspectives presented in Chapter 2 will be linked to specific interpretations of sustainable development.

Different types of methods for policy analysis and implementation, useful to deal with sustainable development issues, are discussed in Chapters 4 and 5. It is indicated how these methods help to increase the insight into economic and environmental effects and relationships, joint patterns of allocation and distribution over space and time, and the use and consequences of specific economic−environmental policy measures. In Chapter 4 indicators, valuation, accounting and modelling of integrated systems are discussed, and attention is given to different positions, definitions and applications. In Chapter 5 policy evaluation, decision support and policy instruments are discussed from the perspective of multiple objectives and indicators. Issues of cost-benefit analysis and discounting also receive attention in that context. The methods of Chapters 4 and 5 may be combined, as discussed in Sections 2.5 and 4.1, and this may lead to a rather complete economic—ecological 'tool-box' for studying sustainable development issues.

In Part Two of the book the methods are applied and tested in various case studies for sustainable development. In Chapter 6 scenario analysis is performed with a dynamic multisectoral macro-level growth model which includes materials flows and economic— environmental interactions. This study demonstrates how various aspects reappearing in economic growth and development theories can be combined with environmental sustainability, renewable and non-renewable resources, materials flows, waste emission, accumulation of pollution, and natural systems' services and processes. In Chapter 7 cadmium flows through the Dutch economy are studied by linking environmental accounts, dynamic materials balances and indicators for sustainable development. Conclusions are specifically focusing on this linking of methods. In Chapter 8 multiple use analysis is illustrated by an extended systems ecology model in a region in the Netherlands, which was used for simulation and evaluation of forests policies and scenarios. It nicely illustrates how a dynamic ecosystem model can be extended with various stress factors and use categories. Chapter 9 presents the results of a study for a Dutch region where agricultural activities conflict with nature conservation of sensitive fen areas. Simulation of a dynamic economic—ecological model was performed to deal with various scenarios. In Chapter 10 the results are shown of a multi-criteria analysis study to evaluate the options for the use of forests and timber resources in Australia. The presentation focuses on the application of the multi-criteria technique, involving problem definition, presentation, choice of indicators, aggregation and sensitivity analysis. In Chapter 11 an account is given of an extensive study that has combined integrated modelling, scenario analysis, multi-criteria evaluation, and spatial analysis. It focuses on interdependencies and conflicts between tourism, local development and nature conservation in an island region in Greece. The model consists of modules describing the interconnected multi-sectoral economies on three islands, and the terrestrial and marine ecosystems of the least developed island. Collectively, the case studies have dealt with very different types of problems and levels of aggregation. The wide range of methods covered by these studies clearly shows the potential of performing analysis for sustainable development.

2. Integration of Economics, Ecology and Thermodynamics

2.1. A SHORT HISTORY OF ENVIRONMENT IN ECONOMICS

Economic scientific perspectives on the relationship between the economy and the natural environment have changed over time. In the early history of economics, the role of the environment used to be regarded mainly in terms of water and land supply, especially in relation to agriculture. After the Industrial Revolution attention grew to cover the physical limits of available renewable resources (e.g., forests) and non-renewable resources (e.g., coal), as well as local air pollution in cities. In recent decades the character of the interest in environmental problems has substantially changed. For instance, the international scale of economic processes, North−South relationships, and global environmental phenomena have now acquired a more central position in the environmental−economic debate (see, e.g., Pearce and Turner, 1990).

In this section we will take a brief look at different economic approaches to environmental problems. The reason for this is that acceptance of the concept of sustainable development does not mean the abandoning or replacement of older ideas in the field of environmental economics, but rather combining many of them in a broader framework. This wider panorama is offered in Sections 2.2 to 2.5. First, in Section 2.2 we present a short survey of the relevance of thermodynamics in the field of environmental and ecological economic analysis. Then, in Section 2.3 critiques on mainstream approaches are shortly mentioned, and a tentative classification is offered of theoretical perspectives or approaches that together make up 'ecological economics'. Relatively much space is devoted to discussing the characteristics of these theories. In Section 2.4 a basic dynamic model, extending the concept of carrying capacity, is presented to illustrate what are considered the essential concepts and issues in economic-ecological analysis. In addition a typology of direct economic-environmental interactions is offered here. Next, Section 2.5 continues with a discussion of methodological frameworks or approaches, focusing on the input – output and systems approaches, also linking to Sections 2.3 and 2.4. Issues like the linking of economic and ecological models, measurement units and scale receive attention. Finally, the classification of theories in Section 2.3.2 is confronted with a number of criteria, including systems' characteristics.

One may search for elements of natural resource and environmental economics in the contributions of classical economics and find that many ideas are invented, forgotten and re-invented. Therefore it seems sensible to assume that classical economics can contribute to or in any case inspire modern research. The classical economic theories may be especially useful in the context of an economic – ecological approach, since they were almost always concerned with integrated views on the pace and direction of, as well as the natural limits to, long-term development. This included especially attention for population growth and the role of resource-based sectors.

The 18th century Physiocrats may be a good starting point for our concise overview, as they were the first to explicitly recognise the importance of nature for the economy. They consider nature as the essential production factor, so that only agriculture and natural resource exploitation were regarded as potentially productive activities. Classical economists, such as Smith, Ricardo, Malthus, Marx, and Mill have touched upon environmental and resource issues in various ways. Adam Smith (1723 – 1790) may be regarded to show a positive view on the availability of natural resources. This optimism can be explained by the socio – economic, scientific and technological change as well as colonialism at the time of the Industrial Revolution. However, when around the year 1800 agricultural product prices increased, economic theorists became more pessimistic about future limits to food production and natural resource availability. Formally, this was represented by the notion of decreasing returns to scale in agriculture, such as in the land rent theory of David Ricardo (1772 – 1823). This deals with the distributional implications of a declining quality of land being put to use in agriculture. Around the same time, the population theory of Thomas Malthus (1766 – 1834) was developed. It states that some part of society will permanently live under conditions below subsistence level. This was thought to result unambiguously from the absolute scarcity of land available for food production in agriculture, and represents the most pronounced classical perspective on absolute scarcity or limits to the scale of the economy. Also the idea of John Stuart Mill (1806 – 1873) of the desirability of a stationary state as a kind of social optimum is based on the perception of a limited ability of agriculture to reach increased production levels. He furthermore introduced the important role of technological advance in relaxing environmental limits to growth. Finally, Karl Marx (1818−1883) regarded nature as heaving only meaning by its functions for mankind. This means that some ethical perspective is adopted which allows for − or even aims at stimulating − human control of resources. It should be noted, however, that in the marxist perspective nature is also regarded essential for long-term continuation of socio−economic activities (for more subtle economic history overviews, see Blaug, 1978; Chaudhuri, 1989; and Rostow, 1990; for more detailed environmental economic perspectives, see Martinez-Alier, 1987; Barbier, 1989; Opschoor, 1989; and van der Straaten, 1990).

After 1870 the up till now most influential economic perspective of neoclassical economics was developed. This represents a more restricted approach towards studying economic phenomena, in terms of adopting a well-defined and delineated framework for each specific question, which is often at the same time general and ad hoc. Associated with this is a more narrow perspective than common in classical economics, although perhaps more flexible to variations in characteristics of systems, situations and problems studied than sometimes recognised by its critics. Relative, rather than absolute, scarcity and resource allocation issues are at the centre of the neoclassical environmental economics (see especially Kneese and Sweeney, 1985; and Siebert, 1987). Of the utmost importance for the development this approach has been the introduction by Marshall of the concept of the external economies. This was clearly founded on the neoclassical perspective of rationally behaving actors in the economy, to which was added the important role of prices − as representing (complete) information − and the optimisation of utility or profits as − in the absence of market failures − guaranteeing a socially optimal functioning of the economic system (in the sense of Pareto efficiency; Baumol and Oates, 1988). An external effect is then defined as a direct effect of one economic actor's actions upon the welfare, costs or profits of another, without a price being charged, i.e. outside the operations of market mechanisms. An example of a positive external effect is that a large activity shifts cost curves of other activities in a favourable direction by the creation of an attractive labour-market environment. The extension to negative externalities is due to Pigou (1932). He was interested in the effects of pollution generated by one economic agent on the welfare or production (functions) of others. The first possible policy reaction focused on the − sometimes confusing − interpretation of 'internalisation' (see, e.g., Verhoef, 1994) via − later known as Pigouvian − taxes, which result in an optimal welfare and associated optimal level of externalities. Subsequent environmental economics of policy instruments has focused much on the criterion of efficiency (Baumol and Oates, 1988; for a fundamental discussion, see Bromley, 1990).

In addition to the tax solution of environmental externalities, a number of other, and sometimes directly related, approaches have been developed as well. The classical paper by Coase (1960) on the relationship between negative externalities and the absence of property rights has initiated a large literature on market solutions based on defining property rights (to polluters or polluted) for arranging ownership of resources or environmental quality. One other important category of instruments is tradeable permits (Dales, 1968), which combine the optimal or desired scale − of emissions, resource use or other negative effects − via direct regulation or an upper limit (i.e. an aggregate standard) applied at the overall or appropriate systems level (sector, region, country, etc.), with optimal or efficient allocation via endogenous prices based on market creation at the same level. It therefore merges the attractive characteristics of price and direct regulatory instruments (see further Section 5.4.2.

A modern rigorous treatment of economic or financial instruments for policy solutions to environmental problems deals also with market imperfections and uncertainty (see Baumol and Oates, 1988). This approach belongs to the field of microeconomics and most of it is focusing on the environment in a strict sense, restricted to emission and pollution problems. In addition, there has been quite some development of microeconomic and macroeconomic (growth) analysis of resources, dealing with extraction and allocation. This has been concerned with issues of (absolute) scarcity and optimal extraction of (non-renewable) resources. The theoretical work of Hotelling (1931) on this subject is the starting point for the large body of literature (see Dasgupta and Heal, 1979; and Neher, 1990).

Finally, with regard to a more macro and multisectoral type of analysis of economy-wide effects of environmental policies, the extension of conventional input−output modelling to include the emission of waste residuals has been important (Leontief, 1970). This approach has been extended and much applied in the seventies and eighties (see, especially the work by Victor, 1972; and for a more recent overview James, 1985). Further discussion of theoretical perspectives and instruments is contained in sections 2.3.2 and 5.4. For original recent overviews see also Batabyal (1995) and Smith (1992). For more policy oriented discussions, a broader spectrum of policy criteria and country-wise comparisons see Opschoor and Vos (1989) and Opschoor *et al.* (1994).

Modern environmental economic research is developing in several directions. First, there is the continuation of the above mentioned neoclassical microeconomic studies. These involve translating and applying results and techniques of microeconomics, such as game theory, imperfect market theory and modern trade theory, to the field of environmental economics. Especially the study of environmental policy in the open economy and international policy coordination attract much attention nowadays (see also Section 5.4). Important is also the work focusing on theoretical and applied general equilibrium analysis, for dealing questions of integrated instruments, indirect effects, international trade and policy coordination (see also Section 4.4.2). One noticeable example in this context is the investigation of the 'double-dividend of ecotaxes' hypothesis, in terms of improving employment and environmental quality (see Bovenberg and de Mooij, 1994a and b). In addition, there is a macroeconomic perspective, which builds on the input–output and multisectoral approaches mentioned, and on (endogenous) growth theory (see van Ierland, 1993 and 1994; and Smulders, 1994).

Finally, interdisciplinary and alternative approaches starting from existing theory and modelling receive relatively much attention at the moment. This pattern does not imply that the different 'mainstream' and 'alternative' perspectives are independent, as may become clear in the next two sections. One should instead regard the pattern as a logical reaction to:

- cycles of specialisation and integration in economic theory, which is fundamental and science driven;
- a need for answers to concrete policy questions, i.e. strategic–applied and issue-driven; and
- the lack of mainstream theories to generate desired answers and insights to pressing scientific and policy issues.

In order to provide a more or less complete basis for applying methods to ecological economic issues and problems, in addition to the historical overview above, critiques, alternative theoretical perspectives, and interdisciplinary or economic–ecological approaches will be dealt with in the following sections, starting with the implications of thermodynamics.

2.2. THERMODYNAMICS AND ECOLOGICAL–ECONOMIC ANALYSIS

It was stated in Section 1.1 that economic–ecological analysis is based on a mix of economic and ecological theories and models. As this implies that physical and monetary units come together, various disciplines may supply theories or insights. One which is especially important and much discussed in the context of integrated economic–ecological analysis is the theory of thermodynamics. It is certainly not the purpose here to give a complete account of writings in this field. However, any text on ecological–economic analysis should devote at least some attention to thermodynamic insights.

Of special importance to the development of the ecological economics' approach have been contributions that take the First and the Second Law of Thermodynamics as a starting point. These laws reflect empirical tests that have not been refuted. The First Law of Thermodynamics states that energy may be transformed, e.g. from chemical to mechanical type, but not created nor destroyed. This implies the conservation of energy, and since energy and matter are mutually transformable, of energy and matter. Under earthly circumstances, where energy–matter transformations are negligible, one may derive two 'approximate laws', useful for operational applications: (i) conservation of pure energy; and (ii) conservation of matter. The latter is referred to as the materials balance principle (for a more extensive discussion, see Ayres, 1978; and Ruth, 1993).

The Second Law of Thermodynamics, the 'entropy law', states that the entropy of the universe is increasing. Entropy is a measure of unavailable energy of a system, defined as energy that is incapable of performing work. Popularly stated, the law entails that heat flows from hot to cold, so that uniformity of energy results and less opportunities remain for benefitting from energy potentiality differences. In the above statement 'the universe' may be replaced by 'any thermodynamically closed system'. This can be defined as a situation where no energy or matter is exchanged with the outside world. However, no known system outside the entire universe satisfies the restriction of being thermodynamically closed (for a clear and interpretative discussion, see Umaña, 1981a). An important corollary of this law is that – for the closed or total system – the entropy process is irreversible.

The notion of low entropy has been linked – both intuitively and formally – to concepts and theories of time and irreversibility, information, non-linear processes, order and chaos, self-organisation, evolution (physical, chemical, biological, economic and social), and teleological processes (see Prigogine *et al.* 1977; Faber *et al.*, 1987; Faber and Proops, 1990; Kay, 1991; O'Connor, 1991; Ruth, 1993; Amir, 1994; Schneider and Kay, 1994; Faber *et al.*, 1995). In this context the important aspect of modern thermodynamics is the notion of a disequilibrium (or non-equilibrium) thermodynamic system. Especially when it is far from equilibrium, such a system requires a continuous inflow of low entropy, and may be characterised by 'dissipative structures' (Prigogine *et al.*, 1977) which go along with self-organised ordered structures, i.e. emanating from disorder in fluctuating or stochastic type of patterns. Some of these issues will be further discussed in the context of specific theoretical perspectives in the next section.

Whereas thermodynamics now receives a great deal of attention from ecological economists, until the early seventies only a few environmental economists seriously addressed this topic. In a short but influential paper Boulding (1966b) stressed the existence of biosphere constraints on the operation of human activities in relation to the openness and interdependence of all subsystems ranging from individual actors to national economic systems in terms of material and energy flows. He proposed a transition from the 'cowboy economy' to the 'spaceship economy', to include the notion of the earth as an approximately materially closed system. This notion implies that the economy and biosphere can only survive if short-term oriented, exploitative, expansive human behaviour is replaced by long-term oriented, conservative and prudent actions.

On an epistemological level Georgescu-Roegen (1971a, 1976) dealt with the meaning of the second law of thermodynamics for economic analysis, specifically that concerned with production processes in agriculture and industry (a short overview is Georgescu-Roegen, 1972). His approach to production theory is very original, based on elementary reproducible short-run processes, changes in quality (entropy process), and typology of production inputs or factors. On the epistemological level his insights are based on a dialectic instead of a mechanical method of reasoning, where it is emphasised that there is continuous change of everything ('being is becoming'), and that it is impossible to choose analytical boundaries in terms of geography and duration. This has also been a reason for him to severely criticise the neoclassical mainstream approach in economics of the environment, and even economics in general. Some of the interpretations and extensions of his work are still being debated, especially the question of how important the openness of the earth is for correctly interpreting thermodynamics as defined in terms of a closed system (see, for instance, Daly and Umaña, 1981; Ayres and Kneese, 1989; Young, 1991; Daly, 1992; Townsend, 1992; Ruth, 1993;

Bianciardi *et al.*, 1993b; Amir, 1994). This is further discussed below, in the context of recycling.

A point stressed by Georgescu-Roegen (1971a) in the context of production, matter and energy — and much referred to by others — is the distinction between stocks, flows, funds, and actors. A fund differs from a stock in that the allocation over time of the services it generates is restricted. A stock, on the other hand, may at any time be emptied or, alternatively, used up as slowly as desired. The exploitation of a stock furthermore gives rise to a flow of the same quality in terms of units of measurement (e.g., matter, products, individuals of a population). Actors are specific funds, which include capital and labour, and may be defined as operating to transform flows. In other words, they are performing tasks for which energy and materials are required. The main difference between an actor (or more generally a fund) and a flow, i.e. all other type of inputs and outputs in production, is that the actor both enters and leaves the process (i.e. it is an input *and* output) whereas the flows only enter or leave. This means that the flows are necessarily derived from, or produced by, the funds. To complete the picture, the entropy law implies that the actor requires maintenance afterwards (food, rest, leisure) and possibly compensation for decay ('investment') in order to regain its original state — in terms of approximately the same quality or potential for services-generation. Materials end up as either (integrated) elements of the product or as waste output. These different categories of inputs allow for a more precise treatment of separate levels or interpretations of substitution between production factors, for instance direct or ex-ante substitution within a category (the *replacement* of one types of material by another) and indirect or ex-post substitution (e.g., the *saving* on materials use by longer working hours or more labour input). In addition, this distinction allows to formulate production functions with environmental variables and satisfying materials balance conditions (see Georgescu-Roegen, 1971b; Gross and Veendorp, 1990; and van den Bergh and Nijkamp, 1994c; see for related issues Smith and Weber, 1989).

The entropy law has been used to derive that materials will become more and more dispersed. In fact, this means that a sort of materials entropy increase is introduced separately from energy entropy, somewhat similar to materials balance as separate from energy conservation (first law).[1] This materials' entropy notion is relevant for a policy issue in

---

[1] Young (1991, p. 169) notes that the entropy law is about energy and 'can be extended to matter only by *analogy*' (italics by Young) and that therefore materials entropy lacks a 'law-like character'.

environmental economics, namely whether complete recycling of matter is possible. Georgescu-Roegen referred to the negative answer to this question as the fourth law of thermodynamics.[2] Some ecologists have argued, however, that natural systems do recycle materials 100% (see Costanza, 1981b). Bianciardi *et al.* (1993a) even conclude that in order for such a fourth law to exist, the second law must be rejected. Young (1991) uses an example to show that materials entropy may decrease in a closed system. Although materials entropy may still be increasing in the long-run, the irreversible character of the (general or energy) entropy law is thus absent. Townsend (1992), amongst other, argues that complete materials recycling might be possible but would require an enormous amount of energy input. It may be pointed out then that the earth is not closed, and that continuous inflow of solar energy can be used for this purpose. Townsend (p. 100) reacts to this by focusing on the negative effect of such a strategy in terms of a 'superabundance of thermal pollution'. Of course, this is another reason against the belief in 100% recycling, and should not confuse the discussion about the correctness of a speculated fourth law of thermodynamics. Daly (1992, p. 92) states that he is '... prepared to believe in common-sense evidence that for all practical purposes complete recycling is impossible ...' but '... not competent to assess the claim that it is physically impossible'. This would seem to hold the wisest position in this debate, until (and unless) physics comes with a definite answer.

There are some other studies dealing with the inclusion of thermodynamic notions and insights in economic analysis. Based on the first law of thermodynamics, Kneese and others (Ayres and Kneese, 1969; and Kneese, Ayres and D'Arge, 1970) formalised the materials balance principle in a general equilibrium framework. Dynamic nonlinear modelling of materials balance in a multisectoral economic—ecological system is studied in van den Bergh and Nijkamp (Chapter 6 in this book). More recently, materials balance is also operationalised in applied studies of 'industrial metabolism' (see Ayres, 1989) and 'materials—product chain' management (see Opschoor, 1994; Kandelaars *et al.*, 1995). In a very abstract study Perrings (1987) combines some of Georgesu-Roegen's ideas with the input—output framework, extended to include and generalise economic and environmental intra- and inter-actions. Further study on the consequences of the two laws of thermodynamics for environmental—economic

---

[2] For curious readers it is noted that the Third Law of Thermodynamics states that the absolute zero (Kelvin) temperature can never be reached (see, e.g., Kestin, 1966).

interactions, focusing on formal model implications, can be found in Ayres (1978), Faber *et al.* (1987) and Ruth (1993). Other studies dealing with economic modelling and entropy are Berry *et al.* (1978), Kümmel (1989), Kümmel and Schüssler (1991).

Concluding, the first law, or in any case the derived approximate and operational materials balance law, seems to be rather straightforward and easily formalised in economic—environmental analysis. However, the relevance of the entropy law is under dispute, while its implication for and application in economic—ecological theories, models and case studies is not always evident. One may simply use it to deal with technical limits (lower bound of energy or work required to operate a system), or to say something about maximum heat exchange of an ecosystem or economic activity with its environment. Some authors have gone further, and relate energy contents or maintenance flows to value (see for various perspectives Daly and Umaña, 1981; and the Biophysical—Energy perspective in the next section). Berry *et al.* (1978, p. 133) conclude that '... when conditions of economic cost minimisation are stated in terms of prices and convex production functions, thermodynamic optimality adds no new insights.' A similar, though more general conclusion is stated by Young (1991). He points out that production relationships based on diminishing returns may be a concrete outcome of the entropy law application to economics. Daly has often stressed (e.g., 1977, 1992) that the entropy law is a formalised expression of the general or absolute scarcity that mankind and its economy are subjected to. Similarly, in Georgescu-Roegen's jargon the entropy law is the 'taproot' of economic scarcity. Whereas traditional environmental economics has not devoted much attention to the entropy law, the ecological economics perspectives have. However, it is not yet clear at all whether this actually means that thermodynamics is useful and can be integrated in relevant analyses. It may be used to derive conditions for specifying production functions in theoretical and empirical work, or to tamper optimism about economic growth and technological progress. Reading of many of the above mentioned writings leaves the feeling that the entropy law may provide in any case a consistency check to both economic and environmental—ecological theories as well as allow for a common ground in their integration.

In the next section economics-based, ecology-based and integrated theoretical perspectives will be discussed, some of which explicitly focus on the interpretation and implication of thermodynamic insights.

2.3. ECONOMIC–ECOLOGICAL THEORETICAL PERSPECTIVES

2.3.1. Critique on the 'Mainstream Approach and Opinion'

Alternative approaches in environmental economics include criticism on 'standard theory' or adopt original theoretical perspectives, based on specific conceptual or analytical frameworks. In addition to the impact of thermodynamics – as discussed above – critiques on the traditional economic approach to studying the relationship between the economy and the environment have been important in the progression to alternative theoretical perspectives. Especially the debate on the conflict between economic growth and environmental quality has been an important catalyst in the development of alternative theories.

Institutional critique on traditional economics in its focus on environmental externalities was first provided by Kapp (1950), who argues that in market economies environmental costs can be shifted to other actors or cost categories, implying sometimes wrong incentives or leading to unfair outcomes. Other institutional criticism comes from Ciriacy-Wantrup (1952), who introduced the 'safe minimum standards' of natural resource use (extraction). Motivated by welfare theory, Mishan (1967) has criticised the need for economic growth by indicating various undesired side-effects that go along with it. Daly (1977, 1980) also mentions ecological limits to growth and proposes to strive for a steady state (where population and economic capital are constant). Hueting (1980) provides a conceptual link between economic growth and the loss of environmental functions. Probably the most widely read – as well as most widely criticised – criticism of uncontrolled economic growth is the 'Limits to Growth' report for the Club of Rome (Meadows *et al.*, 1972; and its follow-up in 1992, 'lethal model 2' in the words of Nordhaus, 1992). Other critiques are based on social and ethical (sometimes religious) perspectives (see, e.g., Schumacher, 1973; Scitovsky, 1976; Hirsch, 1977; Mishan, 1977; Boskin, 1979; for an older overview Phelps, 1969; for a very clear and broad overview at the time, Lecomber, 1975; and for an interesting collection of articles by the most important growth–critics, Daly, 1980). For responses to some of these critiques or approaches, see, for instance, Nordhaus and Tobin (1972), Nordhaus (1973, 1974, 1982, 1992) and Beckermann (1976). Also some of the more recent publications on sustainable development contain discussions of the (im)possibility of and need for (no) growth. These are mentioned in Section 3.1.

Van den Bergh and de Mooij (1995) discuss a number of factors explaining persisting different positions in the growth debate, and conclude that partiality of views (e.g., ethical, physical, economic, technological, historical, institutional), dissimilar purposes (theoretical, statistical–empirical, explanatory, forecasting), and differences in the time horizon implicitly adopted by each approach are essential. As another important factor one may mention the tendency of people to be optimistic or pessimistic rather than neutral, although the latter would, given the complexity and amount of information available, seem a more rational choice.[3] Finally, other recent contributions showing diverse approaches are: den Butter and Verbruggen (1994) on growth, measurement and Green GDP; de Bruyn *et al.* (1994) on empirical testing of the link between GNP and patterns of environmental indicators; and Krautkraemer (1990) and Toman *et al.* (1994) on sustainability in neoclassical growth theory.

It is probably impossible to give a complete account of studies performed in the field of mainstream and alternative perspectives in environmental economics. As Pearce and Turner state in their introduction to 'references and further reading' in environmental economics: 'The literature on environmental economics is massive, something that often comes as a surprise to those who think economists have made little effort to tackle environmental issues' (Pearce and Turner, 1990, p. 361). The same thing might be said for the broader field of integrated environmental and ecological economics studies. Adopting a critical position, however, one may add that relatively few studies have been successful in integrating economics and ecology. It is furthermore difficult to compare different approaches or even classify them in terms of integration criteria. A main reason for this is the wide range that exists of definitions and interpretations of integration (see, e.g., Vedeld, 1994; and Sections 2.4, 2.5 and 4.1).

2.3.2. A Classification of Theoretical Perspectives

Since Plato, any scientific investigation has to go through the step of classifying, and also here an attempt is made to systematically deal with the immense literature that may be relevant for economic–ecological analysis. This is done by presenting a (tentative) list of twelve perspectives that may offer a conceptual and theoretical basis for economic–ecological analyses. An attempt is made to shortly describe the essential characteristics of each perspective. Boundaries are sometimes vague, and it should be noted that certain perspectives overlap

---

[3] Such neutrality of position does not preclude that one adopts a prudent or precautionary approach in formulating policy or management strategies.

conceptually, or in terms of methodological elaboration. This is also reflected by several references appearing at various places.[4]

(i) *Equilibrium—Neoclassical:* This includes a mechanistic, formal approach to economic phenomena, based on assumptions of rational individual behaviour, decisions derived from utility and profit maximisation, interaction via price signals giving full information, and market clearing. It should be noted, however, that this field is most developed of all economic perspectives, so that many variations of assumptions have been investigated, focusing on regulation of industry and market characteristics from the perspective of efficiency. Sometimes it is said that an important difference between the neoclassical and other economic perspectives is that it focuses on the properties of artificial economies in an equilibrium state, rather than on the convergence path to such a state. Furthermore, if dynamic, then it is dealing with gradual and mechanistic change, rather than with innovations, evolutionary and discrete adaptive patterns, uncertainty and surprises, structural changes, etc., that are emphasised in some of the others perspectives.

The environmental economics literature is mainly based on welfare and public economics dominated by the externality concept (Baumol and Oates, 1988; Cropper and Oates, 1992), and nowadays focusing on international and trade issues. Resource economics focuses on (temporal) allocation issues. Ecological—economic issues have been mainly dealt with in neoclassical bioeconomics (Clark, 1976; Wilen, 1985). This was shortly discussed already in Section 2.1 and is dealt with further on in Chapter 3, where assumptions, critique and potential extensions will subsequently be discussed.

An important issue in the welfare approach is the monetary valuation of costs and benefits (see Freeman, 1993). This has seen relatively few applications to ecosystem functions and services, although this is changing (see, e.g., Barbier *et al.*, 1994; and Section 4.4.6.).

An interesting extension of the general equilibrium—welfare approach to ecological economics is Crocker and Tschirhart (1992), who use general equilibrium externality analysis to include externalities occurring via ecosystem functions (see also Crocker, 1995). They show how a simple foodchain can be included in the general equilibrium system, and also try to extend the premise of maximising behaviour to ecosystem

---

[4] Alternative ways of classifying and further discussion on characteristics of the following perspectives are discussed in Section 2.5.4. The classification of this section will later be confronted with approaches to sustainable development (Section 3.2.2).

processes, adopting an energy basis. Ecological theory linking to such an approach should be based on behavioural modelling, prices and input−output systems (see especially Hannon, 1973, 1976, 1986 and 1991). The input−output system has since long been a method for operationalising integration of economic and ecological systems (see next section). General equilibrium systems are generalised input−output systems, where more attention is devoted to non-linear processes (substitution), endogenous prices (allocation and demand−supply interaction), and behavioural objectives.

An issue where neoclassical economics has come the closest to integrated modelling − i.e. in the sense of using a simple description of natural processes − is in growth theory (see Kamien and Schwartz, 1982; Tahvonen and Kuuluvainen, 1991 and 1993; van den Bergh and Nijkamp, 1991b; and Gradus and Smulders, 1993). The modern treatment of this has linked to issues of environmental sustainability (see Toman *et al.*, 1994) and models of climate change (see Nordhaus, 1990 and 1993; and van Ierland, 1994).

Finally, other economic fields using the neoclassical approach, or linked to it, have contributed to environmental economics. Especially Urban and Regional Economics has done this, focusing on spatial systems approaches, also including integrated modelling, project evaluation and conflict analysis (see, e.g., Nijkamp, 1979a and b; Hafkamp, 1984; and Brouwer, 1987). Econometric models have been rarely applied in economic−ecological analysis (see John *et al.*, 1994). Other important fields are Macro-, Agricultural and Development Economics (see, e.g., van Ierland, 1993), often stepping away from the pure neoclassical paradigm, although sometimes using rigid modelling indirectly related to it.

Some authors prefer to set the neoclassical economic approach opposite to the ecological economics' approach (see, e.g., Vedeld, 1994; Sahu and Nayak, 1994). Although this can enlighten some essential features of an ecological economics approach, the treatment here is based on the idea that neoclassical economics has something to offer in the context of ecological−economic issues, both because it has established a consistent and elaborated structure of theory and applications, and since it allows to be linked analytically or heuristically to other approaches.

Finally, it should be noted that the neoclassical approach may be the most anthropocentric of all perspectives discussed here, especially when it is interpreted as a comprehensive approach. However, neoclassical economics is not necessarily aimed or supposed (by its users) to provide a complete world view, as may well be impossible for any '(analytical) scientific approach', but offers theoretically consistent partial views that must be informally integrated with other insights in order to realise, or better approach, the complete world view, if such a thing exists. That particular process may also be referred to as 'interdisciplinarity' (Vedeld, 1994).

(ii) *Neoaustrian — Temporal:* Traditionally, the Austrian stance in economics is associated with subjectivism, apriorism, and a teleological mode of operation (see Blaug, 1991). In the Neoaustrian approach the main focus is the explicit treatment of aspects of time (see Faber *et al.*, 1987; and Faber and Proops, 1990 and 1993). The neoaustrian approach is thus strongly oriented towards intertemporal issues. Time is regarded as a multidimensional concept with particular characteristics not dealt with adequately in the neoclassical model: (i) time asymmetry exists because of irreversibility (entropy law), knowledge asymmetry (past — future) on the one hand, and growth, development, and evolution on the other hand; (ii) (teleo)logical sequences underlie many phenomena, i.e. technology and production before consumption, and price reactions in a logical order (see also Faber *et al.*, 1995).

In an ecology — economy setting such views easily adapt to a model of long-run technological progress as a result of a teleological process of inventions stimulated by resource and environmental scarcity, causing in turn innovations and production technologies which affect the state of the environment. Austrian capital theory aims to incorporate this line of thought, in addition to the following elements: Schumpeterian concepts of innovation and structural change (Schumpeter, 1934); the concept of superiority, stating that the total amount of consumption over the economic horizon can be increased; and the concept of roundaboutness, saying that it is possible to postpone consumption. In summary, in the neoaustrian approach the coordination of activities over time is accentuated, with production techniques not fixed but generated as part of the production processes.

(iii) *Ecological — Evolutionary:* Ecology studies the relationships of organisms with their biotic and abiotic environment at four levels: the individual, the population, the community, and the ecosystem level (see, e.g., Anderson, 1981; Hedrick, 1984; and Odum, 1976). 'Population' refers to a single species. The biotic community is the assembly of different populations in a given area. In an 'ecosystem' ('ecotope' for the spatial — temporal form) the communities interact with the abiotic environment. The study at the latter three observation levels is called synecology, and seems most relevant for the purpose of understanding the economic — ecological interface; its level of aggregation comes closest to that of (regional or macro) economics; and, it is most useful for a description of material and energy flow in and through the ecosystem.

An ecosystem approach uses concepts of trophic levels, food chains (connecting trophic levels), food web (connecting food chains), and key species to describe the flow through the system and relate the species to each other. Trophic levels are groups of species equally far away from the primary producers (the green plants) in terms of 'food steps'. The process of change in the community structure of an ecosystem is called succession. After moving through maturing states a final stage called the climax can be reached. It is characterised by a maximum stability under the given environmental conditions. The process may also be cyclic if it goes through the stages of pioneering, building, maturing, degenerating, pioneering, etc. Evolution can be considered in the wider implication as occurring on the species and ecosystem levels simultaneously, or better interactively. A change in the overall ecosystem means a different composition of species, and ultimately requires adaptation or (local) elimination of a species.

Formal approaches in the field have focused on energy and material flow analysis, species' growth, decay and metabolism, species' interaction and ecosystem relationships (see, e.g., Watt, 1968; Patten, 1971; Maynard Smith, 1974; Wilen, 1985). For a broader recent overview see Roughgarden *et al.* (1989) and Jørgenson (1992). See also the Systems − Ecologal and the Biophysical − Energy perspectives.

On a short time scale, dynamics of controlled or disturbed ecosystems have been studied, dealing with resilience, stability, etc. (see, e.g., Brookhaven National Laboratory, 1969). The well-known four-box model based on creative destruction by Holling (1986) is an example of a simple coherent explanation for such dynamics. It describes a cyclic pattern of colonisation and (re)organisation (abundancy of nutrients and other resources), exploitation (r-strategists, pioneers, opportunists, entrepreneurs, simple ecosystems), conservation (K-strategists, climax and complex ecosystems), and release (fire, storm, pest, mismanagement). This pattern is necessary, i.e. regular destruction is too, in order to have a more resilient system at a higher level.

The evolutionary approach focuses on change in the diversity and adaptation of populations and organisms based on the mechanism of natural selection (Darwin), which includes random production of variation in terms of species and genes, and (more deterministic) selection through survival. Evolution may be applied both on the level of genotypes and phenotypes (see Faber *et al.*, 1995). In ecology, game theory has been used to deal with evolution processes explicitly as interaction between different species (see Maynard Smith, 1982).

Strategies represent then genes and pay-off reproduction success. Such evolution is also integrated and discussed in the technology and economics oriented Evolutionary – Technological perspective.

(iv) *Evolutionary – Technological:* This can be regarded as a combination of neoclassical microeconomic elements, neoaustrian use of time concepts, Schumpeterian ideas on entrepreneurship and innovation (Schumpeter, 1934), and notions of thermodynamic disequilibrium. Central to this stream of thought are self-organisation in dynamic systems, and positive externalities, associated with learning and knowledge accumulation, causing non-convex properties of models. This leads away from the pure neoclassical model as prices have not only allocative and substitution effects, but also influence innovations. Concepts from evolutionary theory, for instance, 'genetic information' and 'diversity' may then be implemented in evolutionary economic models (see Boulding, 1978; Norgaard, 1984 and 1985; Faber and Proops, 1990; Hinterberger, 1994; Gowdy, 1994). From the environmental externality perspective, the difference is one between internalisation and dynamic optimisation – shifting between static equilibria – of technological, positive and environmental, negative externalities. Finally, there are the important related issues of ignorance, randomness, path dependence, irreversibility, phase transitions, and surprise. Their recognition has resulted in a refutation of a deterministic micro-level model, since 'outcomes of innovative efforts can hardly be known ex ante' (Erdmann, 1993, p. 71). Instead, there is a preference for stochastic and chaos-type of modelling approaches (bifurcation and catastrophe theories).

Endogenous technology has in economics regularly been approached from an evolutionary perspective, dating back to Schumpeter (1934), and is almost becoming a standard approach (see, Nelson and Winter, 1982; Dosi *et al.*, 1988). Allen (1988, p. 95) may explain this increased attention: 'What we are really faced with is an evolving complex system, and the creation, acceptance, rejection, diffusion or suppression of "innovations and technical changes" cannot be considered in terms of "economics", separated from history, culture, social structure, the ecological system and so on. That we should have ever attempted to do so is a symptom of our past unwillingness to "grasp the nettle" of the holistic, dynamic, "more than mechanical" nature of the real world.' It also seems that a mix of neoclassical, or at least formal, and evolutionary approaches is taking place here, linking especially to dynamic macro-economics and endogenous growth theory. In other words, the boundary between these approaches is sometimes less clear (see Silverberg, 1988).

Important differences to be noted between the various categories of evolution concern speed and goals. Generally, social evolution is faster than biological evolution. As opposed to biological systems, economic systems may be characterised by Lamarckian characteristics − i.e. a built-in drive for perfection in all organisms (teleological processes; see Faber *et al.*, 1995) −, consciousness of evolution, explicit goal setting, using foresight, and learning at various levels. Furthermore, culture and institutions extend the potential of the body to inherit acquired traits and information, on the level of phenotypes (the brain) as well as genotypes. This is analogous to technology extending the functions of the body, giving rise to exosomatic functions (in the jargon of Georgescu-Roegen, 1971a). Finally, social and ecological systems generally tend to evolve toward higher order and complexity, whereas uncontrolled physical systems tend to be best described by entropy law-like behaviour for closed systems, i.e. towards uniformity and disorder.[5]

(v) *Physico−Economic:* This approach aims at a maximum consistency with the laws of thermodynamics (see previous section; and Christensen, 1989). As opposed to the standard economic view this leads to a dynamic uncertainty and disequilibrium view, where physical characteristics dominate the long-run outcome of economic activities. In addition it means the inclusion of economic−environmental relationships in two directions. When economic activities cannot be sustained by the continuous regeneration and assimilation processes that are based on an incoming flux of solar energy, maintenance of such activities will imply a deterioration in the quality of the natural environment. This in turn may give rise to a negative feedback to the economy. A chain of two-way dynamic interactions between the economy and the environment can be considered as one level of inclusion of the entropy law (see also Faber *et al.*, 1987), and surpasses the standard economic view of a

---

[5] It has been suggested that when the universe 'came into existence' during the first moment of the big bang, an initially unstable situation was created on the fundamental level of matter and energy. This may then have caused a physical evolution until a point of stability was reached and the present physics' laws became effective. This stability is illustrated by the mere fact that such laws have been formulated in various fields of physics: relativity theory, quantum mechanics, thermodynamics, etc. Development of physical systems is, in a way, restricted by the 'real' laws, so that they cannot evolve as freely on a physical level as ecological or economic systems on a biotic or technological level. This is also illustrated by the fact that in ecology and economics there are fewer empirically proven laws. Most existing ecological or economic laws are only qualitative, and can be characterized as 'approximate' or 'quasi-laws', since the may change over time.

circular economy (as criticised by Daly, 1977). In addition, thermodynamic consideration can give more support to implementation of notions of irreversibility, as well as provide information for specifying functional relationships in models and determining numerical values of parameters. Faber *et al.* (1995) discuss issues of disequilibrium and self-organisation in the context of teleological development (see also previous section).

A recent interest in this Physico–Economic approach is the attention for materials and energy flows and transformation, for which sometimes the concept industrial metabolism is used (see Ayres, 1989). This also links to the ecological ecosystem approach in which metabolism may be used at an organism or system level. In the economy it may be used similarly on a systems to sectoral – production or household –, or even single firm level.

As already mentioned in the previous section, an interesting concept in modern thermodynamics is that of a non-equilibrium thermodynamic system. It requires a continuous inflow of low entropy, and is characterised by 'dissipative structures' which may lead to self-organising patterns (Prigogine *et al.*, 1977). According to O'Connor (1991) such 'thermodynamic ordering' may not be easy to detect or apply since most economic and ecological processes are occurring far from thermodynamic equilibrium. Ecologists, more than economists, have worked on providing links between ecosystem theory and disequilibrium thermodynamics (see Günther and Folke, 1993; Kay 1991; see also the Biophysical–Energy perspective). The place of disequilibrium thermodynamics for ecological economics can maybe best be summarised by the following statement: '... the relationship between entropy production and changes in the structure organisation is multi-faceted and situation-specific. Attempts to account for the specificity of societal activities in terms of a generic scalar measure of organisation or dissipation, are largely after-the fact, and in no way do away with the need for analysis of institutional and ethical dimensions in their own right' (O'Connor, 1991, p. 95).

(vi) *Biophysical–Energy:* This approach aims to integrate economic and environmental, ecological processes on a physical scale, by formulating one-dimensional energy variables (Odum, 1983; Umaña, 1981b). The idea behind it is that all systems are constrained by energy availability. This is made clear by material balances, and limits to energy transformation, recycling, and consequently to system structure, growth and development. The method commonly employed is dynamic systems modelling. 'Energy language' is employed to visualise the structure and dynamics of systems, and includes symbols such as energy source, tank, heat sink, consumer, producer, circuit, interaction, amplifier and transaction. Pivotal concepts are Emergy and Transformity, which stand for embodied energy and energy transformation ratio, respectively (see Odum, 1983). Embodied energy is defined as the direct and indirect energy required to produce organised material structures. Finally, Exergy is used as a measure of the difference in physical quality of energy, and the deviation of thermodynamic equilibrium (see Günther and Folke, 1993; Schneider and Kay, 1994).

The applications of these energy-inspired models include populations, ecosystems, production — consumption economies, resource — economic systems, trade systems, global geochemical models, and environment — economy models (see Odum, 1987). An application to a regional system is Jansson and Zuchetto (1978). Finally, an alternative and more economic-oriented example of energy-systems modelling, with a central place for capital, population and investment, is Slessor (1975). A recent application, using the much applied ECCO modelling system (e.g., Gilbert and Braat, 1991), deals with the question of a transition from a world economy based on the depletion of fossil fuel energy sources to a completely solar-based one (King and Slessor, 1994).

In the context of energy analysis, an energy theory of value has been developed, based on the concept of embodied energy (see Costanza, 1981a). The motivation for this theory is that direct substitution between capital or labour and energy inputs in production does not indicate well how much energy is saved. The reason is that the factors are not really independent, since additional capital or labour requires additional energy in turn. Economists will see the analogy with the Marxist labour theory of value, which has been discarded as a too limited and incomplete explanation of the formation of values. Daly (1981) argues that embodied energy is only a necessary condition for deriving relative values, and not a sufficient condition. The latter implies that there can be no such thing as an energy theory of value. The reaction of Costanza (1981b) to this and other criticism can be summarised as: values relate uniquely to embodied energy and not to a general and vaguer notion of energy related to materials; and a measure of embodied energy is insufficient for value in the market sense, because of imperfect and incomplete markets (in terms of ownership and information). Daly (1981) gives a summary of stances in this debate. Sections 4.2.3 and 4.4.6 offer further (economic) explanations and interpretations of value concepts.

(vii) *Systems — Ecological:* An important branch in ecology for the present work is systems ecology, concerned with ecosystem modelling (see

Patten, 1971; Jörgenson, 1992). Ecosystem modelling initially was focusing on interaction between natural components of ecosystems. As environmental problems started to become the reason for performing certain ecosystem studies, also effects of environmental pollution, resource use and other types of disturbance were studied and modelled. Relevant for integrated research is then, for instance, the inclusion of stress factors in such models, giving rise to pollution impact models, eutrophication models and ecotoxicology models focusing on organic pollutants, heavy metals, PCB's and radiation; for various studies of terrestrial and aquatic systems, see, e.g.: Holling (1978); Biswas (1981); Rinaldi (1979); van Steenkiste (1981); Braat and van Lierop (1987); Braat (1992); Latour *et al.* (1994); and Krysanova and Kaganovich (1994). Specific recent development try to link hydrology and ecology, which is particularly relevant for economics of wetlands (see, e.g., Costanza *et al.*, 1989; Lynne *et al.*, 1981; Barendregt *et al.*, 1992; Claessen *et al.*, 1994; White and Wadsworth, 1994). Very closely related to the ecosystem modelling work is resource management ecology which is taking a more interdisciplinary perspective (Watt, 1968; Holling, 1978; Walters, 1986; see related resource economic work by Perrings 1994). One important approach that has been developed in this field concentrates on energy-based ecosystem modelling (see Odum, 1983). Approaches of energy modelling can be found in Odum (1987), Jansson and Zuchetto, (1978), and King and Slessor (1994). Finally, landscape and spatial ecosystem ecology (see, e.g., Maxwell and Costanza, 1994) are an interesting new branch that may link to, for instance, spatial economics, economic geography, urban economics and social geography. Section 4.4.3. includes further discussion of systems ecology in the context of integrated analysis.

Interactive economic−ecological models that use extended economic and ecological model components are rare. The choice of a spatial scale that is relevant from the economic, ecological and environmental problem perspective makes it difficult to built such models while keeping them operational (see Lonergan, 1981; Braat and van Lierop, 1987; van den Bergh, 1991; Ruth, 1993; van den Bergh and Nijkamp, 1994a and d; see also Chapters 8, 9 and 11 in this book). On the other hand, conceptual (analytical or numerical) modelling has been developed for many issues in environmental economics. One topic which seems to have escaped this until recently, however, is biodiversity (see Perrings and Pearce, 1994).

Costanza *et al.* (1993) mention two related issues that provide uncertainties about the further development of ecosystems and economic ecological models, namely predictability and scale (or resolution). To start with the latter, it is clear that models suppose a homogeneity below a certain scale to minimise interactions, and interaction between subsystems or areas at a given scale level, or between different scale levels. This hierarchy of scales is especially relevant for economic–ecological models since these may involve great variety in ecological and economic scales. In addition to the conceptual difficulties, technical issues of prediction, estimation and calibration are raised, which are not solved by data availability, since non-linearities (even chaos and fractal type of issues) may be disturbing. Therefore the problems of prediction and resolution are to some extent of a fundamental nature.

(viii) *Ecological engineering:* This approach focuses on the manipulation of environmental systems for human benefit or for improving environmental quality. It can be more broadly defined as the design, operation and control of human–environmental systems to realise one or both of the mentioned objectives. Ecotechnology may be considered as a specific type of ecological engineering, concerned with technological methods for management of human–environmental systems (see, e.g., Mitsch and Jörgensen, 1989). A more specific orientation exists as well. Odum (1962) has used ecological engineering to refer to situations where energy supplied by human activities is small relative to naturally available energy flows (see Mitsch, 1991).

The interesting role of ecological engineering is that it can generate information for comparison of different options for design, management and control of environmental systems. Comparison may be based on ecological characteristics related to energy characteristics, self-design, self-organisation, recycling, biodiversity and sustainability. Mitsch (1991) states that therefore ecological engineering can be regarded as prescriptive rather than descriptive ecology, which is similar in some respects to engineering, although oriented towards management of nature rather than industrial activities. It is a part of applied ecology in the sense of combining ecosystem theory with empirical and experimental studies dealing with productivity in ecosystems, ecosystem restoration and environmental impacts on ecosystems. This approach therefore clearly leads to an integrated perspective on economic–environmental relationships useful for dealing with complex issues of management and multiple use of (semi-)natural ecosystems.

(ix) *Human–Ecological:* Drawing the ecological perspective somewhat further to economy and man, human ecology results. Economics is seen as a part of ecology according to this view, since man is included in a foodweb (see Hardin, 1985). Furthermore, man's actions are posed to have multiple effects, and there is no such thing as 'side-effects'. Population growth of mankind is regarded as subjected to the same laws as that of other species, and therefore the economic growth models necessarily fall in the same class as biological and ecological growth models. This means that the idea of carrying capacity is relevant, which can be related to numbers of people and their material existence – not to be confused with welfare or happiness – level (see further Section 2.4.1). It is necessary therefore that a trade-off is made between population size and the standard of individual living (see Hardin, 1991), because a positive feedback cannot be sustained and negative feedback is desired.

An economic development model based on an human–ecological oriented systems approach has been pursued by Wilkinson (1973) (see also Duncan, 1959; Common, 1988; Arntzen, 1989; Opschoor, 1989; van den Bergh and van der Straaten, 1994b). Here the economic concept of scarcity is extended to all aspects of the natural environment, and the ecological concept of evolution to all demographics, social and economic entities.

(x) *Sociobiological:* This perspective focuses on the biological basis of all social behaviour, using elements of sociology, biology and ecology. Man is regarded simultaneously in his role as a social being with moral commitment to his society, a biological organism with intuition, and as an ecological component influenced by his natural environment. Social norms are part of genetic information and learned. As societies change, norms change, and behaviour accordingly. The role of spatial overlapping characteristics of environment and society are of crucial importance for establishing the basic elements of how people act in society and interact with their environment (see Wilson, 1975). The theory links to evolution in the sense that it emphasises the survival of genes rather than of species. See for more discussion linking to ecological economics Hinterberger (1993 and 1994).

(xi) *Historical–Institutional:* Institutional approaches to the study of economy and environment are concerned with a holistic instead of reductionist approach, patterns and circular interdependence, based on organic–biological, ecological and biophysical notions rather than mechanical–atomistic and very abstract ones, such as found in neoclassical economics (see, e.g., Martinez-Alier, 1987; Dietz and van der Straaten, 1992; Söderbaum, 1992; and Opschoor and van der Straaten, 1993). This approach is different from the other ones, in that it is not formal and rigid, binding together (many detailed) facts, employing low-level generalisations, allowing for a mix of observed facts and subjective values and convictions (see Blaug, 1991), and employing ad hoc approaches to systems with a focus on specific characteristics. An analysis of particular situations may focus on historical, unique patterns (examples of an environmental—political issue are Martinez-Alier, 1991 and 1994). Sometimes the approaches are also referred to as historical, interdisciplinary, social, or humanistic economics.

Political motives, interaction between pressure groups, and the notion of vested interests play an important role in this, especially when focusing on power, conflict and distributional analyses. Some further elements of difference with neoclassical economics can further clarify this approach. First, the idea that value can be determined by application of objective techniques is refuted, and replaced by a subjective, ethically-based and hierarchical interpretation of individual values and preferences, about which agreement is not necessary, so that in fact diversity and uniqueness are emphasised. Furthermore, scientific analysis is value-coloured and subjective, and one should attempt to alleviate such characteristics, but rather recognise them and explicitly deal with them.

Söderbaum (1992) mentions as a difference between neoclassical and institutional approaches the position with regard to behaviour of institutions. In the neoclassical public choice theory the emphasis is put on individual interests with usual assumptions: politicians maximising votes, or bureaucrats maximising their financial budget. Interaction between these takes the form of negotiations. In the institutional actor-network theory there is (also) more attention for individuals with many interests and ideology. Furthermore, the interactions are (also) based on public (ideological) debates and networking.

The historical orientation has also become popular with respect to considering very long periods of time. Wilkinson (1973), earlier mentioned, used an ecological model to explain historical economic developments related to the industrial revolution (see also Common, 1988; Pezzey, 1992; van den Bergh and van der Straaten, 1994b). Finally, Taylor (1977), Simmons (1989) and Ponting (1991) sketch a very broad picture of the historical development of human societies in relation to their natural environment.

In conclusion, this approach relates to the evolutionary approaches in its process-orientation (see Hodgson *et al.*, 1994), path dependence, and with the Ethical—Utopian stream in its value-orientation. The main distinction with these is the focus on the formation, behaviour and effects of institutions.

(xii) *Ethical—Utopian:* This is a stream of thought that is much concerned with ethical starting points with respect to resource use and interaction with the environment on the one hand, and welfare distribution and equity on the other hand. This leads to the use of notions like 'steady state' and 'minimising throughputs' (Daly, 1977), 'small is beautiful' (Schumacher, 1973), 'blueprints' (e.g., Goldsmith, 1973), 'citizen—consumer distinction' (Sagoff, 1988).

This approach can be found in some of the discussions on sustainable development. This perspective may then be characterised by extreme ecocentric positions of deep concern for 'Nature', sometimes referred to as 'deep ecology' (see Devall and Sessions, 1984; see Section 3.4.1). In the context of an anthropocentric focus, a concern for future generations may be expressed by an extreme egalitarian position (see Section 3.4.2). The difference between the two positions can be regarded in terms of a trade-off between people and other species, and between people now and in the future, respectively. This position has been especially relevant in long-run issues related to growth and development. Thus normative and utopian ideas have been generated about sustainable economies, sustainable economic development, sustainable society, etc. (see, e.g., Proops, 1989; Daly and Cobb, 1989). Most close to this perspective are the Human—Ecological, the Historical—Institutional, and the Socio-biological ones.

Concluding this section, it is hopefully made clear that, despite unique crucial elements, one can find much similarity between various theories. As a result, different starting points — conceptually and theoretically — do not necessarily lead to a conflicting point of view on every issue. One may of course aim for a list of common principles of economic—ecological analyses (see, e.g., Costanza, 1991; Jansson *et al.*, 1994; or Sahu and Nayak, 1994). However, the disadvantage of this may be a downplay of differences between alternative theories. Norgaard (1985, 1989) has forcefully argued for methodological pluralism in ecological economics. His 'plea for pluralism' is based on, amongst others, the following motives: it is too early to limit the methodologies now; there is not a best methodology in dealing with the complex issues; multiple insights carry over a need for careful decision making on a policy level since it expresses that there is no single right solution; pluralism may help foster biological and cultural diversity; and it may promote participation and decentralisation (see Norgaard, 1989). The upshot of this is that ecological economics should not only search for common elements, theories and approaches in the sciences of economics and ecology. It should try to take a broad view encapsulating economic, social, ethical, historical, institutional, biological and physical elements. The main reason for being wary of neglecting one particular method is that the (even discounted) cost of regret later may be extensively larger than the cost of having extra scientific luggage at this very moment.

2.4. A BASIC DYNAMIC MODEL

2.4.1. Endogenising Carrying Capacity

Many traditional economic perspectives focus on a single negative environmental influence of economic activities, for instance, materials extraction, environmental disturbance by artifacts and activities, and chemical or physical pollution. Several writers have proposed to consider simultaneously resource potentials and environmental quality (e.g., Siebert, 1982; and Opschoor, 1987), for which the concept 'Environmental Utilisation Space' has been proposed (see Opschoor and Weterings, 1994), and applied in a formal theoretical analysis (Verhoef and van den Bergh, 1995a and b). This concept is related to that of carrying capacity in ecology. In its basic form it is assumed to be fixed (i.e. constant), so that in fact one-way effects are studied (see Wilen, 1985). In the present context, the existence of a finite carrying capacity would act as a limiting factor to the scale of the economy. Some possible patterns for such a case are shown in Figure 2.1. When one, as here, is interested in two-way interactions between economic and ecological systems, then variations in the carrying capacity should be allowed for. In the latter case one can furthermore endogenise the carrying capacity, i.e. make it dependent on the scale of the economy (see Figure 2.2). A feedback process can then give rise to a variety of patterns: monotonic or cyclic; and convergent, stable or unstable (not indicated in the figure).

The patterns in Figures 2.1 and 2.2 can be illustrated by representing two-way economic−environmental relationships formally as in model (1). It can be considered as an extension of the concept of carrying capacity.

$$\frac{dE}{dt} = H(E,K)$$

$$\frac{dK}{dt} = F(K,E).$$

(2.1)

This model offers a conceptual view on the global and long-term relationship between an economy and its natural environment, each

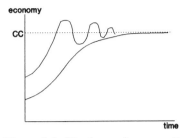

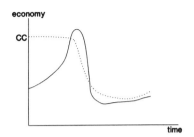

Figure 2.1. Fixed carrying capacity with two possible patterns of economic growth.

Figure 2.2. Variable carrying capacity with two-way interaction between economy and environment.

represented by a single indicator that is changing over time. One may interpret the overall system represented by it as closed. However, most economy−environment systems are not closed, and therefore one can better regard the model as representative of an open system in which internal economy−environment relationships dominate external influences, in terms of their effect on the total system's behaviour.

In order to specify H and F, assumptions have to be made regarding the intrinsic dynamic features of the economy and the environment as well as the general character of influences exerted by the economy and the environment on each other. E and K are non-negative variables which indicate the environmental quality level and the economic activity level, respectively. Both H and F can take positive and negative values. In this way it is possible to include simple and straightforward relationships, such as: the environment (E) is 'necessary' for the economy (K); 'more' of E is 'good' for K; and 'more' of K is 'bad' for E, i.e. positive and negative external feedbacks, respectively. But also more interesting features can be captured. The environment may be assumed to be initially subject to positive feedback and negative feedback for high values of E. The internal economic structure, represented by F, may be chosen to reflect either a similar mechanism, or only a positive internal feedback, or a combination of the two. In van den Bergh (1993) this simple model is analysed for various assumptions (for technical details, see van den Bergh, 1991). One set of assumptions represents a case where both internal (behavioural) and external (sustainable development) negative feedback to economic growth occur. It turns out to lead to one interior stable equilibrium. Furthermore, three general types of pattern characterise all possible behaviour far from equilibrium. These are dependent on the inclusion and intensity of the feedback mechanisms between the economy and the environment. To illustrate this case, consider the following specification of system (1).

$$\frac{dE}{dt} = \alpha(K) * E * (E_c(K) - E),$$

(2.2)

$$\frac{dK}{dt} = \beta(E) * K * (K_c(E) - K).$$

E_c and K_c are carrying capacities of the sub-systems environment and economy. They do not have a constant value, but derive their values from the state of the other sub-system. Several interpretation of these carrying capacities are possible. One may consider, for instance, the amount of available space − or land area − and solar energy inflow as given. This may then determine an upper bound to E_c, e.g., in terms of a maximum biomass level of natural vegetation. Notice however that the amount of available space being fixed implies that 'land' does not appear as a variable in the function E_c. In order to explain the existence of an economic carrying capacity one may apply a similar idea, but with space replaced by potential supply of natural environmental services, and natural vegetation replaced by, e.g., a level indicator of economic activities. In this case, however, the carrying capacity (K_c) is not fixed but instead varies with E. The formulation of a carrying capacity for an economy may be based on two ideas. First, natural systems exert a limit on the use of environmental services and materials by economic systems. This may effectively constrain physical growth potentials. The escape via substitution of growth in the physical scale of the economy by growth of the service sector is also limited. This is the result of the fact that also physical inputs are required directly and indirectly to generate services. Furthermore, services will replace non-economic services (e.g., those presently not included in economic calculations, e.g., of GNP). Second, conscious decisions are made to satisfy environmental sustainability objectives, which may be caught under some type of feedback mechanism aimed at sustainable development in the long-run (see also Section 6.5). This is in fact the political-institutional impact on economic decisions.

It is important to realise that the existence of a carrying capacity essentially derives from a single external and fixed scarcity factor, i.e. the most critical among a number external scarcity factors. In the case of E this may be land. This is included in the model via the carrying capacity E_c. In the case of K the critical scarcity factor determining the carrying capacity K_c is E, which is clearly variable in the context of the model. Since a carrying capacity level will be increasing in its limit (assuming that it is quantifiable) $\partial K_c/\partial E > 0$ holds. The implication of this assumption is a negative feedback from K to K directly and indirectly via E.

It should be emphasised that the impact of K on E_c is of an entirely different nature, i.e is not operating as a regular scarcity factor upon a carrying capacity. This impact namely represents the environmental disruption as a result of extraction and emissions of materials, land use, etc. The consequence is that $\partial E_c/\partial K$ has an opposite sign (< 0). This means, however, that one might interpret the negative of K as a critical scarcity factor, although it is not external nor fixed.

Finally, the internal growth rates of each system, α and β, are also variable in the state of the other system. Since for each equation these parameters are suspected to show a direction of response to changes in their arguments similar to those of the associated carrying capacities we assume $\partial\alpha/\partial K < 0$ and $\partial\beta/\partial E > 0$.

By considering numerical results for several parameter values one can obtain insight into the behaviour both far from the stable equilibrium and close around it. This means that, although the results are less general than in the case of analytical derivations, one can obtain more insight into the nonlinear behaviour of the system, also that far out of equilibrium. Examples are given in phase diagrams of Figures 2.3 to 2.5. They show time patterns of an economy–environment system that – from several extreme initial states (i.e. on or close to the edge of the figure) – converge to an interior equilibrium (0.48, 0.29). The coordinates of the equilibrium are the same in each graph.

Figures 2.3 and 2.4 both show paths that rather quickly tend to a curve along which they slowly move towards the equilibrium state. This assumes that time in the model is linearly related to time in reality, in which case a short distance between points in the graphs indicates a higher speed of change, as time distances between these points are constant.[6] In Figure 2.3 K reacts very strongly compared to E when the system is relatively far out of equilibrium. The movement of the system is then directed towards a central curve leading into the equilibrium state. In this case the economic reactions range from strong collapse to fast growth. This depends on the initial state of the economy–environment system, which can be one of, roughly, four categories, namely combinations of 'small and large sizes or qualities' of the economy and

---

[6] Numerical values were generated at 30 points, at equal distances from each other. The total time period of simulation may be interpreted, for instance, in terms of decades.

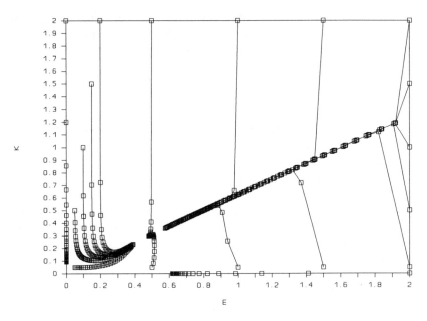

Figure 2.3. Simulated E−K-phase diagram of the model in (2): stable node type 1.

the environment. In Figure 2.4 E is more reactive, and a similar but very differently positioned structure can be recognised. Therefore, the conclusion is that if either K or E is more reactive than the other variable then a nodal type of structure in the phase diagram results, even beyond a close neighbourhood of the interior equilibrium. This can be explained by the fact that the economy in this case is rather stable and for that reason can escape stages of strong growth and severe depression. Figure 2.5, finally, shows the case where K and E are more equally reactive, in which case a shorter way to the equilibrium is taken from most initial states. Then, a spiral type of overall structure is obtained. In this case the economy and environment adjust to one another equally, i.e. the magnitude of changes in one subsystem is in accordance with that in the other. Opposite and similar directions of change alternate until an equilibrium state is attained.

The paths in Figure 2.3, as far as the economy (K) is concerned, are familiar from more complex model studies (e.g., Meadows *et al.*, 1972). Those paths starting in the north-west region represent an economy that faces a fast collapse followed by a slow recovery, after which the stationary state is approached. The patterns starting from the south-eastern part of the graph show an economy that is initially growing

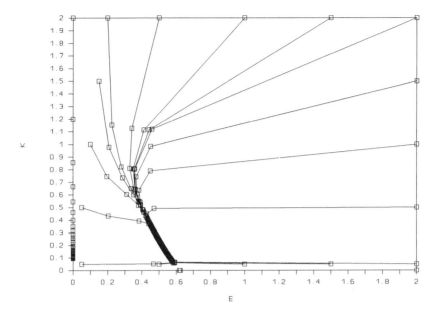

Figure 2.4. Simulated E−K phase diagram of the model in (2): stable node type 2.

rather fast, and then slowly decreases in size to a stationary state. In Figure 2.4 no such familiar patterns are found. There seems to be no obvious reason why this situation could not occur in real world economic − environment systems, so that one should consider a more wide spectrum of possible behaviour than some models suggest. The case represented in Figure 2.5 is in its qualitative character closer to Figure 2.3, i.e. it shows also the familiar − although less extreme − patterns of growth, collapse and recovery. Of course, the recovery was built in by the assumption of two-way negative feedbacks, so the system was forced to remain in boundaries, and not explode so as to finally be completely destructed. This type of catastrophic scenario is not very useful in a predictive sense (too sensitive to parameters), is inconsistent with the many negative feedbacks that exist in reality, and furthermore is not required at all for an analysis of dynamic characteristics of economic − ecological systems.

The above models may be implemented to reflect the behaviour of an economic system which strongly interacts with its environment. The disadvantage of using small open economic systems is that they may be too much dependent on outside environmental support, in which case this interaction will be very weak only. Thus one should focus on a rather

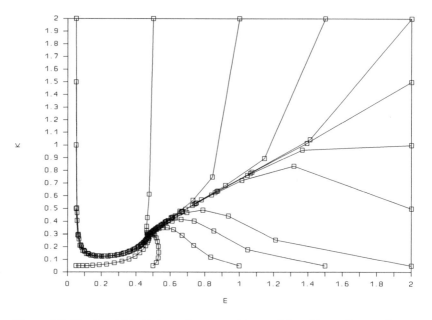

Figure 2.5. Simulated E−K-phase diagram of the model in (2): stable spiral.

closed system preferably. The success of an applied approach depends furthermore on two other factors. In the first place it is necessary to find adequate economic and environmental indicators for each variable in the model. Secondly, one needs data over very long periods of time with values sufficiently varying to test the patterns in the figures.

Alternatively, an application may require that the present stylised form of the model in (2.1) or (2.2) is converted into a more disaggregative formulation, in which variables are more easily interpretable. Several types of models may result from such a step. One example is given in Chapter 6. A classification of economic sectors is then an important issue to be addressed. One may do this on the basis of three criteria: materials flow characteristics of an economy, environmental impacts and influences of activities, and production and welfare sensitivity to environmental factors. The latter two are dealt with now.

2.4.2. A Typology of Direct Economy−Environment Interactions

In order to be able to say something about feedback and other dynamics as discussed above occurring on the boundary of economic and ecological systems, one has to be clear about the direct impacts of

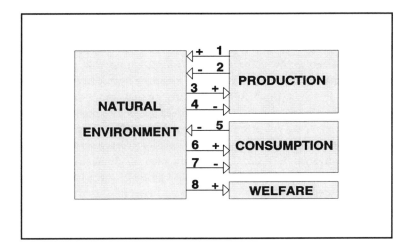

Figure   2.6.   Categories   of   direct   economic — environmental interactions.

Note: '+' and '−' denote positive and negative influences, respectively.

economic on ecological systems, and vice versa. In Figure 2.6 eight types of direct economic — ecological interactions are distinguished by linking a division of the economy into production, consumption and welfare to the natural environment. Four arrows link the environment and production blocks. The first arrow shows the positive effects of production on the environment, for instance, by way of environmental protection activities. The second arrow points to negative effects, caused by polluting, extracting and disturbing activities, for example. The third arrow represents the positive influences of the environment on production, e.g., in terms of soil conditions for agriculture, or marine quality for a fishery. Furthermore, this arrow represents the material flow from the extraction of renewable and non-renewable resources. The fourth arrow shows a negative effect on either productivity (e.g., in agriculture), in terms of the quality or quantity of outputs produced, or a negative health effect. One must think here of the impact of pollution that is flowing into (or accumulating in) the environment (air, water, biotic elements), or the impact of natural disasters. Consumption has three linkages with environment. The fifth arrow originates from the recognition that consumption may have a non-positive effect on the natural environment, via waste generation and disturbing activities (e.g., certain types of recreation and land use). The sixth and seventh arrows indicate the positive and negative contribution of the natural environment to consumption, e.g., via attractive natural areas for recreational activities and polluted seashores along beaches, respectively. Since welfare is no activity, it has no arrow going in the left direction. Arrow 8 denotes the direct beneficial effect of the natural environment on welfare, without the interference of actual production and consumption processes. One may think, for example, of scientific, aesthetic or spiritual values. Most inter-actions mentioned, except arrow 8, occur on a physical−material level.

A related discussion of environmental functions, services and processes is contained in Section 3.3.2. The classification of direct interactions, or effects, is necessary for dealing with indirect uses, in terms of intermediate deliveries and dependencies between activities, delayed effects, cumulative effects, etc. To deal with such indirect effects, various frameworks have been proposed. These are considered in the following section.

2.5. METHODOLOGICAL FRAMEWORKS FOR ECONOMIC−ECOLOGICAL ANALYSIS

2.5.1. The Input−output Approach

Various attempts have been made to formally analyse direct and indirect economic−ecological interactions in a single methodological framework. The input−output framework has received much attention in this respect, and has been applied both as a conceptual and as an accounting framework in economic−ecological studies (see Cumberland 1966; Daly 1968; Isard 1969 and 1972; Perrings, 1987). This approach allows one to deal with interactions between components in economic and ecological systems, as well as between components within each of these sub-systems. This use of the input−output framework should not be confused with the less comprehensive economic input−output models extended with emission modules (Leontief 1970; Leontief and Ford, 1972; Victor, 1972), applied in environmental economics and even ecological economics (see Idenburg, 1993); and neither with input−output accounting of flows in ecosystems (e.g., Hannon 1991), but rather as the integration of these. For this purpose, the scale, units, and disaggregation of the sub-systems should be (made) consistent and complementary.

The input−output framework can be combined with various theoretical perspectives, as already indicated in Section 2.3.2. In neoclassical economics it is generalised to non-linear multisectoral or multi-market equilibrium models. Here two restrictions of the input−output system are removed. First, the assumption of complementarity between inputs or, alternatively, the linear shape of the model, is replaced by the assumption of substitution and an optimal choice of the input mix, based on, for example, cost minimisation. Second, prices are endogenised by linking them to the volumes and allocation decisions in the models. Such extended models have, however, seen almost no applications – neither theoretical nor empirical – to ecological–economic issues. Two noticeable exceptions were mentioned already in the previous section. First, the inclusion of an ecosystem model in a general equilibrium setting (see Crocker and Tschirhart, 1992). And, second, the link between a general equilibrium system and materials flows and accounting (Ayres and Kneese, 1969).

Another important addition to the input–output framework are dynamic relationships. This ultimately moves us into the area of systems' analysis, which in fact covers many other approaches, including nonlinear and even static models. It also is a tool for numerical analysis in the context of the theories of Section 2.3.2, notably those focusing on dynamics. Such a system-oriented methodological approach may be based on extending an economic theory or model; extending an ecological theory or model; combining existing economic theories and models; or a general atheoretical statistical or systems approach, where one can start from data, employing purely statistical models, or from logical processes based on cause-effect relationships.[7]

2.5.2. The Systems Approach

It is useful to consider the systems method somewhat more closely. In the first place, it has been applied in almost all scientific disciplines, largely due to its general character. Its philosophy is particularly appropriate for dealing with structure and behaviour of well-bounded parts of reality, by taking a general, atheoretical, stance to avoid being unnecessarily restricted by assumptions. Consequently, it is often applied to deal explicitly with complexity, in terms of networks, input–output relationship, nonlinearity, linked processes, or hierarchical levels. A systems approach is based on the notion of a set of relationships between

---

[7] For this purpose one may focus on common elements, analogues, or metaphors in economic and ecological systems, that originate from a specific theory (Section 2.3.2). There have been many concepts suggested for this: variety, specialization, equilibrium, optimization, growth, structural change, evolution, stability, threshold, carrying capacity, metabolism, population dynamics, input–output system, feedback, network, etc. (see Hardin, 1963; Boulding, 1966a; van der Ploeg, 1976; Norgaard, 1985; Svedin, 1985; Perrings, 1987; Ayres, 1989; Shogren and Nowell, 1992; Ruth, 1993; Holling *et al.*, 1993). See also the recent collection of 30 'classics' by Hodgson (1995).

elements or variables, some of which are state or level variables capturing all relevant information about the state of the system, and others as flow or rate variables which include inputs, throughputs, and outputs. This is so general that in fact a systems approach covers most other *formal* approaches in applied sciences, so that it allows for dealing at a more general level with identification (estimation), analysis and control of a specific system. This means, for instance, that phases such as formulation, estimation, and analysis may proceed in a consistent, integrated, and interactive manner, not constraining oneself immediately by adopting a specific theoretical, statistical, or methodological construct. An advantage is furthermore that several (mathematical) representations exist of a system (based on: continuous versus discrete; level-rate or stock-flow, differential versus difference equations, Laplace or Z transformations, ARMA models), each attractive for a specific goal, be it identification, simulation, interpretation or generalisation.

Concepts like dynamic processes, feedback mechanisms, and control strategies clearly express the idea that a systems approach can be deal with economic − ecological realities in a unified framework (see also Bennet and Chorley, 1978; Costanza *et al.*, 1993; and Hannon and Ruth, 1994). Extending a systems framework for a particular instance or situation is in principle a straightforward procedure. One can integrate two subsystems, have a nesting of systems, or start with one (holistic) representation. The fixed elements in the system can be considered as black boxes, each of which may be specified, so that one element is replaced by several others; these can then be linked in a consistent way to other elements in the system. One may regard this as adding more detail or disaggregative interpretation to a systems model. Finally, an important phase in systems analysis is setting the boundaries. This is usually done so as to minimise interactions − in terms of influences and flows − between elements of the system and the 'rest of the universe'. This is of course a very, and perhaps the most, important criterion for deciding about how integrated or interdisciplinary a model should be.

Two important characteristics which make systems analytical approaches attractive are non-linear relationships and dynamic feedback processes, and especially combinations of these. Linear models (e.g., input − output models) would only be useful insofar as they are easily solvable, catch the multidimensionality and sign of effects, or are used for short-term analysis. However, alternative heuristic approaches may well do a better job here, by combining nonlinearity and dynamics with numerical solutions. Examples are mentioned in Costanza *et al.* (1993), such as meta-modelling, and employing numerical algorithms. Especially spatial disaggregation would force one to choose such options (see

Maxwell and Costanza, 1994). This is relevant for spatial policy issues, and landscape modelling focusing on micro-level ecosystem processes.

Positive feedback and negative feedback can lead to anything between collapse, homeostasis and explosive growth. Interesting questions may thus be related to stability of the overall system when the behaviour of a subsystem in isolation tends to be chaotic, unstable, or cyclic (see also Section 2.4.1). Holling (1994) distinguishes different approaches in theory and modelling based on the following dynamics' assumptions: (i) smooth exponential growth: optimistic; (ii) hyperbolic and unstable growth: pessimistic, decentralisation, small-scale; (iii) logistic growth: navigate along a sustainable development path; (iv) nested cycles of discontinuous events and nonlinear processes: periods, cycles, long waves; (v) evolution and adaptation: complexity, order out of chaos, self-organisation, integrated studies. As Holling states, none of these beliefs is correct or wrong. They are just like the theories presented in Section 2.3.2 containing partial or conditional truths, and may be complementary in various ways.

Finally, note that the systems' approach is not covering every theory and approach. There are more general or higher-level classifications of 'scientific research'. Georgescu-Roegen (1976), for instance, makes a distinction into mechanico-imaginative, mechanico-descriptive, and analytico-physiological manners of dealing with economic phenomena. The first category includes mathematics which bears no relation to reality, while the second category does only describe but not aim at explaining reality. These two categories are based on arithmomorphic—formal structures. This is said to be incompatible with qualitative change, novelty and surprises. The last category includes 'physiological analysis akin to that of biology' (p. 237). Georgescu-Roegen (1971a) refers then to the economic works of Quesnay, Smith, Marx, Malthus, and Schumpeter as falling into this category. Finally, he distinguishes these three analytical arithmomorphic—formal categories from dialectical approaches. The systems approach is clearly falling into the arithmomorphic—formal category.

2.5.3. Linking of Models, Measurement Units and Scale
The linking of models is restricted by the model type. If economic and ecological models fit in a (general) systems frame, then they may be blended in a single model structure, where compartments or modules may represent the original models, and certain outputs of one module serve as input for another. However, often it is not easy to link models directly. For instance, if both the economic and ecological systems are represented in the form of programming or optimisation models — linear,

nonlinear, dynamic or stochastic — then one should decide what to do: look for a new, aggregate objective; adopt a multi-objective or conflict analysis framework; or, when possible, derive two sets of optimal conditions and solve these simultaneously. However, when the economic and ecological systems are represented by different model types, then it is difficult to suggest how they can be linked to one another. Often economic models have an optimisation or programming format and ecosystem models a descriptive format. This can allow for direct technical integration. Generally, in cases where formats differ, a transformation to other model types may be necessary. This will usually lead to a loss of information, change in assumptions, or even inconsistency with the monodisciplinary study objective. Whether such effects are undesirable depends on the purpose and questions of the integrative study.

Two other aspects of integration may present some difficulties, namely units of measurement, temporal scale, and spatial aggregation. First, monetary units dominate in economic models and theories, and physical units in ecological ones. Of course, both types of theories also employ functional units, such as number of commodities, number of actors, and the size of a population. Direct coupling, however, is because of different units not always unambiguous or even possible, such as valuation of benefits of future services of 'environmental capital', or environmental quality effects on production functions in agriculture or fisheries.

The issue of spatial scale (and levels) is important because economics usually distinguishes between micro, regional (meso) and macro levels: micro may involve one activity (a household, a business), or multiple activities (a market, a country or the world). Regional and macroeconomics are more specifically oriented towards larger real-world spatial entities: actual provinces, states, regions, nations or the world. In ecology, a distinction can be made between approaches linked to various aggregation levels, in turn related to approximate spatial scales: global ecology of the biosphere; ecosystem ecology; population ecology on community and population levels; autecology on population and individual levels; and ecophysiology on the individual level. If one relates these subdivisions of levels or scales with each other, then it seems that economics usually adopts a larger spatial scale. In other words, within one spatial area conceivable or in an economic geographical region, one may find many ecosystem areas. The most useful and likely options for integration would probably imply an intermediate level where some concessions are made in terms of economic and ecosystem comprehensiveness, and consequently in terms of complexity as a result of multiple ecosystems in one economic region.

Economy—environment interactions differ conceptually among various geographical levels, from micro to global. One human being may interact with one plant, for instance, by eating it. The type of interaction between the world population and the global population of birds is less evident, and in any case multidimensional and indirect. Of course, this is a familiar problem, namely of aggregation. But now there is more to it, because one must deal with mutually consistent boundaries, space and time scales, and units. Although sometimes suggested, a holistic approach can not be entirely satisfactory. Instead, disaggregation in terms of identification, description, validation and analysis, and aggregation in terms of performance indicators and evaluation, may be used sequentially, so that the assumptions necessary to arrive at 'holistic' conclusions are in any case explicit.

Finally, the importance of the above issues becomes more evident when the strong connection between issues of measurement, temporal scale and aggregation is noticed. Further discussion of fundamental issues related to this connection were already mentioned under the Systems-Ecology perspective in Section 2.3.2.

2.5.4. Classifying Theories and Models

Classifying theories and models can be done in many ways. The choice made in Section 2.3.2 is to some extent ambiguous, and has therefore a limited value. A systems approach as discussed in Section 2.5.2 allows one to classify the theoretical options differently. For instance, Costanza *et al.* (1993) separate between economic, ecological and integrated approaches on the basis of whether they optimise:

(i)   generality: characterised by simple theoretical or conceptual models that aggregate, caricature and exaggerate (e.g., Section 2.4.1);
(ii) precision: characterised by statistical, short-term, partial, static or linear models with one element in much detail; and
(iii) realism: characterised by causal, non-linear, dynamic—evolutionary, and complex models.

These three criteria are usually conflicting, so that a trade-off between them is inevitable. In Table 2.1 the twelve theoretical perspectives of Section 2.3.2 are compared with the latter categorisation. In addition, four other criteria are included in the table, namely whether the approach is of a formal type, whether thermodynamic considerations have an impact, whether short-term dynamics is included (e.g., dynamic materials balance, accumulation, regeneration, delays), and whether long-run dynamics is included (e.g., 'development', structural shifts in sectoral composition, cycles, 'qualitative change', evolutionary patterns). These are of central importance in the context of the discussions in this chapter on thermodynamics (Section 2.2) and dynamic systems (Sections 2.5.2). Note, however, that Table 2.1 must be regarded as an indicative, rather than an absolute representation of the link between theories and methods.

Table 2.1.   Characteristics of Theoretical Perspectives

THEORY	generality	realism	precision	formal rigid	thermo-dynamics	short-term dynamics	long-run change
Equilibrium – Neoclassical	x		x	x		x	
Neoaustrian – Temporal	x	x		x	x	x	x
Ecological – Evolutionary		x			x	x	x
Evolutionary – Technological		x		x	x	x	x
Physico – Economic	x	x		x	x	x	
Biophysical – Energy	x	x		x	x	x	
Systems – Ecological		x	x	x	x	x	
Ecological Engineering		x	x		x	x	
Human Ecology	x	x				x	
Socio-biological	x						x
Historical – Institutional		x					x
Ethical – Utopian	x						x

Concluding this section, interdisciplinary work, which may be the separating line between economic – ecological analysis and environmental economics or ecology, may involve economists or ecologists taking elements or even theories and models from the other discipline and transforming them for their own purposes. This may require activities such as reduction, simplifying or summarising. The results may not always be very acceptable within the original fields of science, since often it is insufficiently realised outside a specific discipline that its theories and scientific results are subject to certain nuances as well as embedded in a historical pattern of refinement of theories. Furthermore – maybe more relevant for economics – science is not very uniform, i.e. there exist many different opinions on the level of theories, empirical applications and policy implications. Integration may for all these reasons not be straightforward. A more fundamental and extensive discussion of this issue, with epistemological considerations, can be found, among others, in Ruth (1993) and Vedeld (1994).

The issue of integration of methods will be picked up again in Sections 4.1.1 and 4.1.2. Some of the theoretical issues will return in the following Chapter. There we will focus on the conceptual, theoretical and analytical aspects of sustainable development, sustainable resource management, environmental functions and processes, and environmental and inter-generational ethics.

3. Sustainable Development and Management

3.1. ENVIRONMENTAL SUSTAINABILITY AND ECONOMIC DEVELOPMENT

There is some confusion about the meaning of sustainable development. This has on the one hand to do with the various interpretations of the terms 'sustainable' and 'development' that have been proposed in the scientific and policy-oriented literature. On the other hand it results from the fact that the terminology is being used for different purposes in scientific and political realms. It seems reasonable to say that 'sustainable' refers to the ultimate natural environmental basis of human activities, interpreted broadly in a socio−economic sense. 'Development' may be restricted mainly to economic development, leaving out broader social−cultural phenomena. Thus, sustainable development is used here as a shorter way of referring to ecologically sustainable economic development. It incorporates the idea of a development pattern such that the natural foundation of economic activities is maintained (see Opschoor, 1987). In addition, the notion of sustainable growth is used to denote the maintained increase of a one-dimensional indicator of growth, such as GNP. This has given rise to old and much repeated questions of both the feasibility and desirability of continuous growth (the 'growth debate'; see also Sections 1.2 and 2.3.1). In a formal sense this has been dealt with in the field of economic growth theory, extending the neoclassical models with non-renewable resources (e.g., Solow, 1974; Hartwick, 1977; Dasgupta and Heal, 1979), and recently also in the context of endogenous growth theory (see Gradus and Smulders, 1993; and Smulders, 1994). Also in view of conditions of environmental sustainability have 'integrated growth' analyses been performed (see Pezzey, 1989; Barbier, 1990; van den Bergh, 1991; van den Bergh and Nijkamp, 1994c).

Two ethical concerns underlie the quest for sustainable development. One is the anthropocentric objective of intergenerational justice, which is explicitly mentioned in the definition of sustainable development by the

WCED (1987), given in Section 1.1. It implies a long-term horizon for planning and evaluation, although the exact choice is arbitrary. If one wants to take account of future generations in a meaningful way, then one should aim for a period at least long enough to include (part of) the next generation after the present one has disappeared (see further Sections 3.4.2 and 3.4.3). The second ethical concern is based on an ecocentric perspective of biodiversity, especially living nature. It reflects a concern for intrinsic values in nature and leads to the objective of preserving diversity, from species to ecosystems (see World Conservation Strategy, WCN/IUCN, 1980[1]). Such an ecocentric approach can be criticised for being obstructive towards development, and therefore possibly socially costly, especially in developing countries. It may be argued that some human problems are so pressing that they deserve more sympathy than bioethical considerations. Besides, the need for preserving biological diversity − both of ecosystems and of species − and a stable environmental quality can be supported on the basis of concern for future generations and (economic) option values, at least when there are potential economic benefits (WCED, 1987). However, this argument fails to protect species and systems that are perceived as having no instrumental value (Opschoor, 1987). An ecocentric standpoint pays attention to all ecosystems and species, while an economic perspective is more limited because it focuses on ecosystems and species related to specific economic sectors or interests (agriculture, medicine, etc.). It is clear in any case that we have to take the multifunctionality of natural environments into account (see further Section 3.3.4). We may conclude this discussion by mentioning the viewpoint that, in order to be transparent, the objective of environmental sustainability must be complemented by criteria on the quality of life and the integrity of ecosystems (de Wit, 1990; Opschoor and van der Ploeg, 1990).

Some of the important previous events and political actions that have paved the way for the emergence of the concept of sustainable development are: (i) the Stockholm Conference on the Human Environment and the establishment of the UNEP in 1972; (ii) the 'Limits to Growth' report (Meadows *et al.*, 1972); (iii) the 'US Global 2000 Report to the President' (Barney, 1980) and its reaction work 'The resourceful earth' (Simon and Kahn, 1984); (iv) the 'World

---

[1] The objectives of this strategy are: prevention of species extinction; preservation of as many varieties as possible of domesticated animals, otherwise economically valuable species, and their wild relatives and habitats (crop and forage plants, timber trees, livestock, animals for aquaculture, microbes and other); and protection of unique and representative ecosystems (WCN/IUCN, 1980).

Conservation Strategy' (WCN/IUCN, 1980); (v) the IIASA report 'Sustainable Development of the Biosphere' (Clark and Munn, 1986); and, of course, (vi) the previously mentioned United Nations report 'Our Common Future' (WCED, 1987). In general, the reactions to the latter report have been very positive, mainly because of its political effect and stimulus for scientific research. As a critique, the possibility of inconsistency between its growth objective and regard for ecological limits has been noted. According to the Brundtland report growth in both LDCs and developed countries is necessary to overcome poverty, an important cause of environmental degradation. Critics argue that continuous growth in the physical size of an economy is not compatible with the maintenance of environmental quality, and conclude that growth in the South must be compensated by a decline in the size of the economies of the North (see Daly, 1990; and Hueting, 1990).

Much of the literature related to sustainable development has a strong bias towards developing countries (see Bartelmus, 1986; Redclift, 1987, Repetto, 1986; Tolba, 1987; Schramm and Warford, 1989; Pearce *et al.*, 1990; and Simonis, 1990). Some authors prefer a historical, ethical or theoretical economic argument to end with proposals for sustainable development (Goodland and Ledec, 1987; Pezzey, 1989; James *et al.*, 1989; Daly and Cobb, 1989; van den Bergh and Nijkamp, 1990; Barbier, 1990;). Various papers show the variety of opinions and approaches that are possible (Collard *et al.*, 1988; Turner, 1988b; Pearce and Redclift, 1988; Archibugi and Nijkamp, 1989; NAVF, 1990; CLTM, 1990 and 1994; Costanza *et al.*, 1991; Gilbert and Braat, 1991; Jansson *et al.*, 1994; van den Bergh and van der Straaten, 1994). Recent contributions are Klaassen and Opschoor (1991), Opschoor and van der Straaten (1993), Pezzey (1992), Perrings (1991), Common and Perrings (1992), Ayres (1993), Goodland (1995) and Dovers (1995).

3.2. THEORETICAL PERSPECTIVES ON SUSTAINABLE DEVELOPMENT

3.2.1. Ecological Conditions or Economic Goals
Making a distinction between economic goals ('outcomes') and ecological conditions ('principles') for sustainable development is critical to resolving the confusion that often prevails in discussions on sustainable development. Sustainable development may be linked to indicators of economic performance such as income, production and welfare, by requiring that they move along non-declining paths over

time. From this goal one may then derive constraints on actions such as investment, resource extraction, waste emission, and land use. Alternatively, the condition may be imposed on the stock of environmental – ecological assets that it is maintained (the interpretation of 'stock' will be discussed subsequently; see also Jansson *et al.*, 1994 and Section 3.3.1). Constraints on environmental impacts caused by human activity can be derived from these stock conditions, giving rise again to constraints on actions such as investment, resource extraction, etc. Though the two approaches may give rise to different constraints, the overall conclusions are similar: permanently decreasing environmental stocks cannot support increasing or even constant levels of physical, economic outputs in the distant future.

A few remarks are in order about the rationality of the sustainable development goal and conditions. The goal clearly expresses concern for the well-being of future generations. The objective of stock maintenance or environmental conservation may be based on concern both for future generations and for nature, in line with the above discussion. Keeping stocks intact, or even increasing them, may be rational when their levels are in agreement with an intergenerational welfare optimisation perspective. Furthermore, one may interpret such stock conditions as based on risk aversion in the face of uncertainty and potential irreversibility of decreases or qualitative changes in the stock. Ecological understanding confirms that both the quality and quantity of certain natural resources and ecosystems are important for their own continuation and for larger scale natural processes (e.g., biogeochemical cycles) (see Clark and Munn, 1986).

The interpretation of the stock condition for sustainable development depends on how a stock is defined, for instance, as a complex of resources, as an aggregate and abstract concept, or as a single explicit resource. Furthermore, one may refer to the physical size or the economic value or productivity. Pezzey (1989) mentions maintenance of the effective resource base in terms of a constant real price index for virgin materials (derived from Page, 1977) or a constant economic productivity of the whole resource base by balancing resource depletion with capital accumulation and technical progress (from Howe, 1979). The conservation objective can also be specified as maintaining three general functions, namely the formation of useful materials, the storage and assimilation of waste and pollution, and the generation of amenity services. This refers to more qualitative notions of regenerative and assimilative capacities, and environmental quality, respectively. The constraints following from such a conservation objective on economic activities are that resource extraction does not exceed natural regeneration and emitted waste is kept below the assimilative capacity. 'Sustainable use' can be employed to denote a strategy that aims to maintain the renewable resource base, which has the two mentioned implications for extraction and waste emission. However, usually 'sustainable use' refers to extraction only (see, e.g., Clark, 1976). No direct implications follow from the conservation objective for land use and investment. In Section 3.3.3 more attention will be given to the notion of sustainable use of natural resources.

In relation to the stock conditions for sustainable development, a distinction has been made between strong and weak sustainable development (see, e.g., Pezzey, 1989). Two interpretations are possible here. The first of these states that strong sustainability refers to non-decreasing patterns of environmental and resource stocks over time. Weak sustainability allows them to decrease temporarily so long as they return to their initial levels (see Pearce *et al.*, 1990). The second interpretation is based on characteristics related to substitution between and complementarity of different types of environmental and resource stocks. Strong sustainability requires then that each relevant natural stock is kept in its original state, while weak sustainability requires only maintenance of an aggregate measure (e.g., a sum) of all stocks, including non-environmental capital assets. In the latter case single stocks may decrease and even be exhausted, so long as the aggregate condition is being satisfied all the time. Based on this latter notion is the idea of compensation, which states that a loss in one element of the natural environment must be compensated for by an addition somewhere else (see Klaassen and Botterweg, 1976). Taking the two interpretations together, the most stringent condition states that each type of stock is maintained at each point in time. The weakest form requires only that the sum of all stocks must return to its original value at some future time.

Non-renewable resources such as stocks of fossil fuels and ores provide a special problem in the discussion of intergenerational equity and natural resources. While for renewable resources maintenance of stocks is a legitimate objective, for non-renewables the basic question is how much resources should be left available to future generations. Usually, this question is answered by taking the standard of living as a criterion for intergenerational comparison, and assuming that resource materials, man-made capital and technological knowledge are substitutable for one another in production (see, e.g., Dasgupta and Heal, 1979). The notion of stock maintenance can then be interpreted broadly, namely by considering a suitable stock that includes both natural and man-made capital (i.e., weak sustainability). This is an interpretation by Solow (1986) of the well-known Hartwick rule, which is stated as: 'the investment of current exhaustible resource returns in reproducible capital implies per capita consumption constant' (Hartwick, 1977; for a generalization, see Hamilton, 1993). Consumption can thus be regarded as the interest on the suitable capital stock. A criticism on these type of analyses is that they disregard material balance conditions, so that they may mix monetary with physical variables without providing for correct transformations between the two dimensions. For a more complete discussion on complementarity of and substitution between man-made capital and natural resources, as well as for interpretations of the Hartwick results, one may consult Pearce *et al.* (1990) or Pearce and Turner (1990).

A complex choice problem of intertemporal welfare optimisation may result from combining the objective of intertemporal economic efficiency with a description of the dynamics of the economic and natural systems. The discussion above indicates that sustainable development implies the addition of constraints to this general economic evaluation problem, for both the ecological goal approach and the economic conditions approaches. Conditions would be defined by the environmental use space, comprising a generalised set of constraints on resource extraction, waste emission and other environmental stress factors, based on natural resource availability as well as natural regeneration and assimilation. Furthermore, it is noteworthy that many futures may be sustainable, while only a limited number can be optimally sustainable − in the sense of some intergenerational criterion. The constraints will then have to be derived from a combination of ethical and physical−ecological considerations. Finally, one may establish behavioural feedback mechanisms based on these constraints that adjust the direction and pace of economic processes to meet or approximate sustainable development conditions (see Sections 2.4.1 and 6.5).

3.2.2. Alternative Theoretical Perspectives

Many other perspectives on sustainable development than discusssed above are possible. Definitions of sustainable development abound. Some attempts show a systematic approach to construct a definition or framework (e.g., Brown *et al.*, 1987; Ekins, 1994) or to provide a collection of different viewpoints (see the Appendix in Pezzey, 1989; it contains a large number of definitions of sustainable development by economists, ecologists and others). Based on the twelve theoretical perspectives of Section 2.3.2, the statements and keywords listed in Table 3.1 indicate some alternative characterisations or interpretations of sustainable development. They are not necessarily conflicting, although some may be, and offer an interesting combination of viewpoints.

Table 3.1. Theoretical Perspectives on Sustainable Development

Theory	Characterisation of sustainable development
Equilibrium – Neoclassical	welfare non-decreasing (anthropocentric); sustainable growth based on technology and substitution; optimising environmental externalities; maintaining the aggregate stock of natural and economic capital; individual objectives prevail over social goals; policy needed when individual objectives conflict; long-run policy based on market solutions;
Neoaustrian – Temporal	teleological sequence of conscious and goal-oriented adaptation; preventing irreversible patterns; maintaining organisation level (negentropy) in economic system; optimising dynamic process of extraction, production, consumption, recycling and waste treatment;
Ecological – Evolutionary	maintaining resilience of natural systems, allowing for fluctuation and cycles (regular destruction); learning from uncertainty in natural processes; no domination of foodchains by humans; fostering genetic/ biotic/ ecosystem diversity; balanced nutrient flows in ecosystems;
Evolutionary – Technological	maintaining co-evolutionary adaptive capacity in terms of knowledge and technology to react to uncertainties; fostering economic diversity of actors, sectors and technologies;
Physico – Economic	restrictions on materials and energy flows in/out the economy; industrial metabolism based on materials – product chain policy: integrated waste treatment, abatement, recycling, and product development;
Biophysical – Energy	a steady state with minimum materials and energy throughput; maintaining physical and biological stocks, and biodiversity; transition to energy systems with minimum pollutive effects;
Systems – Ecological	controlling direct and indirect human effects on ecosystems; balance between material inputs and outputs to human systems; minimum stress factors on ecosystems, both local and global;
Ecological Engineering	Integration of human benefits and environmental quality and functions by manipulation of ecosystems; design and improvement of engineering solutions on the boundary of economics, technology and ecosystems; utilising resilience, self-organisation, self-regulation and functions of natural systems for human purposes;
Human Ecology	remain within the carrying capacity (logistic growth); limited scale of economy and population; consumption oriented toward basic needs; occupy a modest place in the ecosystem foodweb and the biosphere; always consider multiple effects of human actions, in space and time;
Socio-biological	maintain cultural and social system of interactions with ecosystems; respect for nature integrated in culture; survival of group important;
Historical – Institutional	equal attention interests of nature, sectors and future generations; integrating institutional arrangements for economic and environmental policy; creating institutional long-run support for nature's interests; holistic instead of partial solutions, based on a hierarchy of values;
Ethical – Utopian	new individual value systems (respect for nature and future generations, basic needs fulfilment) and new social objectives (steady state); balance attention for efficiency, distribution and scale; strive for small-scale activities and control of 'side-effects' ('small is beautiful'); long-run policy based on changing values and encouraging citizen (altruistic) as opposed to individual (egoistic) behaviour;

It would seem that especially the Equilibrium—Neoclassical, Neo-austrian—Temporal and Evolutionary—Technological focus on a sustainable development leading to a technologically advanced economy. As opposed to this, a society less concerned with material welfare seems to be supported — at least implicitly — by the Human—Ecology, Socio-biological, Historical—Institutional and Ethical—Utopian perspectives. Associated with such visions of a 'final techno-socio-economic structure' are ideas about the desirability and possibility of economic growth, the type of environmental management (exploitation, conservation, preservation), value systems (basic needs, anthropocentric, intergenerational justice, ecocentric), organisation of life (work, home, recreation, social interaction), and optimistic or pessimistic beliefs about 'nature's resilience' (ecological disaster, demographic patterns, lasting poverty).

The type of sustainability adopted (weak/strong; see previous section) also differs between the various perspectives. The Equilibrium—Neoclassical, for instance, seems to be the closest to adopting 'weak sustainability', allowing for substitutions, such that functions or services rather than specific systems or processes are preserved. Especially the Ecological—Evolutionary, Human Ecology and Ethical—Utopian perspectives would argue for a strong interpretation of sustainability. Uncertainty, irreversibility and instability are implicit in the table. The approaches to such issues are quite diverse. In the Equilibrium—Neo-classical framework, for instance, this may be arranged in terms of adjusted cost-benefit analysis such as implemented in the Krutilla—Fisher algorithm (see, e.g., Porter, 1982). Ecological approaches would focus on resilience characteristics of ecosystems, and on relationships with complexity. Modern theories of dynamic systems would lead to chaos-type of modelling.

Finally, sustainable development policies are also mentioned in the table. It is clear that these should be able to deal with a long-term horizon, about which there may also be disagreement between the various perspectives, i.e. in terms of orientations on technological solutions, changes in preferences, ethics and values, market solutions or direct regulation and legislation. Differences in opinions on this depend much on whether sustainable development is regarded as not far away — requiring only marginal changes, and leading to a similar economy as exists now — or whether it is difficult to reach — and critically depends on structural and drastic changes, while it will go along with an entirely different type of social-economic system. Whatever one believes, the latter can never be excluded as a reasonable possibility. This is also made clear in the following section.

3.2.3. Barriers to Sustainable Development

It is possible to come up with a number of barriers to the realisation of sustainable development. First, there are problems related to the control of the economic—environmental system (see, e.g., Perrings, 1991) and the effectiveness of policies and instruments to keep economic activities within ecological constraints. Realisation of sustainable development depends upon a permanent correction of the market system, instead of only a temporary policy to overcome a transitional period. Providing for the 'right' and permanent corrections is difficult, because of the absence of future markets, uncertainty about values of environmental services, and the public goods and common property character underlying many environmental problems. Second, many political obstacles exist that are related to, for instance, conflicting opinions and the necessity of compromises in the political arena, the prevalence of short-term over long-term objectives, and the absence of powerful political institutions to deal with international economic—environmental issues. Third, there are certain structural processes that give rise to environmental problems. Very important in this respect are economic growth and an increase in distance between causation and effects of environmental change (see Opschoor and van der Ploeg, 1990). Growth is driven by aspirations of individuals, competition between private firms, government policies, technological progress, international differences in welfare (and environmental preferences), etc. The increase in distance, both in time and space, between decisions made and negative environmental effects can often be traced back to the trends of internationalisation and the increasing scale of economic activities. As a last barrier we mention the differing opinions about the ethical foundation of sustainable development, namely whether separate concern for the natural environment is necessary, or whether a focus on economic benefits and future generations is sufficient. This could be an obstacle to international agreements on environmental policies.

3.3. ENVIRONMENTAL FUNCTIONS, SUSTAINABLE AND MULTIPLE USE

3.3.1. Natural Resources

Those environmental components that are subjected to use are referred to loosely as natural resources. In the past, natural resources focused on environmental components from which environmental goods (or raw materials) could be produced for entry into economic processes: such use can be referred to as extractive or quantitative in that a temporary or permanent reduction in some environmental component is achieved. Non-extractive or qualitative use of the environment leaves nature altered; for example, the use of water and air to remove and process wastes, the operation of the hydrological cycle with flood control and provision of drinking water, the pollination of crops (e.g., Folke and Kåberger, 1991a). The use of these services by human societies has gained increased attention in recent decades (e.g., van der Ploeg, 1990). As a result, larger and more complex environmental components such as ecosystems may be viewed as natural resources.

Man's technological development is allowing him a greater influence over natural processes. More environmental components are coming under his control. This is greatest with individual species, such as livestock, plantation forest species, and cultured marine species, which, in being domesticated, have become more dependent on man than nature for their distribution and abundance. Such entities are considered here as economic commodities rather than natural resources. 'Natural resources' may then be defined as 'environmental components which provide goods and services in support of socio-economic activities, and which are dependent for their distribution and abundance on natural (physical, biological, ecological, etc.) processes'.

This definition distinguishes natural resources from the environmental functions which they provide; the former are essentially stocks, while the latter are flows of goods and services. As stocks, natural resources can also be considered as natural capital (Folke and Kåberger, 1991b; Jansson *et al.*, 1994). Two types of natural capital are identified. Renewable natural capital is active and uses solar energy for self-maintenance or renewal; it can be harvested to yield goods but may also yield a flow of services. Nonrenewable natural capital is inactive, yielding no goods or services until extracted, and not capable of self-renewal. Natural capital is required to make man-made capital via economic activity, but it also provides life-support functions which cannot be provided by man-made capital. Natural capital contrasts to man-made capital in often being multifunctional while man-made capital contrasts to natural capital in its generation of pollution.

3.3.2. Environmental Functions and Processes

De Groot, (1992) considers 'functions of the natural environment' as offering a concept for dealing with ecological and other environmental processes from an anthropocentric perspective. A distinction is made between extractive and non-extractive use of the environment. Further specification of environmental functions considers whether or not use is accompanied by a flow of commodities. Three types of flows can be distinguished: from the environment and into the economy (positive flow) and corresponding to extractive or quantitative use; from the economy back to the environment (negative flow); and no flow at all. Figure 3.1 adopts this approach and leads to the following types of environmental functions which are discussed further below:

(i)   production of renewable and nonrenewable stocks and of habitat;
(ii) receiver and purification functions;
(iii) carrier functions;
(iv) information functions.

The first environmental function is production − the environment produces stocks which are used to generate a positive flow of commodities, and it produces a habitat in which human societies can operate − and may be correlated to positive commodity flows. Nonrenewable resource stocks are the result of past production activities; their quantities are finite in that there is no 'reproduction' or regeneration. Regeneration is the primary characteristic of the two types of renewable stocks. The regeneration of renewable natural resource stocks is more dependent on ecological processes such as growth, reproduction and biogeochemical cycling than on man's control or intervention. Renewable man-made stocks are also subject to these ecological processes but man exerts a much greater degree of control over their abundance and distribution. The difference between these two renewable stocks is demonstrated by: natural versus seeded pastures; naturally-occurring populations of fish versus aquacultured populations; wild populations of herbivores versus domesticated livestock; natural forests versus plantations; free-flowing water versus impoundments.

The environment also provides space for human activities. Depending on the kind of use to be made (e.g., infrastructure such as roads and ports, agricultural activities, residential and urban development), use of space may involve the removal of natural habitat and may also trigger a 'one-off' positive flow of commodities as in the case, for example, of strip mining.

The receiver and purification function corresponds to non-extractive use and negative commodity flows. Human societies release a variety of substances and organisms (e.g., pathogens in human waste, species for biological control) into the environment. The release of wastes and surpluses and the accidental release of substances are contrasted to releases associated with the control of environmental performance. Examples of the latter are the use of fertilizers to enhance the service

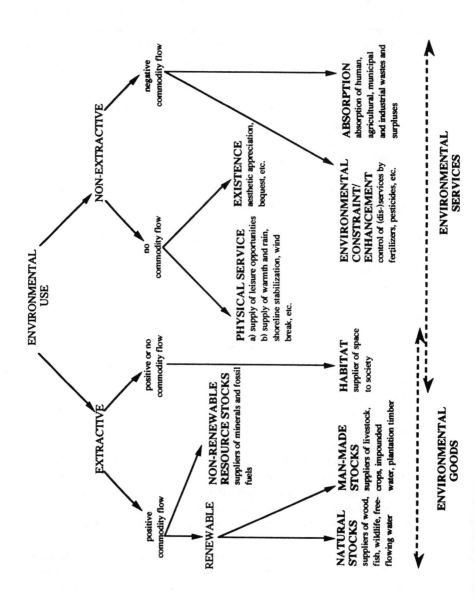

Figure 3.1. A classification of environmental use.

provided by soils in the production of crops and pasture, the release of pesticides in an attempt to prevent or reduce the environmental disservice of pest species, and the fertilisation of oil spills with oil-degrading bacteria in an attempt to accelerate the biodegradation process. These activities also lead to environmental surpluses.

Wastes, surpluses and accidentally released substances are dealt with by the environment in one of two ways: (i) they may be processed and recycled within and between ecosystems; and (ii) they may be reallocated across various environmental components, and in some of these they may accumulate. Purification and absorption functions differ in that ecological (including physiological) processes exist in the former for breakdown and reuse, but not in the latter. Substances in the former category would include animal wastes and carbon dioxide. Within limits, the environment can receive, process and recycle them without any negative effects; in some cases, such as nutrient emissions into oligotrophic (nutrient-poor) environments, there may even be a positive effect. The presence of the ecological processes means that one can talk of the self-purifying capacity of the environment. However, this capacity is constrained: firstly by environmental transportation mechanisms which carry a substance from the point of its release to the environmental component which will be responsible for its breakdown; and secondly by thresholds which, if exceeded, will induce negative effects and ecosystem change. Again using the example of nutrient emissions, the residence time for substances in estuaries is often long due to the intermixing of marine and riverine flows, and so estuaries may bear a greater burden for processing nutrient loads than adjacent marine or freshwater ecosystems; continued nutrient-enrichment of even oligotrophic environments may ultimately produce eutrophic conditions with algal blooms, oxygen shortfalls, and changes in species abundance and composition.

Substances in the category (ii) are subject to limited processing by the environment. Initially they may diluted and dispersed, but they will ultimately accumulate in some environmental component. This is the case for persistent toxic micropollutants (heavy metals, PCBs, dioxin, pesticide residues). Biological activity and associated physical conditions (e.g., aerobic or anaerobic) determine the chemical form of many of these substances and subsequently their mobility between environmental media, their uptake by organisms and even their toxicity. In the absence of uptake, accumulation will occur in an environmental medium such as soil or sediments. In the presence of uptake but absence of metabolic processes for subsequent breakdown and/or excretion, these substances will move through successive trophic levels in food chains to accumulate in higher order predators. For these substances there is no self-purification by the environment and any release leads to accumulation. There are no thresholds with regards to release, only thresholds for subsequent toxic effects.

The term 'sink' is often used in conjunction with the receiving function of the environment, and serves to identify the environmental component(s) where the burden of disposal lies — estuaries in the nutrient example above; sediments, predators and even their ecosystems in the case of persistent micropollutants.

The carrier and information functions are not associated with a commodity flow. The former term is used to describe physical support which the environment provides society. Three types of carrier functions can be identified:

(i)   the supply of natural environments for leisure and recreation;
(ii) environmental stabilisation and regulation;
(iii) communication.

The first function is relatively straightforward. Examples of the second include: plants which bind sediments and inhibit erosion; mangroves and seagrasses which stabilise coastline by dissipating the energy of currents, waves and winds; climate regulation; and, the ozone layer which filters out harmful ultraviolet radiation. Finally, the environment offers both means and constraints to communication between societies for trade and other purposes; river systems, such as the Rhine and the Danube, have long been major channels of communication between human societies; winds as used by sailing vessels and oceanic currents as used by all shipping also facilitate communication; geographical barriers such as mountains and treacherous waters as well as deserts and other inhospitable environments constrain this communication.

The latter function is oriented more towards human psychological and intellectual needs. The knowledge that certain species, ecosystems and/or landscapes exist may provide a psychological benefit to humans; the economics literature refers to 'existence value', and the need for humans to have this value available to future generations is referred to as 'bequest value' (e.g., Pearce and Turner, 1990). All of these functions, together, comprise the life support function of the environment.

3.3.3. Sustainable Use

An older concept than 'sustainable development' is 'sustainable use' of natural resources. The link between the two concepts is 'ecological sustainability'. This was, in conjunction with economic development, highlighted by WCN/IUCN (1980) and WCED (1986). By ecological sustainability we mean: the maintenance and/or prolongation of socially valuable environmental components, processes and systems. It implies sustainable use, i.e. rates and intensities of environmental use which do not lead to long-term or irreversible reductions in the environment's capacity for resource regeneration and waste absorption.

Sustainable use has its roots in the concept and theory of sustainable yield, initiated early in this century by population biologists (see Lotka, 1925; Volterra, 1931; May, 1976). The theory of sustainable yield has been applied to the harvesting of simple biotic (e.g., fish) and cycling abiotic (e.g., groundwater) resource stocks. If regeneration of a natural resource exceeds its loss, then some annual increment is available for harvesting. Harvesting is sustainable and can continue indefinitely if it does not exceed this increment. The theory has a number of shortcomings (e.g., Larkin, 1977) which the concept of sustainable use attempts to avoid. Instead of focusing only on the extractive use of homogeneous resource stocks, sustainable use acknowledges the full range of environmental functions. It also considers larger and more complex environmental entities; for example, one could talk of the sustainable use of the North Sea. Instead of treating the resource stock as if it were in isolation from the rest of its ecosystem and its environment, interactions among the various hierarchies of ecosystems are explicitly taken into account, as is the role of the physical environment and its inherent variability in influencing the size of resource stocks; for example, the sustainable use of rangelands would consider competition (between woody and herbaceous species, livestock and wildlife) and the episodic occurrence of drought.

Human systems encroach on natural resource systems in a variety of ways which may affect sustainable use. Man's impacts on the environment, and particularly those which are spatially or temporally displaced, are explicitly addressed by the concept of sustainable use; for example, mangrove deforestation may affect offshore commercial stocks by removing nursery habitats, the widespread application of fertilizers may affect the sustainable use of surface water bodies and of groundwater stocks, and environmental contamination may adversely affect the regenerative capacity of natural resource stocks and lead to direct economic impacts.

The ultimate test for sustainable use is the ex post observation of preserved resource quantity and quality. This contrasts with sustainable yield where the maintenance of yield levels is of primary concern and the maintenance of stock quantity of secondary concern, while the maintenance of stock quality is not considered at all (Larkin, 1977).

The consequences of unsustainable use can be severe. This can be illustrated by the crash of the anchoveta fishery which caused major disruption of Peru's economy in the early 1970s (Glantz and Thompson, 1981). Estimates of the maximum sustainable yield did not suggest that the catch was excessive, but omitted two factors: natural predation on the anchoveta by guano-producing seabirds, and the oceanographic phenomenon known as El Niño which could radically alter the anchoveta's physical environment. Economic factors were also ignored, such as the role of the fishing fleet, particularly its increase in capacity and efficiency, and pressures on individual fishermen to repay debts. Interactions with other industries were ignored, such as the guano industry which was dependent on the seabirds which in turn depended on the anchoveta. Subsequent recovery of the anchoveta stock after the crash was slow, possibly hampered by ecological factors such as a shift in competitive balances favouring sardines and horse mackerel. Recovery of the stock has occurred, at least to a level which has permitted a resumption of fishing. However, the once lucrative market for the anchoveta industry — feedlot fodder — has largely been lost.

The nature and complexity of ecosystems, the variety of goods and services demanded or functions supplied, and the benefits and costs arising from use introduce trade-offs among alternative uses, alternative patterns of use, and alternative development paths. Making such trade-offs requires consideration of societal and individual welfare, as well as the welfare of future generations. Ecological sustainability and sustainable use are obviously a prerequisite or necessary condition for sustainable development at the global scale. However, it may not be the only condition since broader issues of natural balances could also be considered. Not only the uses (functions) of the environment should be kept intact but also other environmental characteristics.

3.3.4. Multiple Use

Multiple use is the simultaneous use of natural resources by multiple users or by a single user with multiple (social and economic) objectives. The following forms of multiple use can be distinguished:

(i) A single resource population is used in one particular way by more than one user. Example: An open access natural forest with many people cutting firewood or collecting leaf litter.

(ii) A single resource population is utilised in a number of different ways. Example: A forest stand is used, consumptively, by harvesting (part of the) stand and in a non-consumptive manner by biologists studying and recreationists enjoying the trees.

(iii) Several users using different resource populations within a single resource ecosystem, either
  (a) for the same purpose, or
  (b) for different purposes.
  Example: In a forest ecosystem, timber producers are harvesting several stands, while recreationists collect berries and fungi in adjacent stands and biologists study breeding birds in yet another stand. It is possible then that the resource populations are mutually dependent, for instance through foodchain or micro-climatic relationships. The impact of one particular user on his resource population may then be transferred to the resource population of another user.
(iv) The use of common property systems such as air, rivers and groundwater for purposes such as waste disposal, while these systems are essential to the functioning of private property resource ecosystems. Example: the use of air masses to absorb and carry off industrial waste products over a forest ecosystem used for timber production.

Multiple use of renewable resource systems is an issue which is of interest in attempts to expand the number of options and the physical basis for sustainable economic development, but at the same time an issue about which very little is known in a quantitative sense (see van der Ploeg, 1990; Braat, 1992). One of the main challenges for resource managers is therefore the resolution of multiple use conflicts. The central issue is: what is the optimal sustainable combination of the different forms and intensities of use? To address this question properly both economic aspects (e.g., demand, competition between users) and ecological aspects (e.g., supply rates, competition between producers) must be analysed.

Exclusive single purpose land use for a single user does probably not exist at any scale of interest. In large countries such as the United States and Canada large parts of terrestrial renewable resource systems (groundwater aquifers, soils, marshes, savannas, forests) are however used by a single dominant user for a single dominant purpose. In most countries in North-Western Europe, which are all much smaller than the two mentioned above, the common situation is, however, that ecosystems are used in several ways at the same time by a number of different users. This almost always leads to conflicts of interest and damage to the environment. The consequences range from suboptimal use, due to unregulated access, to degradation of recourse systems due to limited knowledge of the ecological processes involved (see, e.g., Hardin, 1968).

In North-Western Europe, the land has historically been used in several ways at the same time by a number of different users. The United States multiple use has been an explicit objective in forestry since the Multiple Use—Sustainable Yield Act. Compartmentalisation has been the major policy in reducing multiple use conflicts. In the Netherlands, multiple use has only recently become an official forest policy objective.

Compared to single use situations, the economics of multiple use situations are a lot more complicated (see Bowes and Krutilla, 1985; Howe, 1979). Analysing cost and utility aspects of resource management belongs to the realm of resource economics. The criteria used to determine utility (or 'function performance') levels may range from strictly monetary benefit—cost rations to species diversity and embodied energy. The choice depends on the way the manager prefers to evaluate the total and individual user's utility and what type of information he prefers to the base trade-offs on. The price mechanism is considered an effective instrument for allocation if efficiency is the only criterion considered; otherwise regulation is necessary. If in a multiple use situation each of the individual users receives less benefits than in comparable single use situations, but can sustain the flow of benefits, the uses are called competitive but compatible. Otherwise they are called incompatible.

Most economic studies of resource use involve a single resource population, and one user, usually harvesting the resources. The most common situation in reality can however be more adequately described as a complex network of relationships between users and resources. In the Netherlands, almost all ecosystems on sandy soils are simultaneously used for biotic production (timber, crops or grass), aquifer recharge, outdoor recreation and conservation of wildlife.

The professional literature on the economics of multiple use is scarce, and most of it deals with theoretical models and hypothetical examples. Sandstrom (1989) identifies a number of challenges for economists in this area (see also Bower and Krutilla, 1985; and Mendoza, 1988).

The analysis and prediction of forest ecosystem performance levels under various combinations of use, which involve removal of ecosystem components, trampling, destruction, and disturbance, are part of the realm of applied resource ecology. Given that different users appreciate or consume different parts and aspects of a forest ecosystem, it follows that a resource regenerative system approach in multiple use management implies the analysis of a number of (most likely partially overlapping) regenerative systems.

Conceptual, qualitative and verbal models of compatibility and competition in multiple use situations are available (van der Maarel and

Dauvellier, 1978; Arntzen and Braat, 1983; de Groot, 1992; van der Ploeg, 1990). Empirical studies about the mechanisms of interactions between the various forms of use are however rather scarce (see van der Ploeg, 1990; Braat, 1992; and Chapter 8).

Multiple use resource management can be viewed as a multi-objective optimisation problem, which can be divided into a number of separate problems of maximisation of a single objective, with the other objectives constituting the constraints approached as tentative minimum values (see Section 5.2.2). By repeating this formulation process a solution space can be defined in terms of minimum requirements of resource ecosystem structure and functioning.

In principle a solution can be arrived at in two ways:

(i) An optimal ecosystem structure and process, which serves all users at once, in a homogeneous spatial structure, the composition of which has been calculated from the requirements of each of the users.

(ii) A spatial mosaic of sites, composed of segregated spatial units each maximising a single objective, but together being multi-purpose.

However, as most resource ecosystems are dynamic systems, the solution for one period may not be optimal for a later period. This holds for both approaches. The first approach is likely to produce unsatisfactory results for consumptive users, as the restrictions resulting from conservation (i.e. non-consumptive use) requirements are rather limiting as to harvesting. In the second approach the values of each of the sites for each of the users will change through time.

3.4. NATURE, FUTURE GENERATIONS AND ETHICAL CONSIDERATIONS

3.4.1. Ethical Roots of Sustainable Development

As has already been stated in Section 3.1, there are two ethical dimensions relevant to the notion of sustainable development. One is the anthropocentric dimension of intergenerational justice. The other one is the ecocentric dimension of concern for 'Nature'. The difference between the two positions can be regarded in terms of a trade-off between people now and in the future, and between people and other species, respectively. Pearce and Turner (1990, Chapter 15) stress the link between 'value' and ethics. An assigned value derives from interactions between a subject (that holds and/or assigns values) and an object (to be valued); a subject has preferences (held values) which give rise to assigned values; these may be distinguished by use, option, and existence values. Value systems emphasising ethical concern for (elements or parts of) the natural environment evolve more from the perception of additional values than those that derive from private preferences. Possible additional values can relate to public preferences or intrinsic (inherent) values of nature. People capture some of the intrinsic value by expressing preference on behalf of species and habitats through existence values (see Pearce and Turner, 1990).

Why should we show an interest in the well-being of future generations apart from those with which we have a family tie? Such an attitude is motivated by a sense of solidarity with our fellow men, the awareness of being part of one humanity. One may argue that the temporal distance between us and members of future generations is not very different from the spatial and social distance between us and other members of the present generation, for whom we show (little) concern. Hilhorst (1987) states that the manageability of our future implies that it becomes a moral issue (and not a matter of metaphysics). Manageability must be understood as the conscious guidance of our actions which − by way of causality − will always influence the future, irrespective of whether or not the outcome meets the objectives. We may thus regard future generations as our liability already because we create their (potential) existence. From such a point of view, they should get even more attention than our contemporaries, for whose existence we do not bear any responsibility (see Hilhorst, 1987; Maclean and Brown, 1983). This responsibility is also felt in the interest shown by each generation in the next, which is the result of parental concerns and overlapping generations. Still, it seems that the concern for our offspring is of another moral category than concern for generations in future time that we are separated from by time. That either category of concern does not guarantee prosperity for future generations is shown in Arrow (1973a and b) Dasgupta (1974), Solow (1974), and Norton (1989), depending much upon the social welfare function which can be regarded as an implicit preference for investment (i.e. foregone consumption).

An alternative ethical underpinning of sustainable development exists, namely a non-anthropocentric ethic (or an 'interspecies ethic'). This may arise from an extension of moral consideration to non-human individual beings, dependent on whether they satisfy certain characteristics; these may range from 'fulfilling reciprocal duties', 'having the capacity to suffer' (moral sentience), 'having interests', or 'being alive'. Moral considerations may result in acknowledging natural or basic rights. In general, moral concern for nature may derive from regarding nature and man/culture in a partnership, or as both having their own goals (Gaia; see Lovelock, 1979), or as not separated at all ('Deep Ecology'); spiritual, aesthetical, and physical origins of moral concern for nature have been mentioned as well. An environmental ethic may extend to populations and systems rather than only to individuals. The radical 'Deep (as opposed to shallow) Ecology' movement (Devall and Sessions, 1984) can be regarded as showing the most extreme of all positions since it supports equal rights for all species ('bio-egalitarianism') and considers it essential that solutions to environmental problems are approached by a broader, longer-term and sceptical view on the source of these problems. Glasser (1995) gives a quite complete account of all the work of Naess who proposed this idea (Naess, 1973), and also develops implications for policy.

3.4.2. Intergenerational Equity

Three main ethical systems may provide a framework for an intergenerational comparison: utilitarianism, libertarianism, and contractualism [2,3] (see, e.g., Kneese and Schulze, 1985). In classical utilitarianism the evaluation of human actions takes place by checking whether the consequences are good or bad on the whole, i.e., all individuals having been taken into consideration. The criterion used for this is the sum of individual utilities, each representing the amount of net individual happiness. State x is regarded as being better than state y if for x the value of this criterion exceeds that for y. With such a criterion trade-offs can be made between qualitative and quantitative aspects, i.e., the quality of an individual's life and the population level. Apart from discounting in the utilitarian framework, individuals in future generations are, in principle, as important as those in the present generation. Average utilitarianism aims at maximising average utility, which may give rise to a different optimum population level. Both systems rely on the existence

---

[2] A basic difference between these systems is related to their ethical starting point: teleological or deontological. The first implies that the goodness (morality) of an action is determined by the goal that is strived for. The second characterizes a good action as one which itself satisfies certain conditions (such as universality). Of the three systems mentioned, only the last one is deontological.

[3] Some 'minor' theories are mentioned by Wright (1988), e.g., (natural) rights, maximizing intrisic values, satisfying needs rather than maximizing net happiness, an extension of the Lockean standard for ownership, equal opportunity, and membership in our moral community.

of a cardinal utility function that admits interpersonal comparability of utility units. In an extended libertarian or Paretian system, increases in the welfare of one generation are judged positively as long as another one is not made worse off. This Pareto efficiency criterion only allows for an incomplete ranking of alternative intergenerational distributions. Contractualism regards social moral decision-making as based on an agreement between individuals in a society, i.e., a social contract. The most widely known contractual theory is proposed by Rawls (1972). He sets up a hypothetical situation in which individuals of a society have to agree to principles of justice 'behind a veil of ignorance', i.e., having no knowledge of their effective place in society, possession of abilities and assets, etc. The principle agreed upon in such a 'fair situation' is likely to be the 'maximin principle'. This aims at maximising the position of the worst-off individual. Opinions differ however as to whether this system can be extended to intergenerational comparisons (see, e.g., Arrow 1973a and b; Solow, 1974; Opschoor, 1987; Pearce and Turner, 1990). If it is extended, the implication is that each generation should determine how much to invest and how much to save for the next generation, on the basis of the maximin procedure (see Solow, 1974). The practical difficulty in an intergenerational setting is, however, that the present generation not only knows its place in society (and hence is not behind a veil of ignorance) but also cannot even conceive of being placed behind an intergenerational veil. It thus is fully aware of the fundamental asymmetry in position *vis-à-vis* future generations, and of the power in terms of access to resources that this entails (see Opschoor, 1987). This means that although one may perform an individual thought experiment of the kind proposed by Rawls, it will be impossible to do the same on the level of the present generation, and thus influence the public opinion. All these ethical systems use the concept of welfare of a generation, based on preferences with regard to economic output, natural environment, pollution, etc. The main problem that arises is that we do not know the preferences of future generations, but only their basic needs. The preferences may be highly influenced by economic, technological and environmental changes. Therefore, simple constraints on basic needs, or non-decreasing levels of economic and environmental assets, seem to offer a more realistic perspective than optimising a function based on the welfare of many generations, or requiring non-decreasing levels of welfare over generations.

Finally, it is noted that the discussion on sustainability ethics has also lead to criticism on traditional valuation methodologies. Blamey and Common (1994), for instance, distinguish between four bases for deciding about social action required to modify the operation of market forces in natural asset management, which they summarise as: efficiency, equity, ecological and philosophical schools. They argue that pseudo market valuation of the contingent valuation type has been based on the efficiency school, and propose an alternative approach based on the philosophical school. For this reason they adapt the hypothesis of Sagoff (1988) about the citizen – consumer distinction, where people are supposed to have a choice in acting as an egoist consumer or as an altruistic citizen. The latter seems especially relevant for environmental issues beyond those which may be cast in the neoclassical externality framework, in particular global and long-term (sustainability) issues.

3.4.3. Discounting and Future Generations

The relationship between future generations and discounting has to be addressed here since it is a persistent issue in the discussions of intergenerational equity (see for instance Lind, 1982). Ethical objections against high or positive discount rates have focused on effects (see Opschoor 1987): shifting costs to later generations, and fewer incentives for long-term projects (especially environmentally favourable projects). However, a third consequence of low discount rates is a low development as a result of little investment in general. This may be environmentally beneficial because of its negative impact upon the demand for resources and emission of residuals (see Markandya and Pearce, 1988). So here the intergenerational equity and environmental objectives do not seem to completely agree.[4]

Discounting can only be applied if an additive, separable utility function is the criterion for multigenerational evaluation (benefit – cost analysis in an operational context). Therefore classical utilitarianism is at the basis of discounting. Discounting cannot be combined with a minimax criterion or social welfare functions with nonlinear or interaction components.

The basis for choosing a social discount rate has three dimensions: time preference, investment opportunities and uncertainty considerations. If a social rate of time preference (consumption rate of interest) and a social opportunity cost rate can be determined, the social rate of discount can be derived as a weighted average of them, adjusted for risk by adding a 'social risk premium'. Two problems then arise. First, it is not

---

[4] Furthermore, if the total social outcome of private and social investments is evaluated by using a social rate of discount, a consistency problem may arise, as private investors will usually base their decisions on project evaluation on market rates of interest. Only for specific government projects a social rate may be used. Therefore, it is difficult to apply a social discount rate beyond the single project level.

evident how a specific choice of weights should be justified. Second, the estimation of the social time preference rate, the social opportunity cost rate, and the social risk premium poses some conceptual and practical difficulties.

The social time preference can be assumed irrelevant, when a community is not seen as showing impatience. Then individual pure time preferences are regarded as not transferable to communities. Furthermore, conceptually there is a difference between discounting over relatively short periods (smaller than the average life-time) and over multigenerational time periods.[5] However, one may state that expected growth rates in consumption should be taken into consideration, as well as elasticity of the marginal utility of consumption, so that a positive time preference may result.

The opportunity cost will tend to be equal to the time preference rate in a perfect market, i.e. the market interest rate. This is one reason for concentrating on opportunity costs. A reason for focusing on the opportunity cost rate for social discounting derives from the difficulty to deviate from it: a higher rate will imply that fewer projects will be accepted; a lower rate may cause too many projects to be financed. The opportunity principle may also provide a relationship between the discount rate and the means of financing investments for a specific project. The discount rate may thus be set equal to: (1) The social opportunity cost rate, corrected for market imperfections and externalities, if the funds for a project are obtained from the capital market; or (2) the social time preference rate (consumption rate of interest) when consumption is sacrificed (taxes). Alternatively, costs and benefits with possibly varying social rates of time preference may be used (see Gijsbers and Nijkamp 1988). However varying rates over different investment projects may cause the problem of financial crowding out. Finally, the opportunity cost principle may apply only to small-scale, short-term projects, while if extended to big-scale, government or long-term projects it should only be compared with other long-term projects, so that lower values of opportunity cost rates result. For, both types of projects have to be carried out and should not compete too much with each other, which may imply a minor role for the discount rate.

Including 'pure' risk in the discount rate is very restrictive (and stronger for other types of uncertainty), as it offers only one way of

---

[5] A positive discount rate implies a finite horizon. This is usually too large to be of any importance for short period considerations. However, over multigenerational periods it has much relevance.

handling risk, namely as a negative exponential course (see Markandya and Pearce, 1988). Even if risk 'increases monotonically', it is very unlikely to be compatible with a negative exponential pattern. Therefore, more flexible frameworks are necessary.

The above discussion indicates that there are potentials to minimise the attention to discount rates in discussions of intertemporal and intergenerational distributions. Then we have to agree that time preference applies only to individuals, not to communities or in any case not for multigenerational evaluation. Risk can be dealt with more appropriately in other ways than by adjustment of discount rates. Thus, only the opportunity cost principle has to be regarded, thereby taking notice of the remarks made above with respect to its use. The other aspects mentioned can be left out or incorporated in other ways, including possibly also external and intangible effects. The major advantage of a multi-purpose discount factor is that it simplifies the model structure.

3.5. SPATIAL ASPECTS OF SUSTAINABLE DEVELOPMENT

In the context of sustainable development especially the spatial dimension has received little attention. The importance of the spatial element arises from a reciprocal relationship: (1) local processes have global impacts; and (2) global trends give rise to local effects. For example, the loss of ecosystems in some regions may have a large impact on global climatological conditions and geochemical cycles. Over-grazing and deforestation may lead to large-scale soil erosion, downstream sedimentation, flooding and salinisation (see, e.g., Clark and Munn, 1986). Furthermore, environmental processes do not uniformly and smoothly impact on all regions, but may have important different consequences at a regional scale (see, e.g., Alcamo *et al.*, 1990). The specific regional environmental and economic structure determines the sensitivity of a region to external environmental and economic forces (see Siebert, 1985 and 1987).

The integrated study of economic and natural systems at a global scale is complicated because of the variety of economies, ecosystems, and political interests. Performing this study at a regional level has a number of advantages. First, it allows one to analyse less complex systems. This is the result of a smaller number of different types of ecosystems and economic systems at a regional than global level, and subsequently fewer interactions that have to be taken care of in one's analysis. In addition, the use of indicators and models can be more easily accomplished at such a meso level (see Ikeda, 1987). Aggregation of information into global-scale indicators may lead to a significant loss of information. A second advantage is the easier access to (or collection of) regional than global data, and avoidance of some of the problems of data incomparability and aggregation that will occur at a global scale of analysis. Third, a region may be chosen such that it is congruent with a uniform policy. Related to this, a region may further show strong uniformity of political and public interests. Finally, a regional scale allows for easier identification of the source of environmental problems.

Regional sustainable development is a concept which has received only little attention (an early treatment, focusing on international trade issues, is Daly 1989a). This is somewhat strange in view of the large literature that did evolve on (general or global) sustainable development (see Section 3.1). When the term 'region' is used in the context of sustainable development it usually refers to case studies with a local or single ecosystem level of analysis (e.g., Kairiukstis *et al.*, 1989). Two regional characteristics are responsible for the difference between sustainable development and regional sustainable development (RSD); they are: (i) cross-boundary flows of environmental and economic goods and services; and (ii) external determinants of regional development. A realisation of regional sustainable development can therefore be regarded as based on the sustainable provision of natural resources in the region and the sustainable import and export − from the viewpoint of regional sustainable development in other regions − of resources, goods, services and waste.

In order to discuss the sustainable development of a region it has to be made clear what the problem is and how solutions can be found. The problem of unsustainable development of a region is linked to the fact that the size of a regional population and economy are not checked sufficiently by the region's carrying capacity, and therefore overshooting may occur. In many cases this may be acceptable if at a higher level of spatial aggregation overall sustainability was ensured. A second reason for unsustainable development of a region may be the existence of the negative external impact of regional development, cross-boundary pollution and global phenomena (e.g., climate change) from which regional control is separated. Both the regional cross-boundary flows supporting the economy, and the cross-boundary pollution cause the regional carrying capacity to be exceeded for a while, from which the environment may be harmed permanently. This has negative consequences for the carrying capacity itself and thus for the long-run performance of the regional economy (see Nijkamp *et al.*, 1991a; van den Bergh and Nijkamp, 1994a and b). Consequently regional sustainable development has to fulfil two goals: (1) it should ensure an acceptable level of welfare for the regional population, which can be sustained in the future; and (2) it should not be in conflict with sustainable development at a supra-regional level (see van den Bergh, 1991).

Studying sustainability in a multi-regional system may be useful to deal with the spatial implications of global sustainability, in terms of regional activities, and inter-regional trade flows. Verhoef and van den Bergh (1995a and b) present analytical and numerical results of such a type of investigation, in the context of sustainable transport. Based on an extended spatial price equilibrium model, an optimal trade-off can be made between mobile and immobile sources of pollution, between regional production (with autarky as an extreme case) and trade dependence, and between volume reductions and technological solutions. The model also allows to consider to what extent partial — such as isolated, single sector — policies can lead to sustainability goals. Although transport is pre-eminently linked to issues of spatial sustainability, one can also translate the results to other types of open systems, such as countries, sectors and ecosystems. A similar issue is studied in Van den Bergh and Nijkamp (1995), now in an explicit dynamic simulation modelling context where economic and environmental processes of two regions, and their trade and environmental interactions, are dynamically specified. The resulting model is used to trace, among others, sustainable growth in an open economy, the effect of dissimilarity between regional environmental processes, and the role of technological progress and diffusion. Essential for the outcomes is the endogenous pattern of interregional trade in the model.

Especially the trade-off between efficiency and sustainability in a multi-sector production—consumption system is interesting in the above examples, since it can be analytically linked to a trade-off between the absolute volume or size of each sector, its relative size in the economic structure, and the level of 'environmental technology' adopted in each sector. In an operational sense this may be done by using indicators for efficiency and sustainability. The next two chapters present methods for analysis and evaluation of these and other kinds of trade-offs to be made for sustainable development.

PART TWO

Methods for Analysis and Evaluation

4. Analytical Methods and Techniques

4.1. THE NEED FOR INTEGRATION OF METHODS

4.1.1. Motivation

The purpose of this book is to make a first step in filling up the gap that exists between the conceptual considerations and theoretical analysis of sustainable development on the one hand, and the operational analysis and implementation of systems and policies for various real world situations on the other hand. In order to be able to do that we have to pay attention to methods and techniques that can be used in performing the analysis and implementation phases. In Chapter 5 we will be concerned with the implementation part, while in the present chapter the attention is focused on the descriptive and analytical methods and techniques.

It will be evident to the reader that we cannot restrict ourselves to just one method or tool, for two reasons. First, since the issues discussed in Chapter 3 are diverse, one has to be able to either pay specific attention to each of them, one at a time, or to use a framework that allows several issues to be dealt with simultaneously, e.g., temporal and spatial processes or dynamics of multiple use. Second, various techniques and models will have to be used in view of the diversity in: regions, systems and problems, data availability, and specific policy questions and solutions. For example, the case studies in Part Three of this book will cover different types of problems and regions, ranging from ecosystem to national levels, from using temporal to spatial data, from single to multi-sector systems, from optimisation to scenario analysis type of studies, etc. In general, it will be wise to have a toolbox available from which one can choose the required technique or adequate combination of techniques. This holds even stronger for studies in the context of sustainable development, at least when they go along with a consistent and comprehensive approach.

It is worthwhile to emphasise at the beginning of this chapter that one may expect studies for sustainable development taking place at very different levels in between purely conceptual and applied. The reader should understand that, although sustainable development is a key notion in many reports of governmental institutions nowadays, it does not necessarily follow that only applied research is relevant. For instance, the objectives of sustainable development studies may be related to obtaining fundamental insights about long-term environment and development relationships, or to separating clearly between subjective (e.g., ethical) and objective (empirical or theoretical) elements. As a consequence of the broad spectrum of questions arising around sustainable development one will find many different approaches, and more so because the subject is merely in a developing stage.

Data and measurement are generally essential to empirical research. It seems logical therefore to begin our discussion of methods here by devoting attention to such issues. This is particularly relevant within the context of this book, since the combination of economic, environmental, spatial and temporal data involves very fundamental questions of measurement as well as specific problems of observation, measurement and aggregation. In Section 4.2 the choice of indicators for sustainable development will be discussed. This includes a general discussion of purposes and features of indicators, characteristics of sustainable development indicators, and the issue of valuation. In Section 4.3 we will be concerned with databases for sustainable development, in specific with Natural Resource Accounts (NRA's). Different methods are presented, including natural resource accounting, economic accounting, depreciation accounting and the user-cost approach. In Section 4.4 we discuss the use of integrated models for sustainable development analysis. Here particular attention is given to economic, ecological and integrated approaches. Issues of long-term dynamics and valuation are also discussed. Finally, in Section 4.5, we will review techniques for analysis with spatial data sets, generally classified as Geographical Information Systems (GISs). The combination of these tools provides a rather complete box for analysis of sustainable development and management.

4.1.2. Integration of Methods for Policy and Management

The ultimate goal of economic−ecological analysis is aimed at formulating and implementing environmental management and policy instruments and institutions for solving or trade-off of objectives such as economic efficiency (i.e. optimal externality levels), environmental quality, ecosystem performance and sustainability. In the Chapter 1 it was already noted that environmental−economic analysis not only requires integration of models, theories and information from economics and ecology, but also a synthesis of methodological steps which finally lead to the information necessary for management and policy formulation. Such steps are often separately being developed as well as applied. In order to indicate how their integration can be realised, it is important to consider which steps are to be taken. The following list of possibly interactive aggregate steps indicates a quite general sequence of steps:

- a description of problems and systems, preparation of data, and choice of performance indicators;
- forecasting or analysis of static, spatial or dynamic characteristics of systems, under different behavioural, strategy, and policy assumptions;
- impact analysis, monetary or multi-criteria evaluation, or optimisation;
- a policy formulation and choice of instruments.

Some steps may be related to specific methods. However, there is certainly not a one-to-one link between these steps and methods. In the field of economic—ecological analysis one can consider a number of useful methods:

(i) Valuation methods can provide links between values on the one hand, and uses and functions on the other hand.
(ii) Systems methods linking available ecological models, spatial models and economic models can be used to link the use and functions of ecosystems to the internal structure of all relevant subsystems: economic, institutional, ecological.
(iii) Scenarios can be used to deal with management alternatives, exogenous parameters, or system-external events or processes; prospective scenarios are based on desired future states of the system (normative); and projective or 'forecasting' scenarios are based on extending the present from the initial state of the system.
(iv) Social evaluation methods such as Cost-Benefit Analysis and Multi-Criteria Analysis can finally serve to evaluate the economic values and the multi-dimensional system indicators.

In integrating some of the steps one can perform a partial policy—strategy analysis to estimate costs and benefits of specific policies taking only their immediate effects into account, and assuming away indirect effects (for example, as a result of relative price changes). These costs and benefits may be evaluated via benefit—cost evaluation. A general or economy-wide policy—strategy analysis on the other hand can deal with economic incentive systems, such as environmental levies, ecological tax revision, or tradeable permits, and incorporate a considerable amount of the complexity present in market systems. It allows, therefore, for cost shifting effects being transmitted in a multisectoral market equilibrium setting. An optimisation–integrated policy–strategy analysis is based on a constrained optimisation model and integrates economic and environmental variables and constraints, to incorporate physical effects, processes and restrictions as well as economic–environmental interactions. A scenario–integrated policy–strategy analysis can be based on a (dynamic) integrated economic–environmental model that generates values (over time) of performance indicator variables. These values can serve as an input of evaluation methods, notably focusing on multi-criteria evaluation. A scenario–optimisation analysis of policies and strategies combines features of the last two options in a heuristic, possibly iterative, procedure which may use an integrated system of descriptive models, scenario simulation, and optimisation procedures. Multiple dimensions may imply the use of separate, sequential constrained optimisations, or be evaluated in a more integrated multi-criteria method. As will be clear, some of these options focus on traditional economic analysis, and are useful to decide about economic efficiency, least cost measures, and optimal tax systems. Other methods can be considered as operations research type of methods – from a technical perspective anyway – while from a contextual perspective they may be regarded as valuable for dealing with management of uncertain processes in well-defined systems. A special category of methods deals with (long-run) growth and development issues, regional or even lower spatial levels of processes, and analyses on a material–physical level.

For many applications of integrated systems of methods in the field of economic–ecological issues one cannot leave out spatial dimensions. It is important to stress that new developments are relevant in the present context, notably the emergence of Geographic Information Systems. Few examples, however, are available of applications of questions to environmental policy on a regional, meso scale (e.g., Despotakis, 1991; Maxwell and Costanza, 1994). Although not central to this study, this topic will receive some attention (see Section 3.4 and Chapter 11).

Finally, it should be noted that the concept of integration can be technically or mathematically operationalised in different ways. Some models or methods combine optimisation of an objective function with a description of a system. The system may then be represented by linear constraints (Linear Programming), by nonlinear relationships (Nonlinear Programming), or by dynamic relationships (Dynamic Programming). If the interpretation of the constraints is (also) spatial, then the programming model integrates optimisation with systems and spatial descriptions. Such operations research models are very suitable for well-understood systems and one-dimensional goal functions. In the case of complex, dynamic and nonlinear economic – ecological systems combined with multiple indicators and goals, however, one is very limited by such strict models. An alternative then is to integrate different models or techniques sequentially, for instance, a systems model, a spatial model and an (multiobjective or multi-criteria) evaluation model. The results are less powerful then, of course, but one is forced to make this trade-off when pursuing a comprehensive analysis of multidimensional complex dynamic systems as in this study.

Finally, the 'multidimensional methods' seem most adequate in the context of economic – ecological analysis. They differ from the other methods in that they deal with multiple units of measurement in description, analysis and evaluation. However, these other methods, though more narrow from this perspective, can offer strong results useful for comparison or complementarity reasons. In a pluralistic approach one should, therefore, take into account all the mentioned options.

4.2. INDICATORS FOR SUSTAINABLE DEVELOPMENT

4.2.1. Purpose and Features

All of us use indicators in making ordinary decisions. Cloud cover is commonly used in deciding whether to take an umbrella; a patient's temperature may imply illness and, in conjunction with other indicators or symptoms, even suggest what kind of illness; the number of stars which a hotel or restaurant is given indicates not only the quality of the meals and associated services, but also price levels. Indicators used in daily life are selected, often not even consciously, for their known or suspected information content and their easy digestibility. The information may also be assumed to have predictive power, an assumption which is rarely tested for its accuracy. However, with time, proper training and growing experience, most of us manage to sustain our lives based on such uncertain information flows.

In measurement theory the term 'indicator' is used for the empirical specification of concepts that cannot be (fully) operationalised on the basis of generally accepted rules (Vos *et al.*, 1985). Indicators represent components or processes of real world systems. The primary function of indicators lies in simplification, such that they are a compromise between scientific accuracy and the demand for concise information. Good indicators may be identified on the basis of their adequate representation of complex processes combined with effectiveness in aiding decision-making (Vos *et al.*, 1985). The purpose of their use may be:

(i) planning − problem identification, allocation of socioeconomic resources, policy assessment; or,

(ii) communication − notification (warning), mobilisation, legitimisation of policy measures.

Four features of indicators have been identified in the literature (Vos *et al.*, 1985; Liverman *et al.*, 1988; Braat, 1991; Kuik and Verbruggen, 1991). First, the indicator must be representative for the chosen system and have a scientific basis. Ideally, indicators should be based on an empirically tested model. If this is not possible, they should be based on available scientific knowledge for which there is consensus among experts or correlation calculations have been performed. Indicators should be uniquely representative of the problem under consideration.

Second, indicators must be quantifiable. Data for the indicator must be available or obtainable with present technology and should meet current technical requirements as to reproducibility and reliability.

Third, the indicator must represent reversible and manageable processes. This requirement is disputed. The purpose of sustainable development policy is to reverse and manage unsustainable development. However information on irreversible or unmanageable processes may still be useful, for example to formulate mitigating or adaptive strategies.

Fourth, a part of the cause−effect chain should be clearly represented by the indicator. All processes are the result of cause−effect chains. While an indicator may not be able to represent all causes and all effects accurately, it should be clear what part is represented and what not.

Finally, indicators should offer implications for policy. Policies may be implemented, at least in theory, at all stages of the cause−effect chain. In its representation of some part of this chain, an indicator should offer insights, either on the effectiveness of past policy or on options for future policy.

Some observers may attribute a special meaning to an indicator that goes beyond its numerical value or form; e.g., the number of predator birds may be used to represent the vitality of a landscape including forest ecosystems. The change over time in the value or form of the indicator is usually the features which provides this insight or special meaning. A classic example is the change in value of Gross National Product which provides insights into economic growth and, by association, societal welfare. It is this additional information, embodied in or implied by indicators, which is of use in decision making.

Our understanding of the dynamics and complexity of economic−ecological systems is still quite limited. However, the idea for management of these systems is more or less the same as in other management areas and even in everyday life − follow proper training, acquire experience and develop methods for quick but reliable assessments of forthcoming opportunities and problems. One of the challenges of sustainable development is to find indicators which can be assessed easily and reliably.

Information obtained from monitoring networks and special studies may serve as a basis for retrospective evaluation of currently operative policies in achieving their objectives. Indicators used for such policy evaluations must closely resemble the character of the policy objectives to be evaluated. The same type of data may be used to detect historical development trends or sudden shifts in the past − retrospective evaluation in a more general sense. In situations where policies are absent or a number of policies are interacting, data series for sensitive indicators may be more useful. The selection of these indicators should primarily be based on the identification of sensitive social groups and sensitive components of natural ecosystems.

It is becoming more common to express the state of the environment and development trends in so-called policy indicators (Vos *et al.*, 1985; Kuik and Verbruggen, 1991). They are defined as variables which are representative for an environmental policy area, for a part of the natural environment, or for a socioeconomic sector which causes changes in the quality of the environment. Examples are 'total H^+ equivalents per hectare per year' as an indicator for the acidification problem and 'the weighted sum of nitrogen and phosphorus input' as indicator for nutrient enrichment.

4.2.2. Indicators and Sustainable Development

As with environmental accounting, there has been much discussion and even dissension as to the type(s) of indicators required for the assessment of the ecological sustainability of economic development. Conventional economic analysis uses economic aggregates which are derived from the System of National Accounts, the predominant method for national economic accounting. Much effort is being directed towards modification of these aggregates so that they better reflect environmental use and repercussions of this use. Section 4.3 on environmental accounting in this chapter discusses these approaches.

The issue of valuation, as with environmental accounting, is central to the approach adopted to indicator development. This is also discussed briefly in the Section 4.3. There is widespread, although perhaps not unanimous, agreement that indicators in physical units are desirable as a complement to the conventional economic aggregates, and that the economic aggregates should not be compromised by the subjectivities inherent in placing a value on environmental goods, services and capital (Opschoor and Reijnders, 1991; Kuik and Verbruggen, 1991; Victor, 1991; den Butter, 1992).

Three types of essentially physical indicators have been recommended for development in the Netherlands (Opschoor and Reijnders, 1991; Kuik and Verbruggen, 1991):

(i) *pressure indicators*, showing the development over time of the pollutant burden being placed on the environment by man's activities;

(ii) *impact indicators*, showing the development over time of environmental quality levels; and,

(iii) *sustainability indicators*, relating pressure and/or effect indicators with pre-determined criteria for sustainable use.

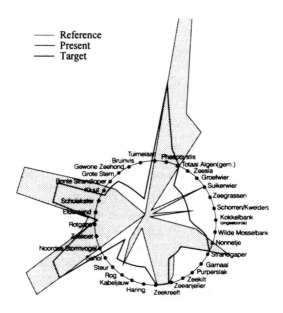

Figure 4.1. The AMOEBA indicator.

Source: ten Brink (1991).

The AMOEBA is offered as a preliminary example of the latter (see Figure 4.1). This indicator addresses the issue of biodiversity and sustainability of the North Sea ecosystem. It combines a reference population size for a range of marine species, current populations size, and target sizes. The reference sizes predate environmental deterioration and so may be equated to a sustainability context. The target sizes reflect policy objectives to move the system towards a better balances of species abundance.

There is considerable effort being invested into further work on this approach. It should also be noted that the approach is not without its critics. Questions have been raised as to how representative of the state of the ecosystem such a species list really is. Further, the format of the indicator of information has been questioned (Janssen, 1992). Connecting the populations sizes of each species is not legitimate, and it implies an area which has no real meaning and distracts attention from the central issue of biodiversity (see, e.g., Barbier *et al.*, 1994).

Further work on the development of sustainability indicators has tended to focus on individual environmental policy issues (Second Chamber, 1989). Pressure, impact and sustainability indicators have been proposed within the issue 'diffusion' which covers the movement of persistent pollutants into the environment and subsequent diffusion and accumulation. This is reported in Gilbert and Feenstra (1992).

4.2.3. Valuation

A crucial issue in environmental accounting is that of the measurement unit. Monetary units offer consistency and direct access to policy-makers. The diversity of physical units provides problems, particularly for aggregation, and may have less of an impact on policy-makers. However, most environmental stocks and flows are 'free' goods in that they are not marketed, and so no price exists to assess their value. The question that environmental accounting must address is: how much of what we want to be valued can be valued in practice?

Environmental valuation has now some 20 years experience. Early Dutch economic damage studies did not lead to very optimistic conclusions regarding the possibilities of finding monetary equivalents of welfare changes (Opschoor, 1974; James *et al.*, 1978; Hueting, 1980). These studies mentioned gaps in knowledge, lack of data and biases in the perception of the consequences of environmental changes. The ethical aspects of valuation based on individual utility were also questioned. The development of valuation methods was further stimulated during the 1980s, largely as a result of more widespread use of cost−benefit analyses. Figure 4.2 indicates the relative ease of valuation. An essential

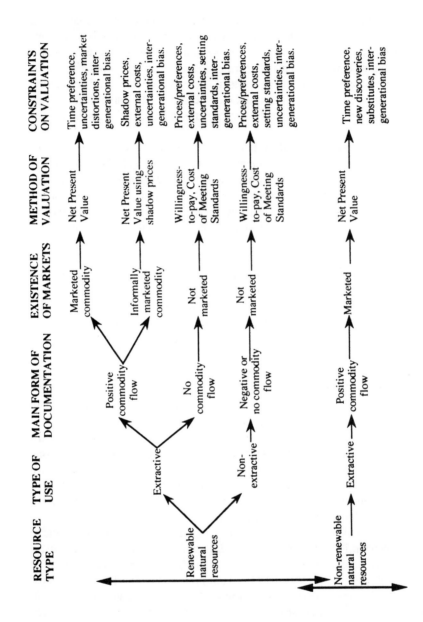

Figure 4.2. Guide to the valuation of environmental assets.

Source: Adapted from Gilbert *et al.*, 1990.

difference in valuation method stems from the presence of a marketed commodity; where no market exists, use of the environment tends to divide into production of commodities in the informal sector, or the provision of services in the public sector of the economy (Gilbert *et al.*, 1990).

The answer to the above question revolves around a number of points. The first questions whether it makes sense to value all goods, services and stock changes. Peskin (1989) identifies a number of natural resources such as air, potable water, plant and animal species, and beautiful vistas as 'vital and irreplaceable', and argues that they are beyond economic valuation. This point was also made by Hueting (1980); Hueting also points to the potential bias if only some environmental goods and services are valued and others not.

The use of a monetary valuation of environmental goods is meaningful and sufficient only when five conditions are satisfied (see Hoevenagel, 1994). The first condition − information − requires that there be sufficient information as to the consequences of environmental changes, so that subsequent effects on welfare can be estimated by individuals. The second condition − scale − requires that the environmental changes should not be too large, as this constrains their useful translation to welfare changes. The third − reversibility − condition refers to the presence of large existence or bequest values which tend to reduce the reliability of valuations. The difficulty of placing values on irreversible environmental changes has been already mentioned. The fourth condition − preference − emphasises that valuations based on willingness to pay (WTP; see Johansson, 1987; Freeman, 1993) only make sense if it is individual preferences which are relevant, raising the question of additivity to a societal preference, and whether government actions should only follow such stated preferences. Finally, environmental changes with impacts on future generations do not tend to be reliably valued. This is related to the inclusivity condition which confines the type of issue being tested to those with relatively immediate impacts. Further, these authors argue that the exclusive use of monetary valuation is insufficient for decision making when the preference and inclusivity conditions are not met.

Costanza *et al.* (1991) accept that well-functioning markets offer the means for the expression of individualistic human preferences for goods and services with few long-term impacts and for which there is adequate information. However, environmental goods and services do not conform to this, tending to be long-term by nature and not traded in markets; also information about their contribution to individual's well-being is usually poor. The quality of valuations in which people are asked how much they would be prepared to pay for environmental goods and services in hypothetical markets is then suspect and dependent on how well-informed they are. In addition, long-term goals are not adequately incorporated because future generations are excluded from bidding.

The second point with regards to the question at the beginning of this section expands on this, and relates to the current capacity of valuation methods. No single valuation method yet exists which provides satisfactory valuations across the full range of environmental goods and services. Opschoor and Reijnders (1991) concluded that attempts to value environmental change, while numerous, are partial, unsatisfactory and hence unconvincing. The following reasons were offered:

(i)   the relationships between physical changes in stock levels or environmental quality, and the resulting economic damage, is insufficiently known, and, in the case of many health effects, even challenged;

(ii)   even where estimates of total current damage (with reference to some base level) are available, their interpolation to equivalent, annual changes in the environment, is highly dubious; and,

(iii) subjective elements, such as the significance of species, ecosystems, etc., must also be valued, and current methods, such as contingent valuation (CVM) for extracting estimates of individuals' WTP, are not well tested and cannot cover all the required ground − Costanza *et al.* (1991) prefer contingent referenda (willingness to be taxed as a citizen along with other citizens) to ordinary WTP studies, largely because it is difficult to induce individuals to reveal their true WTP for natural resources when the question is put directly.

4.3. NATURAL RESOURCE ACCOUNTING

4.3.1. Definition of Environmental Accounting
Environmental accounting attempts to parallel (national) economic accounting. It aims to provide a structured and consistent framework for the presentation of environmental and economic data, and thereby facilitates analysis of environmental−economic interactions. A number of approaches have been taken to environmental accounting. United Nations (1993 − see Figure 4.3) identifies six possible types of environmental accounting on the basis of the unit used and the part of the spectrum between the environment and the economy reflected. Approaches to environmental accounting fit within five of these six areas; satellite accounts (e.g., United Nations, 1993; de Boo *et al.*, 1991)

attempt to incorporate all of these approaches within one framework, maintaining close and explicit connections with conventional economic accounting.

A description of each of these types of approaches is not presented here. Readers are referred to Ahmad *et al.* (1989), United Nations (1993), and Lutz (1993) for overviews, and Common and Norton (1994) for a discussion on the link with biodiversity. Accounts, whether the conventional economic accounts or environmental accounts, are a framework for the presentation of statistics. Issues such as sustainability, growth, and welfare are reflected, not so much in the framework, but in what is done with the statistics. Economic statistics in the System of National Accounts (SNA) input to various modelling activities and scenario analyses, and are also used to generate aggregate indicators of economic performance such as Gross Domestic Product. The same can be expected of environmental accounting – the accounts will comprise environmental–economic statistics and, via their use and interpretation, will contribute to insights into the sustainability or otherwise of economic development. This section focuses on this use and interpretation, addressing the question of what insights environmental accounts can provide for sustainable development.

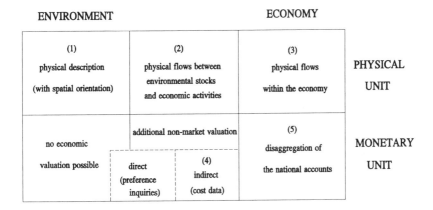

Figure 4.3. Approaches to environmental accounting.

Source: Adapted from United Nations Statistical Office (1993).

4.3.2. Introduction to Natural Resource Accounting

Natural resource accounting, and in particular its use of stock balances to document economic use of natural resources, corresponds to categories 1 and 2 in Figure 4.3. A general stock balance is given by:

$$S_0 + \sum N_t + \sum R_t = \sum M_t + \sum C_t + S_1 ,$$

where

S_0, S_1 = stock of natural resource at the beginning and end of the accounting period;

N_t = additions to stock due to natural processes (growth, reproduction, biogeochemical cycling, immigration or import)[1]; and

R_t = additions to stock as a result of human activities (e.g., exploration and development, reafforestation, environmental rehabilitation) and including revaluation of stock assessments;

M_t = subtractions from stock by natural events (e.g., mortality, fire and storm damage, death caused by pollution); and,

C_t = extractions from stock by human activities (e.g., mining, harvesting), both intentional and unintentional.

Such stock balances provide the basic information on which the sustainable use of natural resources use can be assessed.

In theory, renewable natural resource stocks are used sustainably when losses to economic extraction and natural causes are balanced by their inherent capacity for regeneration. In practice, the data are rarely available for all elements of the stock balance. For example, stocks of wild populations (e.g., fish) can rarely be measured directly; average regeneration rates tend to be used, but these may fluctuate widely in reality as a result of the influences of climate, presence of pollutants, and even the extraction process itself; natural losses (e.g., predation/grazing by other species, storms, fires) as well as man-induced losses (e.g., oil spills) are often difficult to estimate, particularly for mobile species; extraction for economic purposes may be underestimated as a result of multiple use, presence of informal and formal markets, and unintentional extraction (e.g., drainage of groundwater into mines).

---

[1] Rates of these processes can be (indirectly and unintentionally) influenced by human activities.

Nonrenewable natural resources have no regeneration capacity and so cannot be used sustainably. However, the rate of use can, in theory, be controlled to accommodate the development of substitutes, or alternative or more efficient technologies. Stocks of nonrenewable natural resources, which comprise mineral and fossil fuel stocks, require geological surveys for estimation. These tend not to be conducted on a regular basis and there are inherent uncertainties in the estimation procedure. Of more interest, however, is that portion of the total stock available for extraction as a result of resource development or that portion which is economically recoverable. These two factors may lead to different stock estimates. The Norwegian System of Natural Resource Accounts uses the following system for documenting nonrenewable stocks:

$$V_t + G_u + D = M + V_{t+1}$$

and

$$W_t + G_d + M = U + W_{t+1} \, ,$$

where

V_t	$=$	undeveloped reserves at time t;
W_t	$=$	developed reserves at time t;
G_d, G_u	$=$	revaluations during the period of developed and undeveloped reserves, respectively;
D	$=$	discoveries during the time period t;
M	$=$	development of mines during the time period; and,
U	$=$	extraction from developed reserves in the period t to $t+1$.

Note that the dynamics of nonrenewable resources stocks are generated by exploration activities, whether or not reserves are developed. The driver(s) of exploration, such as price and scarcity, are not captured in such stock balances. Such information needs to be coupled to stock balances to provide a better view of resource use.

Stock balances can also be used to document the accumulation of substances in environmental components such as soil and even organisms. They can be coupled to materials balances which trace the movement of substances into, through, or out of the economy in physical terms. Further discussion is contained in Section 7.5.1, and applications in Section 7.5.2.

4.3.3. Economic Accounting

Within economic accounting, the answer of how to reflect sustainability issues has focused on the measurement of true or sustainable income (El

Serafy, 1981 and 1989; Daly, 1989c; El Serafy and Lutz, 1989a and b; Hueting *et al.*, 1992). El Serafy and Lutz (1989b, p. 14) describe sustainable income as 'the maximum amount a recipient can consume in a given period without reducing possible consumption in a future period', a concept which encompasses not only current earnings, but also changes in the asset position of the income earner − capital gains are a source of income, capital losses reduce income. This is essentially a return to the Hicksian view of income (Hicks, 1946): a nation must invest in new capital goods to offset the depreciation of existing assets if the future income-producing ability of the entire capital stock is to be preserved.

The emphasis on gross production as a measure of income, largely a function of widespread implementation of the System of National Accounts, has triggered a shift in the meaning of 'income'. Further, conventional economic accounting does not treat the environment as a capital good; the consumption or depreciation of natural capital is not recorded and does not affect income measures. Failure to extend depreciation to the capital stock embodied in the natural resource base of resource-based (often developing) economies leads to a distortion of evaluations of economic performance and estimates of macroeconomic relationships (Repetto, 1986; and Repetto *et al.*, 1989).

An essential issue is the use of net or gross measures of income. Various authors, such as Daly (1989c) and Repetto *et al.* (1989), argue that net measures should receive more attention in economic policy planning since, by incorporating the depreciation of capital assets, they approximate sustainable income. This requires extension of depreciation from structures and equipment to the natural resource base. Currently, capital consumption is underestimated and the future income-producing capacity overestimated. An important constraint to this argument is that calculation of net measures is plagued by the problem of selecting a depreciation rate for environmental assets as well as for produced capital. Therefore net measure incorporate elements of subjectivity while gross measures are relatively 'pure'.

Two environmental accounting approaches are briefly described below to illustrate this debate. The first is that of Robert Repetto of the World Resources Institute. Repetto can take credit for the first fully elaborated environmental accounting approach which gave clear signals to policy-makers as to environmental−economic performance.

4.3.4. Depreciation Accounting
Depreciation accounting, developed by Robert Repetto and his colleagues, offers a means of including environmental depletion in

aggregate measures of economic performance. It may be placed within category (5) of Figure 4.3. Depreciation of environmental capital is equated with the value of net changes in resource stock. Stock balances in physical units are constructed to derive the this change, which is then valued using the Net Price Method. The approach has been applied to natural resources with marketed products in Indonesia (Repetto *et al.* 1989) and Costa Rica (Solórzano *et al.*, 1991). Its application to non-marketed uses of natural resources has not been demonstrated.

Indonesia's economic performance is generally judged to have been successful. Over the period 1971 to 1984, Repetto estimated the adjusted average annual growth rate of GDP at 4.0% instead of 7.1% (see Table 4.1). If investments are corrected for depletion, they show strong fluctuations and even drop below replacement investment level in 1980 (Repetto *et al.*, 1989). The overstatement of income and its growth may actually be much more than these estimates indicate since only three resource sectors and only their associated activities on Java were treated.

Table 4.1. Comparison of GDP and 'NDP'

YEAR	GDP[b]	Net Change in Natural Resource Sectors[a]				NDP[b]
		Petroleum	Forestry	Soil	Net change	
1971	5,545	1,527	−312	−89	1,126	6,671
1975	7,631	−787	−249	−85	−1,121	6,510
1980	11,169	−1,633	−965	−65	−2,663	8,505
1981	12,055	−1,552	−595	−68	−2,215	9,840
1984	13,520	−1,765	−493	−76	−2,334	11,186
Average Annual Growth	7.1 %					4.0 %

Notes:
a. Positive numbers for resource sectors imply growth in the physical reserves of that resource during the year;
b. in Billion Constant 1973 Rupiah

Source: Repetto *et al.* (1989).

Other important nonrenewable resources, such as natural gas, coal, copper, tin and nickel, were not included. The depreciation of other renewable resources, such as non-timber forest products and fisheries, is also not considered so that complete depreciation accounts would probably show an even greater divergence between the growth in gross output and net income.

Table 4.2 summarizes the results of the Costa Rican case study. Natural depreciation within three resource sectors — forestry (deforestation), agriculture (soil erosion) and fisheries (overfishing) — was estimated.

Over the study period, natural resource depreciation grew at an average rate of 6.4% per annum. It was initially smaller in value than the estimated capital consumption allowance of buildings and equipment, but by 1989 natural resource depreciation had become three times as large. It grew from 5-6% of GDP in early years to 8-9% in the late 1980's. The growth rate of net domestic product fell from an average of 4.9% per annum to 4.7% when natural resource depreciation was subtracted (Solórzano *et al.*, 1991).

Table 4.2. Gross, Net Domestic Product and Adjusted
Net Domestic Product, Costa Rica

	Gross Domestic Product	Net Domestic Product	Net Capital Formation	Natural Resource Depletion	Adjusted Net Domestic Product	Adjusted Net Capital Formation
Year	**GDP**	**NDP**	**NCF**	**NRD**	**ANDP**	**ANCF**
1970	93,446	87,495	13,240	4,982	82,513	8,233
1975	125,393	118,738	20,481	7,583	111,155	12,898
1980	161,894	153,365	34,846	8,233	145,132	26,613
1985	169,299	164,605	39,136	11,231	153,374	27,905
1989	231,289	225,966	n.a.	20,604	205,362	n.a.

Note: In million 1984 colones.

Source: Solórzano *et al.* (1991).

The depreciation approach, while a relatively simple and practical method, suffers from a number of theoretical constraints. The net price method is used in the depreciation approach to derive a proxy for the net present value of an environmental asset (valuation is further discussed in Sections 4.2.3 and 4.4.7). The current net price is only equal to the true present value if future increases in the net price are equal to the interest rate and thus cancelled out in the discounting process. Any rate of increase in the net price that is greater than the interest rate yields excess profits in resource extraction relative to returns on alternative investments (the interest rate). In perfectly competitive markets, the excess profit results in entry and increases in the rate of extraction until the net price increase is equal to the interest rate and excess profits are eliminated. Since natural resource markets are not perfectly competitive, the use of the current net price valuing natural resource stocks will be subject to error. Depletion will be overvalued (undervalued) when the rate of increase in the current net price is less (greater) than the interest rate (Foy, 1991).

Subtracting all of the resource operating surplus from income measures implies a zero income from natural resource extraction (El Serafy, 1989). This contradicts the obvious fact that countries with marketable natural resources enjoy a higher income, and could enjoy a higher sustainable income, than countries without such resources.

The depreciation approach adjusts income measures at the level of net product. While net measures are, theoretically, better measures of income (see previous discussion), they are also beset with subjectivities due to the need to select a rate of depreciation for man-made capital. The absence of subjectivity in gross measures accounts, in part, for their extensive use. Further, the depreciation approach makes it possible for NDP to exceed GDP if the value of new discoveries are greater than extraction and produced capital consumption allowances. The Indonesian case study showed that the depreciation approach was extremely sensitive to new discoveries and revaluation of oil and gas reserves, making it more difficult to identify clear trends in economic performance.

4.3.5. User Cost Approach

The user cost approach (El Serafy, 1981, 1989 and 1991) differs from the depreciation approach. Firstly it does not place a value on the natural resource and so avoids the difficulties inherent in natural resource valuation; secondly, the income advantage which possession of natural resources confers on a country is retained in national income measures; and thirdly, adjustments are made at the level of gross product.

The user cost approach derives a measure of depletion (or user costs) by dividing net receipts as a result of extraction into income and capital consumption components, and then deducting capital consumption from the gross domestic product of the extractive industry. The result is an adjusted measure of gross income. A simple depreciation formula which relates depreciation to the life expectancy of the resource (reserves-to-extraction-ratio) and the discount rate, given constant commodity prices and under certain assumptions, is used:

$$X/R = 1 - 1/[(1+r)^{n+1}]$$

where

X = true income;
R = total receipts (net of extraction costs);
r = discount rate; and,
n = the number of periods of which the resource is to be liquidated.

The difference between R and X is equated with depletion and corresponds to the amount that should be set aside as a capital investment. The procedure depends only on the interest rate and the life expectancy of the reserves. The life expectancy of the reserves is calculated as a ratio of known reserves to current extraction. The choice of discount rate is somewhat arbitrary, but should reflect an available real return on alternative investments. The income percentage of net receipts is greater the higher the interest rate and also the longer the lifetime of the reserves. New discoveries or downward adjustments in reserves change the income percentage through changes in the reserve life expectancy.

Foy (1991) used both the depreciation and user costs approaches to construct, for Louisiana, adjusted state production measures which included net depletion of oil and gas. The adjusted net state product, derived from the depreciation approach, is the more volatile, being directly tied to changes in physical reserves. The gross measures adjusted by the user cost approach were not only more stable, they were always less than Gross State product. Foy concluded that, unless the interest rate is changed regularly, the user cost method should yield a more stable time series than the depreciation approach. The lower variance from this method was considered a point in its favour because of concerns that inclusion of resource depletion in GDP estimates would increase volatility and make identification of trends more difficult and uncertain.

4.3.6. Conclusions

The monitoring of changes to natural resource stocks is vitally important if we are to detect whether an economy is or is not 'living off its capital', and whether the development path is sustainable or not. The national economic accounts, and the most commonly-used indicators of national income, focus more on flows than on stocks and so are inadequate for this purpose (Repetto *et al.*, 1989). Historically, it was thought that resource depletion was balanced by resource-increasing factors such as discoveries of new stocks, recharge and natural growth of renewable natural resources. This mutual neglect of depletion and increase was thought not to have any adverse social consequences.

The current perception is that sources of increase are not matching depletion. Moreover, the potential for new discoveries and rapid increases in growth are slim for stocks of environmental capital such as clean water, clear air and natural forests. If maintaining the stock of these resources is considered essential to sustained growth, the neglect of their deterioration in conventional national economic accounts is especially serious (Peskin, 1989).

Environmental accounts provide the basic statistics on environmental use and the quantity and quality of environmental stocks (natural capital) for the assessment of how sustainable an economy is developing. This assessment requires the development of aggregate measures of performance (parallel to the economic aggregates) and the input of these data into analytical techniques such as models for policy development and assessment. Current knowledge of environment–economic interactions and environmental performance constrains this assessment. Consequently a pluralistic approach to both environmental accounting and to environmental–economic analysis has been advocated (e.g., Norgaard, 1985, 1989; Friend, 1991). Numerous case studies, resulting from both national and international (e.g., OECD, UN) initiatives, are being undertaken to develop and demonstrate the use of environmental accounts. Assessment of these activities should be possible in the near future.

4.4. INTEGRATED ECONOMIC–ECOLOGICAL MODELS

4.4.1. Introduction

Studying sustainable development with formal models can be helpful for the integration of economic and environmental aspects in a single framework of analysis. In this section we aim to give a concise overview of past integrated modelling studies, in addition to what has been said in Sections 2.3.2 and 2.5, and to discuss some implications of sustainable development issues for long-term modelling. The power of modelling is that it offers a simplified, comprehensible representation of a problem or process with a formal or numerical solution. The greatest difficulty is usually to select such simplifications, aggregations and assumptions that predictions, implications and prescriptions are acceptable.

In Section 4.4.2 and 4.4.3 we address the integration issue from the perspective of economics and ecology, respectively. Since the study of sustainable development implies a long-term viewpoint − irrespective of whether it is being conducted on a theoretical or an operational level − the discussion in Sections 4.4.4 and 4.4.5 proceeds by combining both the integrative and long-term positions. This allows for the formulation of a list of model considerations that limit the range of relevant models for sustainable development. Case studies in Chapters 6, 8, 9 and 11 deal with applications of the type of approach discussed here.

4.4.2. Integration: An Economic Perspective

One may distinguish a number of approaches to economic analysis and models of the environment and ecological systems. A possible classification is as follows:

(i)   Calculation of admissible economic activity levels in view of environmental 'safety' limits;
(ii) describing costs, benefits and behaviour (decisions) for adjustment actions to meet environmental standards; and
(iii) description of dynamic physical−material interactions between economic and ecological systems.

The first approach is based on given 'safety' limits to resource extraction, residuals emission, or any other type of environmental pressure, which can be based on biological or health considerations. This approach describes either physical economic relationships between inputs and outputs, different activities and sectors, or relates physical interactions with the environment in terms of resource extraction and waste emission to output levels measured in monetary units. Examples are the input−output model approaches following the original Leontief (1970; and Leontief and Ford, 1972) proposal (see for an overview e.g., Briassoulis, 1986). The inputs or outputs may be used in combination with constraints and objectives, so that these models can be extended to include linear-programming and multi-objective modules (see James *et al.*, 1978; Hafkamp, 1984; an example of a policy study is WRR, 1987). A drawback of this approach is that it leaves out descriptions of substitution between sectors and products (by way of relative price changes) or technological progress (by way of cost functions).

The second approach considers prices of using materials and fuels, or takes into account the cost of performing activities like waste abatement, treatment, introducing resource efficient techniques, and recycling materials (see, e.g., Jantzen and Velthuijsen, 1991). Economic efficiency as an objective on a micro level (maximising profits or minimising costs), or on a macro level (maximising social welfare, national production or national income, or economic growth exceeding some minimum rate) gives rise to dynamic considerations of costs, substitution, capacity and income effects. The resulting level of interaction with the natural environment is optimal from the economic objective (efficiency) point of view. Alternatively, this approach can be combined with the previous one by appending an input – output model. This approach can be used to include taxes, subsidies or tradeable permits (see Section 5.4.1). Examples are macro-economic models with a sectoral disaggregation (see, e.g., den Hartog and Maas, 1990; van Ierland 1991), or computable general equilibrium models, in which each actor's (theory) or sector's (applications) behaviour is formally described and linked to the system via prices and market interactions (market clearing conditions). See for some applications, e.g., Stephan (1989), Bergman (1991), Conrad and Schröder (1991) and OECD (1991). Models of this second type have the advantage of allowing for substitution between and interdependence of different sectors, but the models are much more difficult to quantify and validate.

A disadvantage of both the first and second approach is that the environment is regarded as providing static constraints for economic activities. Modelling for development and environment requires a different type of attack. The third approach is interdisciplinary in that integration is implemented at four levels of economic – environmental relationships: (i) material flows between economy and natural environment based on materials balance conditions, especially focusing on links between products, markets and materials flows (see Ayres and Kneese, 1969; and Kandelaars *et al.*, 1995); (ii) effects of human systems (economy and population) on environmental quality through immaterial or less-tangible categories of impact such as land use, noise, and soil exploitation; (iii) effects of environmental conditions on economic production, consumption and health, including, for example, negative pollution effects (see Faber *et al.*, 1987); and, (iv) production functions with a mix of economic and natural factors, such as can be found in renewable and non-renewable resource extraction, recreation, and agriculture (see van den Bergh, 1991). Such an approach requires many different inputs from various disciplines and is therefore time-consuming. The main advantages of it are that external effects can be dealt with explicitly, in addition to economic effects occurring through price processes. Therefore this type of modelling can be insightful for long-term issues of environment and economic development. See for further discussion the Equilibrium – Neoclassical perspective in Section 2.3.2.

4.4.3. Integration: An Ecological Perspective

There has been much attention for ecosystem processes in relation to human activities, both theoretically and empirically. Ecological approaches to the inclusion of human actions in ecological analysis are in general aimed at lower aggregation levels than economic models as discussed in the previous section. This is because the field that is concerned with the ecosystem level, systems ecology, is only a young branch of science. Most ecological studies have considered lower levels of organisation than the ecosystem. It is useful here to classify such approaches with respect to the nature of the human impact (see Braat and van Lierop, 1987, Chapter 1): (i) ecological impacts of resource use; (ii) ecological impacts of pollution; and (iii) ecological (system) management issues.

The first type of approach is usually directed at single use of natural resources or ecosystems, for instance fisheries, forests, groundwater and agriculture. Well known studies have focused on fisheries management (Gordon, 1954; Scott, 1955; Clark, 1985; Walters, 1986; Flaaten, 1988) based on early biological models of fisheries (Beverton and Holt, 1957; Ricker, 1954; Schaefer, 1954). Other well known studies regard timber production. Much of this is based on the simple clear-cut rotation problem as an extension of the Faustmann problem in which a fixed optimal rotation period is determined by maximising the present value (see, e.g., Clark, 1976, Bowes and Krutilla, 1985). So both the fishery and forestry models are similar to (optimal) investment problems in economics (capital theory; see Wilen, 1985). For an optimal control model of sustainable resource use in a semi-arid environment, focusing on overgrazing issues, see Perrings (1994). Models for water (quantity) resources arise from a different background, using more sophisticated system theoretical and optimisation methods (see, e.g., Biswas, 1976; Hamies, 1977; Bogardi, 1987). They cover various types of water resources such as aquifers, lakes and rivers. Finally, resource modules of agricultural models include physical crop production models (see, e.g., Harnos, 1987), in which the problem is to statistically relate (geographically) the yield of specific crops to a mix of inputs such as water supply, soil type, rainfall, irrigation, fertilisation and use of pesticides. Negative ecological impacts involved in this area are soil erosion in terms of the soil content of organic matter, nutrients and moisture.

Approaches of the second type are very diverse, including various types of pollution impact models for specific ecosystems, both marine and terrestrial. Theoretical analyses that combine resource extraction with waste emission on the level of a single resource or ecosystem are given in Siebert (1982) and Tahvonen and Kuuluvainen (1991 and 1993). Operational models are focused on the pollution impact on the quality of water (Orlob, 1983), soil, and vegetation (see Alcamo *et al.*, 1990). Air quality is also a common terminology but can be regarded as a derivative of the other qualities and human health standards. Such environmental pollution impact models are at the basis of many regional economic – environmental studies using input – output models (see, e.g., Isard, 1972; Kneese and Bower, 1972 and 1979; Ikeda, 1987). Other approaches linking ecological pollution impact to economic models can be found in Lonergan (1981), Biswas (1981) and Rinaldi (1979).

The third approach uses more elaborated models of ecosystems. Theoretical backgrounds for these are given in Watt (1968), Maynard Smith (1974), May (1976), and Walters (1986). Here attention is paid to such diverse elements and processes relevant to ecosystem representation as growth, metabolism, interspecific processes (e.g., predation, competition, mutualism), and foodchain relationships. The interactions between human – economic activities and ecological processes include the various categories of resource extraction, residuals emission, and other forms of environmental disturbance. The objectives of such a model may be linked to multiple use of the ecosystem, including goods as well as services, and take an multiobjective simulation or optimisation format (see, e.g., Braat, 1992). Furthermore, this may include both economic and environmental conservation objectives. A mix of ecological and economic models partly based on energy analysis can be found in Zuchetto and Jansson (1978 and 1985). See for further discussion the Ecological – Systems perspective in Section 2.3.2.

4.4.4. Economic – Ecological Integration
Much of what was stated in Section 2.5 for economic – ecological integration in general is relevant here for integrated models with a long-term perspective. It is important to stress that what the term 'integration' actually means in a methodological and operational sense is often not very clear. The term 'economic – ecological' has been used to denote approaches that use very different concepts of integration. It has for instance been employed for economic process models which include some environmental variables (e.g., waste emission or resource extraction), and for ecological process models with a few economic variables (e.g., activity levels). The considerations mentioned above indicate that much more intensive integration is necessary in order to deal with sustainable development: some combination or synthesis of both economic and ecological processes instead of an economic process and an isolated exogenous ecological variable (or the reverse).

The economy and ecosystems are different objects of study, and the disciplines that study them (i.e. economics and ecology) are very apart indeed: their theoretical concepts and methods are different from one another; also, techniques used to operationalise theoretical concepts, or to perform empirical studies, and test hypotheses are not always used with the same frequency. For this reason, a rational approach to integration seems to be by way of using formal models, in which processes of both fields are described and related to each other.

One example of accomplishing economic–ecological integration on a theoretical or even an operational level of modelling is to include materials balance conditions (see Section 2.2). The combination of non-linear models and materials balance conditions is rare, both in theory and application. In order to formalise the materials balance principle in economic–ecological models, the following requirements must be met: (i) related variables should be in material units; (ii) transformations must be modelled between (variables in) material units and other units, notably functional units; and (iii) materials balance conditions can be specified for economic variables in the economic system, for ecological or physical variables in the environmental system, or as a supplement to descriptions of economic–environmental interactions (which include both economic and environmental variables). The use of materials accounting frameworks provides a good example of combining process descriptions for economic and ecological systems in a theoretically consistent frame (Section 2.2) and can be empirically linked to NRA accounts (Section 4.3; see for more discussion Chapter 7).

4.4.5. Long-Term, Dynamic Models for Sustainable Development

Sustainable development is unconditionally related to a long-term perspective. Therefore, we start with some general observations regarding long-term, dynamic models. An important notion in the context of long-term modelling is causality. Statistical methods combined with data may establish correlative relationships between variables. One is likely to ask the question how long will these remain unchanged. An answer requires unravelling the relationship between variables into mechanic or causal relationships. It must be added that causal relationships are understood not merely as one event having one cause, but also as one event having more causes. Causal relationships mean that variables at a certain point in time are affected by others, at earlier points in time, in a physical (e.g., material flows) or psychological way (e.g., behavioural adjustment). Since the reflection of 'real causality' in long-term models is impossible, causal relationships should merely be regarded as approximations of the 'real processes' or as representations of teleological phenomena or necessary sequential patterns (see Faber and Proops, 1990). Correlative relationships can still be used to replace complex relationships.

Since for the purpose of sustainable development one is concerned with long time horizons, future generations, economic growth, environmental processes, and dynamics of resource extraction and pollution, it is necessary to restrict sustainable development modelling to dynamic economic—environmental modelling. Several types of such dynamic integrated models have been developed. One is analytical with an emphasis on economic aspects, i.e. economic growth models with ecological variables (see Mäler, 1974; Kamien and Schwartz, 1982). Also modern growth theories are now applied to environmental issues (see Gradus and Smulders, 1993; Smulders, 1994). A second type is computer-operational, and includes both programming and simulation models (with econometric, input—output or stock-flow structures). Examples are the global models which try to represent global economic—social—environmental relationships over long periods of time (see Forrester, 1971; Meadows *et al.*, 1982). Other examples are computer simulation of 'macroscopic mini-models' that are derived from energy language diagrams (see Odum, 1983 and 1987).

A long time horizon in dynamic models means that one focuses on long-term rather than short-term processes, in order to minimise on model complexity given the specific modelling purpose. However, this does not necessarily imply that models of long-term processes are the opposite of short-term models, since some elementary repetitive processes, such as production, consumption, regeneration, emission and recycling, may be relevant for both short and long-term outcomes. Especially in an integrated model the interactions between economic and environmental sub-systems should receive adequate attention, and they can only be made explicit in terms of interfacing short-term processes.

A long-term horizon also implies that linear models will not be always adequate, since variation over longer term will be large and consequently reach ranges of nonlinearities for specific processes. Scenario analyses may be used for dealing with various possible strategies and policies, and external circumstances. Furthermore, comparative static and dynamic analyses are relevant in the context of sustainable development. For instance, changes in tastes may be reflected by shifts in parameter values in the welfare function, biological and ecological evolution by changing ecosystem parameters, or technological progress by changing economic production parameters.

In order to study sustainable development as a normative reference case for long-term development of economic—environmental systems, one can choose a number of explicit interpretations of sustainability or sustainable development conditions. One can distinguish between constraints on the level of welfare (for a whole generation or per capita) over generations and restrictions on physical—ecological stocks and flows. In the first case one may choose between the following types of conditions[2]: (i) requiring welfare always to exceed some minimum level (e.g., a subsistence level); or (ii) requiring a monotonous non-decreasing movement of welfare over time.

A second type of conditions may involve constraints on stocks or on flows in and between economic and environmental systems. For instance, the notion of stock constancy (or non-decreasing stocks) may be applied to the sum of man-made economic and natural stocks, to a stock concept such as environmental quality or environmental degradation, to the sum of all natural stocks (compensation principle), or to each stock separately. Instead of directly applying such stock conditions to a model one may use derived flow conditions. Feedback mechanisms may be included to connect sustainable development conditions to economic decisions (see van den Bergh, 1991, Chapter 2; and Section 6.5).

Modelling for sustainable development requires that many relationships are specified. First, it involves subjective decisions with regard to crucial variables. Second, as a result of lack of knowledge and data each relationship is surrounded by uncertainty. With many relationships, this may then severely impact upon the reliability of the whole model in a negative way. It is also clear that the combination of long-term and integrated modelling in practice is an extremely difficult process that uses up much time and effort, and furthermore requires that sufficient data can be made available. Finally, it is worth mentioning that some phenomena and problems inherent to sustainable development cannot be dealt with properly by way of analysis with mathematical models. However, in many cases where well-performed modelling studies fail to augment our insight, other approaches often suffer from the same failure. Further discussion on models for sustainable development can be found in de Vries (1989), Ayres (1989), den Hartog and Maas (1990), and Perrings (1991).

---

[2] Pezzey (1989, p. 13) gives a systematic account of possible simple formulations in this respect. He further links it to the distinction between combinations of on the one hand growth, development and resource use, and on the other hand survivability and sustainability.

4.4.6. Valuation and Systems Analysis

Systems analysis and economic valuation can generate different, often complementary information to integrate in decision-making. Valuation methods hinge on a comparison by present agents of alternative static states of the system. Systems methods actually trace its change in continuous time, for a number of scenarios containing information about external events, exogenous processes and economic and environmental policy and management strategies. In addition, systems analysis may provide insight about instability of behaviour under uncertainty, especially useful in the context of wetlands. These are interesting for scientific research because of their internal complexity and critical dependence on global environmental conditions, the lack of information about their processes and functions, and the many threats to their existence (see Williams, 1990). It also allows for explicit modelling of sustainability conditions and externalities. Furthermore, it can handle multidimensional indicators and be followed by multi-criteria evaluation. One can compare the results, under different regimes, of multi-criteria and monetary evaluations in which increasingly more aspects are incorporated. More specifically, in the monetary evaluation sequentially less tangible, less certain and less instrumental aspects will be included.

Environmental economic analysis of ecosystems has focused on the application of economic valuation methods (Hanley and Spash, 1993; Freeman, 1993) to capture the different types of values: use and non-use values (see, e.g., Turner, 1991). Use values include: Direct use values (associated with directly consumable commodities and services, including food, biomass, recreation and health); indirect use values (associated with environmental support and protection of economic production and property, including nutrient cycles, flood control and storm protection); and, option values (reflecting preferences for future use). Non-use values include: Existence values (reflecting current preferences for the continued existence of natural environments, associated with intrinsic and ethical values, including the existence of species, habitats and biodiversity); bequest values (leaving an environmental legacy, e.g., stemming from feelings of responsibility or stewardship on behalf of future generations).

There are three types of methods can deal with specific value (sub)categories (see, e.g., Johansson, 1987; Hanley and Spash, 1993; and Freeman, 1993; see also Section 4.2.3). One set of indirect methods is based on the identification of surrogate markets using either quantity information (household production functions such as the travel cost method; see Mäler et al., 1994) or price information (hedonic price methods). Other indirect methods use conventional market prices to calculate the value of damage (based on dose-response relationships), replacement or defense measures. Finally, direct methods (stated preferences) include questionnaires or experiments (contingent ranking and valuation).

Both use and non-use values derived vary with the methods applied. Experience in applications seems to indicate that some methods are more robust and relevant for specific value categories in the context of complex systems (Hanley and Spash, 1993). Moreover, whereas use values of ecosystems' products such as fish or amenity values can often be estimated in a relatively easy way, it is difficult to link these to underlying ecological processes and functions of the relevant ecosystems, and to deal with certain indirect use values. The term primary value (or: value of ecological infrastructure) has been introduced (see Gren *et al.*, 1994; Perrings and Opschoor, 1994; Ruitenbeek, 1994; Barbier, 1994) to refer to processes in ecosystems that cannot be captured adequately by use and non-use values. These infrastructural values can be analysed by incorporating the ecological systems parameters and physical—ecological indicators, in a systems dynamic context.

An interesting category of ecosystems for studying the interface between systems' behaviour and valuation is wetlands. These are complex ecosystems on the boundary of water and land ecosystems, which are relevant for scientific study as they generate a range of important functions, are complex, sensitive, and overlap often with areas suitable for human residence and activities − recreational as well as productive. Ecological studies have focused on stress effects. Most of the economic studies on wetlands have concentrated on valuation of ecosystems and wetland services in particular (e.g., Gupta and Foster, 1975; Thibodeau and Ostro, 1981; Turner, 1988a; Turner and Brooke, 1988; Bergström *et al.*, 1990; Costanza *et al.*, 1991; Folke, 1991; Hanley and Craig, 1991; Turner and Jones, 1991; Mäler, 1992; Turner *et al.*, 1993; Hanley and Spash, 1993; and Barbier, 1994). Systems studies are either integrating economics and environment (e.g., Braat and van Lierop, 1987; van den Bergh, 1992; van den Bergh and Nijkamp, 1994b and d) or focusing on modelling hydrological—ecosystems under pressure; (Barendregt *et al.*, 1992; Claessen *et al.*, 1994; Latour *et al.*, 1994).

Concluding, in the context of complex systems the relevance of valuation as well as the interpretations of results of application of methods of economic or monetary valuation to esimate policy benefits or environmental damages are not as clear as in usual categories of economic valuation (see, especially on the issue of complexity, also Hanley and Spash, 1993). It seems insufficient to use, for instance, contingent valuation studies and ask people about what they would like to pay for maintaining a complex ecosystem when the system can develop in many directions given external circumstance, multiple use regimes, and management scenarios. Interaction on various levels between systems analysis in combination with scenario analysis on the one hand, and economic valuation on the other hand, can lead to more satisfactory and informative results.

4.5. GEOGRAPHIC INFORMATION SYSTEMS[3]

4.5.1. A Brief Introduction

In view of the fact that sustainable development has to be implemented on a low level of aggregation, as was made clear in Section 3.4, a system is needed which can process spatial and non-spatial data in an integrated way. Geographical information systems can be useful to that extent, and may even serve as operational tools in policy-oriented applications.

Geographical information systems (GIS) are techniques for transformation, analysis and visualisation of spatial data and/or information (Burrough, 1983; Openshaw 1990; Scholten and Stillwell, 1990; Fischer and Nijkamp, 1992). Recent advances in GIS link dynamic models to spatial information so that integrated spatio–temporal analysis may be achieved (see Despotakis, 1991; Fedra 1991). Computers play an essential role in forming such systems (see Dangermond, 1990), for which reason proper transformations of spatial data into digital form are required.

A strict mathematical definition of any process in space and time requires that at least four parameters are defined for each point to be monitored: its three spatial coordinates and the time coordinate. A series of attributes may then be linked to each spatial point in order to specify characteristics that are considered relevant for the purpose of the study. It is obvious that such a process can turn out to be very complex and time-consuming. Therefore, one may choose to employ several simplifying assumptions based on discretisation in space, discretisation in time, and discretisation in assigning attributes (see Despotakis, 1991).

A geographical information system enables one to perform four functions: preparation, analysis, management of geographical data, and display. Preparation includes such aspects as data collection, digitisation, rasterisation, editing and compression. The purpose of the analysis function is to examine and process the data with the aim of producing

---

[3] This section is based on Despotakis (1991).

information. Display includes all operations relevant for generating graphical outputs. Management is the handling of geographical data transformed into geographical entities (e.g., raster and vector forms) aimed at performing specific operations between them (e.g., additions, overlays, classifications, etc.).

It is noteworthy at this stage to recall that GIS has originated from two complementary sources. First, there is the field of graphical design systems (e.g., Computer Aided Design (CAD) systems), which are meant to aid in the visualisation and graphical design objects in two- or three-dimensional space (see Laurini and Thompson, 1991). For planning purposes such CAD systems have been very helpful, witness the great many applications in the area of infrastructure management, land use management, etc. They allow for connection of large (non-spatial) data bases to cartographic (spatial) representation possibilities.

The second origin of GIS can be found in spatial analytical systems that are used in spatial data analysis and planning (see Burrough, 1983). Such systems have developed in a direction which is suitable for the generation of spatial decision support systems. The main challenge in developing such systems is to ensure a consistent use of both mapping and modelling techniques. A marriage is necessary between the model-based methods and the techniques from GIS to provide adequate tools to assist decision makers. One may distinguish techniques for: transformation of data, synthesis and integration of data, updating information, forecasting, impact analysis, and optimisation. The two approaches (non-spatial models and CAD systems) have rarely come together in the past because of different historical traditions and research focuses. A number of examples, however, can be quoted in which the power of this integration has started to be used (see, e.g., Fedra and Reitsma, 1990).

The spatial component in GIS modelling is present in a very pronounced way in overlay tools of analysis. The main analytical question is whether it is possible to ensure a one-to-one correspondence between GIS overlay and non-spatial model input and output. In this context a relational data base system is necessary, for instance, the package SPANS (1988) in which the user can enter geographic data from digitisers, manually or by types of information from point, line or areal data in vector or raster form. The spatial resolution of the data depends then on the a priori established scale of the area and the data precision. Digital data sources such as digital elevation data, digital base maps and remote sensing data are necessary for a proper treatment of data input and output functions (by using, e.g., scanning and manual digitising). Both vector and raster technologies can be used for GIS colour monitor displays. Finally, it may be worthwhile to call attention for error analysis for all the different GIS functions (see Heuvelink *et al.*, 1989). Error sources come from various categories, for instance numerical integration errors, locational and attribute errors in overlaying procedures, and mathematical model errors.

4.5.2. GIS Models for Sustainable Development

A modelling framework for a specific region should incorporate two major dimensions. First, models should be included to represent economic, ecological and social phenomena. Dynamic models may be used to deal with such phenomena (see Section 3.4). In that context, environmentally sustainable economic development is an important (social) objective. Second, the specific spatial characteristics of the region, both the physical—environmental and socio-economic ones, must be considered when dealing with a policy-oriented micro-scale of analysis. Geographical information systems can assist in sustainable development planning for such policy-oriented purposes, by combining the two dimensions (see Despotakis, 1991).

A number of researchers have been involved in the development of spatial non-dynamic dispersion and diffusion models. Some examples are the Hägerstrand model (Morril *et al.*, 1988), gravity models (Haynes and Stewart, 1988; Trevor and Munford, 1991), transportation models (Werner, 1988; Hagishima *et al.*, 1987). In all these models the processes are not developing over time, i.e. the object propagation in space due to this motion is calculated by the deterministic models at any specific time point. Spatial flow models that used only the distance as a spatial parameter indicate strong spatial correlation of the model residuals. Therefore, model mis-specification may occur when not every spatial aspect is sufficiently taken notice of. On the other hand, several studies that aimed at using GIS for monitoring urban development have also been carried out (Méaille and Wald, 1990). These approaches, although giving very useful results for monitoring urban motion, do not incorporate scenario generation techniques. This implies that regional sustainability criteria cannot be applied. Finally, pioneering studies in applying GIS to environmental database generation have also been conducted in the past (see, e.g., Ahearn *et al.*, 1990), but again, the spatial dynamics was not considered.

The above discussion indicates that a connection between GIS and non-spatial sustainable development analysis is missing. This would have to integrate spatial with non-spatial description (e.g., model-building) and scenario analysis. The link between GIS models and long-term models for sustainable development, as discussed in Section 4.4.5, can be established by taking the following steps (see Despotakis, 1991):

(i)   integration into a GIS of the non-spatial modelling concepts of sustainable development in forms of a set of differential equations;
(ii) aggregation of areal totals and other GIS quantities to arrange correspondence and exchangeability between GIS and non-spatial model results; and
(iii) linking the GIS−economic−ecological system to a decision support system for evaluation of the spatio−temporal alternatives.

In Chapter 11 a modelling study is discussed presenting an example of how one can deal with some of the above mentioned ideas about integration of dynamic, sustainability and evaluation issues in a spatial context. The following chapter contains a detailed overview of methods that can be used to evaluate sustainable development projects or policies, based on multidimensional, monetary or spatial criteria.

5. Methods for Policy Analysis and Implementation

5.1. SUPPORT OF ENVIRONMENTAL POLICY AND MANAGEMENT

As was made clear in Section 4.1 removing the distance between the theory and implementation of sustainable development requires that methods for analysis and implementation are acquired and applied. In Chapter 4 we were concerned with methods for general types of analysis for sustainable development, i.e. for the purpose of obtaining insight in economic–environmental relationships, based on suitable indicators, economic–environmental databases, and accounting and modelling techniques for handling spatial and temporal data. In the present chapter we will deal with methods for policy analysis which embrace those techniques necessary to perform the last part of analyses, namely the evaluation phase. Available evaluation methods are considered in Section 5.2, with particular emphasis on multiobjective methods. These evaluation tools can be used to obtain results on required decisions when evaluation is performed on the outcomes of applications of the techniques of the previous chapter to case studies as in Part Three of this book. In Section 5.3 we discuss the use of decision support for policy making for sustainable development. Since the number and variety of participants in environmental decision processes and the complexity of information related to environmental problems is usually large, one has to pay specific attention to adequate and accessible forms of decision support. Finally, the actual policy that decision-makers may choose, based on the information coming through the decision support process, can be approached from various policy orientations. Therefore, we discuss in Section 5.4 the theory behind the use of environmental policy instruments for implementation of sustainable development. Special attention will thereby be devoted to economic instruments for sustainable development.

5.2. EVALUATION METHODS FOR DECISIONS

5.2.1. Introduction

This section gives a concise overview of evaluation methods for decision support with regard to environmental problems. Broader overviews can also be found in Janssen (1992), Munda (1993) and Munda *et al.* (1993).

An evaluation method is a procedure that supports the ranking of alternatives using one or more decision rules. It is important to know what type and level of support is required and which decision rule is most appropriate for specific problems. Choosing an evaluation method is in itself a decision problem where a trade-off has to be made between comprehensiveness, objectivity and simplicity.

As a start it is necessary to define some basic concepts. A decision rule is a set of rules that facilitates the ranking of alternatives (Chankong and Haimes, 1983). An evaluation method is any procedure that supports the ranking of alternatives using one or more decision rules.

Let *A*, *B*, *C* and *D* indicate different alternatives for the decision to be made. Then an evaluation method can generate:

- a complete ranking   : $A > B > C > D$
- the best alternative   : $A > (B,C,D)$
- a set of acceptable alternatives   : $(A,B,C) > D$
- an incomplete ranking of alternatives : $A > (B,C,D)$ or $(A,B) > (C,D)$
- a presentation of alternatives.

A decision rule is included in the wider concept of a decision strategy. A decision strategy refers to the total set of procedures needed to reach a solution. An attribute is a measurable quantity whose value reflects the degree to which a particular objective is achieved. An objective is a statement about the desired state of the system (Chankong and Haimes, 1983). To assign an attribute (or set of attributes) to a given objective, two properties should be satisfied: comprehensiveness and measurability. An attribute is comprehensive if its value is sufficiently indicative of the degree to which the objective is met. It is measurable if it is reasonably practical to assign a value in a relevant measurement scale. Note that if the relationship between objectives and attributes is not usually specified, comprehensiveness can only be empirically tested by confronting the decision maker with results. Measurable refers to any measurement scale that allows ordering of the alternatives for a particular objective. The ratio, interval ordinal and binary scales qualify as suitable scales of measurement for attributes; the nominal scale does not qualify because it does not allow an ordering of the alternatives (Nijkamp *et al.*, 1990b).

5.2.2. Classes of Multiobjective Decision Support

The elements of an evaluation method are the decision rule, the set of alternatives, and the set of rules by which the value of each attribute is evaluated for a given alternative x. Evaluation methods differ in the type of decision rule applied, the characteristics of the set of alternatives they can handle and the type of rules used to value the attributes.

A typology of evaluation methods is presented in Figure 5.1. It is clear that the choice of a method depends to a large extent on the characteristics of the available information. However, the choice of a method is also dependent on other elements of the problem such as the characteristics of the participants involved and the type of result required. For each class a representative, but certainly not exhaustive, set of methods is included and described in the remainder of this section. It is not possible to include all methods in the enormous set of available methods. A selection is made from various classes of methods with particular relevance to environmental problems. Extensive reviews are given in: Hwang and Masud (1979), Rietveld (1980), Nijkamp and Spronk (1981), Chankong and Haimes (1983), Voogd (1983), Faludi and Voogd (1985), Nijkamp (1986), Winterfeldt and Edwards (1986), Anderson *et al.* (1988), Nijkamp *et al.* (1990b), Janssen *et al.* (1990).

1. The set of alternatives: discrete versus continuous problems
All multiobjective decision problems can be represented in J-dimensional space. Discrete decision problems involve a finite set of alternatives. Continuous decision problems are characterised by an infinite number of feasible alternatives. The selection of a nuclear plant site from nine possible sites is an example of a discrete choice problem. The allocation of nuclear, coal and natural gas resources for the production of electricity is an example of a continuous decision problem.

The emphasis in this section is on discrete evaluation methods. Continuous problems can in principle be translated into discrete problems by selecting an appropriate finite subset from all possible alternatives. Methods to generate such subsets can be found in: Charnes and Cooper (1977), Cohon (1978), Rietveld (1980), Spronk (1981), Zeleny (1982), Chankong and Haimes (1983), Yu (1985), and Steuer (1986).

2. The measurement scale of the attributes: quantitative versus qualitative attribute scales
Most evaluation methods are designed to process quantitative information on attributes. Some methods process qualitative or mixed information. Evaluation by graphics can be used on quantitative, qualitative and mixed decision problems.

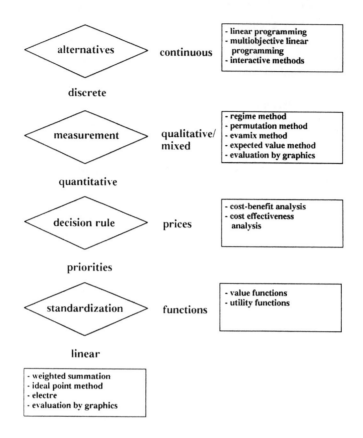

Figure 5.1. Classes of multiobjective decision support.

3. *The decision rule: priorities, trade-offs or prices*

The decision rule is specific to each method. Examples include: maximise total utility (Decision Analysis), maximise the ratio of benefits over costs (Cost−benefit Analysis), minimise the distance to the ideal solution (Ideal Point method; see also Chapter 10) and create a pattern in a diagram (evaluation by graphics). In Cost−benefit Analysis priorities are reflected in (corrected) market prices or through the willingness of individuals to pay. This is in contrast to multi-criteria analysis where priorities reflect the trade-offs of decision makers among objectives.

4. *The valuation function: standardisation versus valuation*

Quantitative scores can be measured in a variety of measurement units. To make these scores comparable, they must be transformed into a common dimension or into a common dimensionless unit. Scores can be transformed into standardised scores using one of the available standardisation procedures or into value or utility indices by defining specific value or utility functions for each effect.

5.2.3. Discrete Quantitative Methods

In this and the next two sections the most well-known multi-objective decision support methods are reviewed. The problem addressed in discrete evaluation methods is to judge the attractiveness of alternatives on the basis of two elements:

(i)   The consequences of the alternatives in terms of the decision criteria. Consider $i(i=1,...,I)$ alternatives and $j(j=1,...,J)$ decision criteria. Let x_{ji} denote the effect of alternative i according to criterion j. The matrix $\mathbf{X}$ of size JxI includes all information on the performance of the alternatives. In this study this matrix will be called the effects table.

(ii) The priorities assigned to the decision criteria are denoted in terms of weights $\mathbf{w}_j$ $(j=1,...,J)$ which are contained in the weight vector $\underline{\mathbf{w}}$.

Discrete evaluation methods differ with respect to the elements in $\mathbf{X}$ and $\underline{\mathbf{w}}$. This section includes short descriptions of the Weighted Summation method, the Multiattribute Utility model, the Ideal Point method and finally the Electre method. These methods require quantitative information on the scores of the criteria as well as on priorities. However, if only qualitative information on priorities is available, several procedures can be applied to produce quantitative weights from these qualitative priority statements. These procedures are described in Section 5.2.5. Important aspects of all methods are their information requirements, the efficiency of the use of information, and the effectiveness of the method in terms of the results.

In *Weighted Summation* an appraisal score is calculated for each alternative by first multiplying each value by its appropriate weight followed by summing of the weighted scores for all criteria. If the scores for the criteria are measured on different measurement scales, they must be standardised to a common dimensionless unit before weighted summation can be applied (Voogd, 1983). The final ranking may be dependent on the type of standardisation applied.

Multi-attribute Utility Analysis is a generalisation of weighted summation. An appraisal score is calculated for each alternative by first multiplying the result of a utility function applied to each value by its appropriate weight followed by summing of the weighted scores for all criteria. In contrast to weighted summation — where a fixed, usually linear, function is used to transform scores — in utility analysis a value or utility function is assessed for each criterion separately. The shape of this function is dependent on the specific characteristics of each criterion. Non-linear, multiplicative or multilinear utility functions are proposed in the extensive literature on utility analysis (Keeney and Raiffa, 1976; Keeney, 1982; French, 1988). These functions are generally believed to provide a good theoretical foundation for describing the utilities of decision makers. They are, however, seldom used in practical applications: firstly due to computational problems and secondly due to the lengthy assessment procedure (Winterfeldt and Edwards, 1986; French, 1988). If the effects of alternatives are uncertain, utility functions can be assessed using, for example, the certainty equivalent or the variable probability method (Keeney and Raiffa, 1976; French, 1988).

In the *Ideal Point Approach* the alternatives are ranked according to the distance that each alternative is removed from a hypothetically ideal situation. Environmental policy is often concerned with removing threats to the environment trying to reach a certain desired state of the environment rather than maximising the overall results of alternatives. This is a useful decision rule for environmental problems. Assuming that alternatives cover all extremes of the solution space, the ideal point can be found by selecting the single objective maximum for each criterion. This is similar to the concept of pay-off matrix as used in relation to mathematical programming (Rietveld, 1980). It is also possible to define the ideal point by the set of policy goals held by the decision maker, if this set is known. The ideal point is defined as the best score on each criterion within this set of criteria. Various distance measures can be applied to establish the distance between the ideal point and each alternative. Chapter 10 contains an application of this method.

The *ELECTRE Method*, also known as concordance analysis, is widely used and especially popular in French-speaking countries (Roy, 1985; Gershon *et al.*, 1982). It is based on a pairwise comparison of the alternatives, thus using only the interval character of the scores in the evaluation of the effects table. The basic idea is to measure the degree to which scores and their associated weights confirm or contradict the dominant pairwise relationships among alternatives. A dominance relationship for each pair of alternatives is derived using both an index of concordance and an index of discordance. The concordance represents the degree to which alternative i is better than alternative i'. The discordance reflects the degree to which alternative i is worse than alternative i'. Beyond a certain level, bad performance on one criterion cannot be compensated for by good performance on the other criterion.

Thresholds supplied by the decision maker, in combination with the concordance and discordance tables, are used to establish a weak and a strong outranking relationship between each pair of alternatives. A procedure of step-by-step elimination is used to transform the weak and the strong graph representing these outranking relationships into an overall ranking of the alternatives. As opposed to the aforementioned methods this one does not always result in a complete ranking, and no information on the differences between alternatives is provided.

5.2.4. Discrete Qualitative or Mixed Methods

Having discussed now quantitative methods for multi-criteria analysis, in this section an overview is given of qualitative methods.

The *Regime Method* can be viewed as an ordinal generalisation of pairwise comparison methods such as concordance analysis (Hinloopen and Nijkamp, 1990). The starting point of the Regime method is the concordance index $c_{ii'}$. The focus of this method is on the sign of $c_{ii'} - c_{i'i}$ for each pair of alternatives. If this sign is positive, alternative i is preferred to i'; and the reverse holds if the sign is negative. Ordinal weights are interpreted as unknown quantitative weights. A set S is defined containing all sets of quantitative weights that conform to the qualitative priority information. In some cases the sign will be the same for the whole set S and the alternatives can be ranked accordingly. In other cases the sign of the pairwise comparison cannot be determined unambiguously. The distribution of the weights within S is assumed to be uniform and therefore the relative sizes of the subsets of S can be interpreted as the probability that alternative i is preferred to alternative i'. Probabilities are aggregated to produce an overall ranking of the alternatives. The Regime Method requires qualitative information on scores and priorities. The method provides information on the relative certainty of the results within the limits of the qualitative information.

The *Permutation Method* (Paelinck, 1974, 1977; Ancot and Paelinck, 1982; Ancot, 1988) addresses especially the question which, of all possible rank orders of alternatives, is most in harmony with the ordinal information contained in the effects table? In the case of I alternatives the total number of possible permutations is equal to $I!$. Kendall's rank correlation coefficient is used to compute the statistical correlation between the $I!$ rank orders and the J columns of the effects table **X** (Kendall, 1970). This results in $I! \times J$ rank correlation coefficients. This method is most suitable for problems where only qualitative information is available on scores and priorities, but can also be used for problems with mixed qualitative/quantitative information on scores and quantitative information on priorities. The method does not always result in a complete ranking but the ranking provided is certain within the limits set by the qualitative information.

The *Evamix method* (Voogd, 1983; Nijkamp *et al.*, 1990b) is designed to deal with an effects table containing both ordinal and quantitative criteria. The set of criteria in the effects table is divided into a set of ordinal criteria O and a set of quantitative criteria Q. For both sets dominance criteria are calculated. The method requires quantitative weights but can be used in combination with any of the methods dealing with ordinal priority information described in Section 5.2.5. A total dominance score is found by combining the indices α_{ij} and β_{ij} calculated separately for the qualitative and quantitative scores. To be able to combine $\alpha_{ii'}$ and $\beta_{ii'}$ both indices need to be standardised. Voogd (1983) offers various procedures for this standardisation.

5.2.5. Priority Information

Weights can be perceived as trade-offs: how much of attribute x is a decision maker willing to sacrifice for the benefit of attribute y. This approach is used in Multiattribute Utility models. In most applications weights are used as a representation of the relative importance of the attributes. Direct estimation of this relative importance by assigning a value to each attribute or by allocating a fixed number of points among the criteria (Voogd, 1983) turns out to be a very difficult task for the decision maker. Therefore in this section two types of methods are included that use ordinal information on priorities in ranking the alternatives.

Trade-off Assessment is closely related to utility analysis and can be used in situations where a linear utility function applies, or can serve as an approximation for a more complex utility function. In this method the decision maker is asked to indicate values for weights by answering questions of the type: how large should c_{12} be in order to guarantee that an improvement of one unit of x_1 is equally attractive as an improvement of c_{12} units of x_2. By repeating this question for all pairs of alternatives all weights can be determined. In practice decision makers have great difficulty answering questions on trade-off or indifference relationships. Jacquet-Lagrèze (1990) proposes to derive weights through direct evaluation of alternatives. The decision maker is asked to rank a small subset of strongly differing alternatives. The information obtained on this subset is used to estimate the weights of the attributes, assuming a linear additive utility function.

The aim of the method known as *Analytical Hierarchy Process* is to derive quantitative weights from qualitative statements on the relative importance of criteria obtained from comparison of all pairs of criteria.

Saaty (1980) proposes a nine-point scale to express differences in importance, ranging from equally important to extremely more important. If the judgements supplied by the decision maker are completely consistent, one row of the comparison matrix **A** would be enough to produce all relative weights. Complete consistency implies that relationships of the type $a_{13} = a_{12}*a_{23}$ hold for all sets of three criteria. This is almost never the case. Therefore an approximation of the weights needs to be made that makes optimal use of the (inconsistent) information available in the comparison matrix.

Ranking Methods can be used if the decision maker is able to rank the criteria in order of importance. Ranking methods treat this ordering as information on the unknown quantitative weights and try to make optimal use of this information. Examples of this type of method are: the Expected Value Method (Rietveld, 1984a and b); the Extreme Value Method (Paelinck, 1974 and 1977); and the Random Value Method (Voogd, 1983).

Expected Value Method assumes that each set of weights within S has equal probability. The weight vector is calculated as the expected value of the feasible set (Rietveld, 1984b). This method gives rise to a convex relationship between ordinal and quantitative weights: the difference between two subsequent weights is larger for more important criteria.

The Extreme Value Method uses the weight vectors on all extreme points of the set *S*. Rankings are determined for each of these weight vectors. Only orderings of alternatives that are found for all of these weight vectors are included in the final ranking. The final ranking therefore holds for all feasible values of the weight vector within the set *S* and no assumption on the distribution needs to be made. In combination with any of the multi-criteria methods described in this chapter, this procedure usually results in an incomplete but certain ranking.

Similar to the Expected Value Method, the *Random Value Method* assumes that the unknown quantitative weights are uniformly distributed within the set of feasible weights *S*. Different vectors of feasible weights can result in different rankings of the alternatives. Using a random generator the ranking of alternatives is determined for a great number of points in *S*. This results in an estimate of the areas in *S* that are linked to a certain ranking. A summation procedure (Voogd, 1983) is used to translate the probabilities assigned to rankings to probabilities that a certain alternative will obtain a certain rank number.

The three ranking methods use the qualitative information on priorities to derive a ranking of the alternatives. The Expected Value Method is straightforward and results in a complete ordering but is dependent on strict assumptions concerning the distribution of weights. The Extreme Value method supplies all possible rankings but therefore often results in an incomplete ranking. The advantage of the Random Value Method is that information is provided on the probability of the rankings, given the qualitative information on weights.

5.2.6.   Cost–benefit Analysis and Discounting

Social Cost–benefit Analysis originates in neoclassical welfare economics. Contrary to Cost–benefit Analysis as used in private enterprise, social Cost–benefit Analysis is based on the concept of consumer surplus (Dasgupta and Pearce, 1972; Mishan, 1988). In CBA all criterion scores that enter the decision rule are transformed into a common monetary unit. Prices need to be determined for criterion scores measured in non-monetary units. These prices can be market prices if available, or corrected market prices. Since no market exists for most environmental stocks, environmental effects need to be priced using valuation techniques (see Sections 4.2.3 and 4.4.6). Qualitative criterion scores and quantitative scores that cannot be priced cannot be included in the various decision rules. Priorities are reflected in (corrected) market prices or through the willingness to pay of individuals. This contrasts with multi-criteria analysis where priorities reflect the trade-offs made by decision makers between objectives.

Scores are transformed into a common time point using a discounting procedure which reflects 'time preference' or the opportunity cost of capital as prevalent in society. This procedure puts a relatively high weight on short-term effects and a relatively low weight on long-term effects (see Section 3.3.3 for a discussion of discounting over multigenerational time periods).

Three decision rules are generally used in CBA:

(i)   the net present value (NPV) of an alternative, defined as the balance of discounted benefits and discounted costs;
(ii) the benefit–cost ratio (BCR) of an alternative, defined as the ratio of discounted benefits to discounted costs; and
(iii) the internal rate of return (IRR) of an alternative, defined as the discount rate that results in equality of discounted benefits and discounted costs.

The choice of a decision rule is dependent on the decision problem. The NPV is most appropriate for problems when one alternative must be selected from mutually exclusive alternatives and no other investment opportunities are available. The BCR and IRR are appropriate if alternatives can be combined and other investment opportunities are available. If costs do not set constraints to the decision all three rules can be used to decide whether an alternative should or should not be implemented (Mishan, 1988).

5.2.7. Conclusions

In Janssen (1992) characteristics of environmental problems have been confronted with characteristics of evaluation methods. It was shown that multi-criteria methods for quantitative, qualitative or mixed information in combination with procedures to process ordinal information on priorities meet the demands of the majority of environmental problems. For application to environmental problems it was recognised that most methods were insufficiently capable of including the time and spatial dimension of priorities and scores in the evaluation and that most methods were insufficiently capable of integrating uncertainties on scores and priorities in the evaluation.

Only Cost−benefit Analysis includes an explicit procedure to integrate the time pattern of effects in the decision rule, namely discounting. But this procedure is not suitable for many environmental problems. For most environmental problems the time pattern of effects can be included by specifying evaluation criteria that reflect the different time spans of the effects. In this case short- and long-term effects appear in the same effects table and are included in a decision rule as separate entries.

The spatial dimension of effects can be dealt with through adequate graphic representations. In most cases it is possible to deal with the spatial dimension through an adequate problem definition. Including a range of methods in a decision support system offers the opportunity to select a method according to specific requirements determined by the problem, stage of the decision process and the decision maker and to switch between methods according to changes in these requirements.

5.3. DECISION SUPPORT OF POLICIES AND MANAGEMENT

5.3.1. Decision Support Systems

The number and variety of participants in environmental decision processes and the complexity of information related to environmental problems call for more adequate and accessible forms of decision support than are presently available. In Section 5.2 an inventory was made of evaluation methods suitable for environmental problems. Such methods can be included in a Multiobjective Decision Support System that supports both the development and the selection phase of an environmental decision process. This will be illustrated in the case studies of Chapters 8, 10 and 11.

Playing is the best and fastest way of learning the most complex things in life. An important reason is that it allows for experimentation under safe and protected circumstances without fatal consequences (Gagné, 1984). The complexity of environmental problems, the time scale and the diversity of environmental effects is such that the implications of decisions affecting the environment are beyond the imagination of most people involved. Instead of trying to explain all the ins and outs of a problem to people involved in a decision, one may offer a learning device to enable them to play around with the problem. In the context of 'serious decisionmaking' such devices are usually referred to as Decision Support Systems (DSS). A MultiObjective Decision Support Systems (MODSS) is then a DSS which puts specific emphasis on using the results of experiments in decision environments characterised by multiple objectives and/or multiple participants. It is an instrument that makes complex environmental problems manageable by coupling the intellectual resources of individuals with the capabilities of the computer. In addition, it provides assistance in interpreting and communicating results and in using the results to invent new ideas and creative solutions.

We regard a decision support system as a computer program that: assists individuals or groups of individuals in their decision processes; supports rather than replaces judgement of these individuals; and improves the effectiveness − rather than the efficiency − of a decision process.

Literature in computer science describes decision support in terms of information processing and according to the various functional elements (Ginzberg and Stohr, 1982; Ariav and Ginzberg, 1985; McLean and Sol, 1986; Sprague and Watson, 1986; Keeney *et al.*, 1988). From management science and planning theory DSS literature adopted the idea of decision making as a process with various stages. Specifically the division of a decision process in intelligence design and choice, as introduced by Simon (1960), and the concept of a decision process as a cyclical process (Faludi, 1971) can be found in almost all literature on decision support. In contrast, economics and psychology focus on the normative aspects of decision making; given a certain definition of optimality decision rules are developed that result in an optimal solution according to the stated rule (Simon, 1959; Keeney and Raiffa, 1976; Rietveld, 1980; Nijkamp *et al.*, 1990b). The way people deal with problems, problem situations and decision aids is the domain of behavioural and cognitive psychology (see, e.g., Neisser, 1976; Keen and Scott Morton, 1978; Huber, 1983; Beach and Mitchell, 1987; Beach, 1990; Yu, 1990). A vast amount of tools for decision support, such as multiobjective optimisation techniques, are available within the field of operations research (Zeleny, 1982; Steuer, 1986).

The number and variety of participants in environmental decision processes and the complexity of information related to environmental problems call for more adequate and accessible forms of decision support than presently available. A Multiobjective decision support system for environmental problems includes methods for decision support − such as multi-criteria analysis, cost−benefit analysis, computer graphics and sensitivity analysis − that are combined with other instruments such as simulation models in a single computer program.

We support the idea that at least for an important subset of environmental problems multiobjective decision support systems can be effectively used to support decisions on these problems. The following steps are necessary to accomplish this: classification and description of environmental decision problems and processes; identification of potential and requirements of multiobjective decision support for these problems; development and implementation of an instrument to support environmental decision making; demonstration of the use of MODSS as applied to important environmental problems; evaluation of the effectiveness of MODSS for environmental problems.

5.3.2. Environmental Decision Problems and Decision Processes

A problem can be defined as a situation where an individual or group perceives a difference between a present state and a desired state, and where: (i) the individual or group has alternative courses of action available; (ii) the choice of action can have a significant effect on this perceived difference; and (iii) the individual or group is uncertain a priori as to which alternative should be selected (cf. Ackoff, 1981).

A decision is a specific commitment to action, usually in conjunction with a commitment of resources. A decision process is a set of actions and dynamic factors that begins with the identification of a stimulus for action and ends with a specific commitment to action (Mintzberg *et al.*, 1976). Decision makers are individuals or groups of individuals who, directly or indirectly, provide value judgements or opinions on the decision process necessary to define and choose between alternative courses of action (cf. Chankong and Haimes, 1983).

Simon (1960) defines three phases in decision processes: (i) searching the environment for conditions calling for decision (intelligence activity);

(ii) phase-inventing, developing and analysing possible courses of action (design activity); and (iii) selecting a course of action from those available (choice activity). Mintzberg *et al.* (1976) redefine the Simon trichotomy into identification, development and selection and describe these phases in terms of seven central routines (see Figure 5.2).

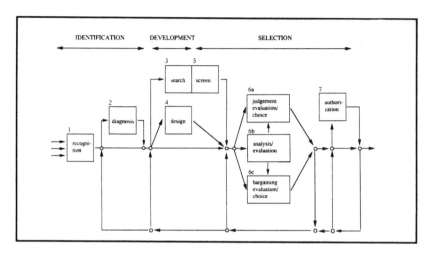

Figure 5.2. A general model of decision processes

Source: Mintzberg *et al.*, 1976.

The identification phase consists of the central routines: (1) Recognition, in which opportunities, problems and crises are recognised and evoke decisional activity; and (2) diagnosis, in which management seeks to comprehend the evoking stimuli and determine cause—effect relationships for the decision situation. The development phase contains: (3) a search routine to find ready-made solutions; and (4) a design routine to develop custom-made solutions or to modify ready-made ones. The selection phase involves: (5) a screen routine when search is expected to generate more ready-made solutions than can be intensively evaluated; (6) an evaluation—choice routine; and (7) an authorisation routine to obtain approval throughout the hierarchy and from outside parties, if necessary. The evaluation-choice routine is considered to operate in three modes: judgement, bargaining and analysis. In judgement (6a), one individual makes a choice in his own mind with procedures that he does not, perhaps cannot, explain; in bargaining (6c), selection is made by a group of decision makers with conflicting goals; and in analysis (6b), factual evaluation is carried out generally by analysts, followed by managerial choice resulting from judgement or bargaining.

A decision process is not a simple sequence of steps. Inherent in a decision process are factors causing the decision makers to return to earlier phases of the decision process. A distinction is made between comprehension cycles and feedback cycles. A comprehension cycle improves the decision maker's understanding of a complex problem by cycling within or between routines. Feedback cycles occur when solutions fail to meet minimal standards and new solutions need to be designed or found.

5.3.3. Objectives of Multiobjective Decision Support

Simon (1976) distinguishes between the substantive and the procedural rationality of a decision process. A decision process is substantively rational if the decision process results in selection of the best solution. A decision process is procedurally rational if the procedure to reach the best solution is appropriate. The aim of a decision process is of course to select the best solution. Unfortunately it is impossible to know a priori whether the solution selected is the best solution since it is impossible to know whether all relevant solutions are included and whether the information on the available solutions is complete. It is equally impossible to decide afterwards whether the best solution has been selected since the decision environment changes over time. It also turns out to be impossible to provide a definition of the quality of a decision in more general terms (Edwards *et al.*, 1984).

The function of a decision process is to transform information, which is the input, to a decision, which is the output of the decision process. This study focuses on the procedural rationality of a decision process. The quality of the decision process is determined by the way inputs, such as information, human resources and models, are used to produce a decision. Therefore, the overall objective of decision support is defined as improvement of the procedural rationality of a decision procedure in order to improve the quality of the decision process. This overall objective can be described by the following three objectives of decision support and therefore of MODSS.

First, effective generation of information on the decision problem from available data and ideas. Information is a function of ideas held by individuals and of available facts. Information is therefore subjective and personal: ideas create information from facts (Roszak, 1986). This objective can be specified as: to maximise the value of the information in making a decision, given the available data and time and processing constraints of the individual making the decision.

Second, effective generation of solutions (alternatives) to a decision problem. Yu (1990) distinguishes between zero, first and second degree expansion of the actual domain of an individual: the space from which an individual can select solutions to a problem. Zero degree expansion occurs when new combinations of elements from the actual domain result in new solutions: expansion through combination. First degree expansion occurs when previously unrecognised information is recognised as relevant to the decision. Second degree expansion occurs when new information is added. This objective of MODSS is specified as follows: to stimulate zero degree expansion by systematically combining what is available, and to stimulate first degree expansion by providing adequate methods to process and present data. Since new ideas are a function of information the provision of the right information can stimulate second degree expansion.

Third, provision of a good understanding of the structure and content of a decision problem. Understanding of a problem can be provided through explanation or by experimentation. The third objective of MODSS is to use experimentation to provide insight into the qualities and limitations of information generated and of the methods to do this.

5.3.4. Functions of Multiobjective Decision Support

An instrument performs functions. To meet the goals listed in the previous section the instrument MODSS must perform certain functions. The following five main functions of MODSS are distinguished:

First, support of the selection phase: by cycling of results of analysis and evaluation repetitively the influence of priorities and assumptions can be analysed.

Second, support of the development phase: cycling through the system supports elaboration of the problem; one idea activates a whole set of ideas; it also supports selection: identifying the key issues of the problem; this may result in an adjustment of existing alternatives, the development of new alternatives and the deletion of irrelevant alternatives; the purpose of this function is to obtain a more complete and adequate set of alternatives.

Third, support learning by doing: by using a DSS decision makers no longer need to communicate with models through an analyst but can have direct access to models and information that are available to support the decision; this allows for 'playing with the problem' and so for learning by doing.

Fourth, support integrated use of judgement, methods and data: how effective is the system in extracting and processing judgement and how well it integrates this with, but also separates it from, other information.

Fifth, support information processing: in MODSS information processing is further supported by combining instruments in one system such as procedures for data management, simulation models, evaluation methods and procedures for sensitivity analysis.

Effectiveness of MODSS for environmental problems will be measured by the performance of the functions of MODSS when applied to environmental problems.

Recent trends in the development of environmental databases (Thomas *et al.*, 1988), Geographical Information Systems (see Section 4.5.1), integrated simulation models (see Section 4.4) and Environmental Management Information Systems (Zoeteman and Langeweg, 1988) result in an increase of information to support decisions.

Effectiveness has been defined in the previous section as the level of achievement of three objectives of decision support. Effectiveness of MODSS for environmental problems will be measured according to the level of performance of the five functions specified in this section in applications to environmental problems. Effectiveness can only be measured in relation to a reference situation. A decision process supported by a single appropriate evaluation method is chosen to be the reference situation. The totally unsupported situation is not chosen, to exclude the effectiveness of the use of an evaluation method by itself from comparison. The added value of a MODSS can be assessed by comparing the situation supported by a MODSS with the situation supported by a single evaluation method.

The disadvantages of MODSS lie mainly in the considerable costs and time involved in developing the systems. As a result the design of a system will be dependent on the size of a problem and on the number of times a problem occurs. Furthermore a flexible design is required to be able to adapt the system to changing circumstances.

5.4. POLICY INSTRUMENTS FOR SUSTAINABLE DEVELOPMENT

5.4.1. Environmental Policy Instruments

In seeking to ensure a sustainable use of natural resources and maintenance of environmental quality, environmental policy can make use of a mix of two basic approaches (see Figure 5.3):

(i) public projects and programs aimed at preventing, compensating and eliminating environmental degradation, such as: collective treatment facilities, environmental sanitation and (re)construction programs;

(ii) influencing decision making processes at the micro level, i.e. economic actors such as consumers, producers, investors.

The latter approach could be regarded as an attempt to implement one particular strategic notion from the Brundtland Commission's report (WCED, 1987), namely merging environmental and economic concerns in private and public decision making.

Environmental policy instruments aimed at sustainability are the policy maker's tools in attempting to alter societal processes to become and remain consistent with environmental sustainability. Such instruments may include, e.g., bans of certain products or processes, charges, deposit–refund systems, education and transmission of information.

Assuming decision makers are rational, decisions of environmentally relevant actors can be influenced via three routes (see Figure 5.3):[1]

(a) alteration of the set of options open to decision makers;
(b) alteration of the relevant cost–benefit ratios of these options;
(c) alteration of the sensitivity or preference for environmental aspects of the options.

Route (a) means: providing new alternatives or forbidding (or licencing) old ones. Typically, this 'command-and-control' approach has been the route followed by environmental policy in most industrialised countries. 'Direct' regulations (i.e. regulations by an external authority directly influencing behaviour) are involved, such as: standards, bans, permits, zoning, quota, use restrictions, etc. These instruments will be referred to here as regulatory instruments.

---

[1] A more elaborated classification of policy and management options is:

1. direct regulation by a public authority: physical standards, permits, norms, zoning;
2. environmental legislation: property rights; arrangement of liability for environmental damage and risk; obligation of environmental impact assessment for large projects;
3. economic or financial instruments: levies, charges, taxes, subsidies, tradeable permits;
4. providing the conditions or supporting R&D: infrastructure, social R&D (universities and research institutes), large investments or projects and loans to private organisations;
5. consistent or complementary policy in other fields:
   a. land use policies, particularly for resource based activities;
   b. nature policy: nature conservation and preservation, restoration of ecosystems, etc.;
   c. economic policy: sectoral subsidies and regulation, direct financial support;
   d. budgetary and finance: ecological tax restructuring (ecotaxes).
6. stimulating voluntary agreements of market participants: environmental covenants, eco-labelling of consumer products;
7. moral suasion via conveying information to the public: direct communication, education;
8. launching temporary public projects aimed at development, restoration, equity, etc.

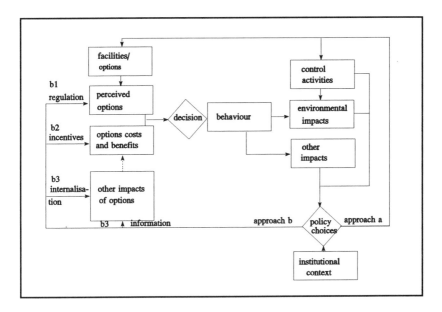

Figure 5.3. Options for environmental policy.

Route (b) leads to the application of economic incentives or market stimuli. The mechanism relied upon here is that if environmentally more appropriate behaviour is made more rewarding in the eyes of the decision maker (or agent) involved, then his/her decisions will 'automatically' shift to these socially more desired alternatives. Options can be made more or less (financially or economically) attractive by applying, among others, charges or levies, granting subsidies and implementing tax differentiation. Such instruments will be referred to below as economic instruments. Note that in this way the environmental concerns have, in a certain sense, been 'internalised', although by altering the direct decision parameters of agents and not in terms of changing preferences structures.

Route (c) would entail approaches such as education, information extension, training, or even social pressure, negotiation and other forms of 'moral suasion'. Here the mechanism is a change of perceptions and priorities within the actor's decision framework, or an 'internalisation' of the environment within the preference structure of the agent. These instruments could be referred to as suasive instruments.

In the following, we shall mainly be concerned with economic instruments, since these will be considered most appropriate for guiding economic systems of production and consumption to a sustainable development path as well as for keeping them on such a path.

5.4.2. The Emergence of Economic Instruments

In the past, environmental policies typically employed the use of regulatory instruments in a 'command and control' strategy. Two major developments, however, have been responsible for changing perspectives on desired policy strategies: (i) growing, experience-based doubts as to the optimality of traditional regulatory instruments (e.g., enforcement costs), and (ii) changes in policy contexts leading to a search for instruments more in concordance or compatible with the post-Brundtland situation. Furthermore, the growing interest in economic instruments is not only stimulated by environmental policy theory (e.g., Baumol and Oates, 1988; Pearce and Turner, 1990) but also evident from empirical studies (see Opschoor and Vos, 1989; Opschoor *et al.*, 1994).

Economic instruments provide incentives to economic actors inducing them to behave in an environmentally more appropriate or acceptable way. Their potential merits include: effectiveness, efficiency, flexibility, incentives for innovation (Baumol and Oates, 1988; Bohm and Russell, 1985; Dietz and Heijman, 1988; Opschoor and Vos, 1989; Bromley, 1990; Opschoor *et al.*, 1994; Portney, 1990; Tietenberg, 1988). If properly chosen, they will ensure that enforcement efforts are minimal. In so far as they apply to sources of environmental degradation, economic instruments are more appropriate in a policy context that places priority on prevention.

The incentives provided may take the form of:

(i)   direct alteration of price or cost levels (as with charges and subsidies);
(ii) indirect alteration via financial or fiscal means (as with, e.g., depreciation allowances for clean installations, deposit−refund schemes, non-compliance fees);
(iii) market creation (as with damage liability extensions and with emissions trading) and market support (as when bottom-prices are guaranteed for secondary materials).

There are a number of reasons for using economic instruments:

(a)   charges or subsidies may be used to correct for market distortions, which are due to government or market failures, to effectively impose the internalisation of environmental maintenance and replacement costs;

(b) they may be used to provide behaviourally relevant incentives to polluters and resource users in order to arrive at some allocative optimum;

(c) they can also be used to provide funds for public or private investment schemes or environmental programs;

(d) they are increasingly being advocated as an appropriate base for general taxation, to replace existing labour oriented schemes based on income, profit or value added (see, e.g., Bovenberg and de Mooij, 1994a and b). in situations where environmental quality and natural resources have become scarcer means of production than labour or manmade capital.

It should be noted that several disadvantages exist as well, notably (see Cumberland, 1994; and Dietz and van der Straaten, 1992): pollution taxes represent a license to 'pollute', have less certain environment effects than direct regulation, may cause undesirable economic effects (barrier to market entry in imperfect markets), have unintended distributional implications (but so does direct regulation), are difficult to assess optimally because of missing data on damage and abatement costs, are based on the unknown optimum equilibrium, cannot be applied to all types of pollution issues (toxic, nuclear), and are − if regulatory and optimal − subject to considerable opposition by various economic and environmental interest groups.

If we define economic instruments loosely, i.e. if we include financial and fiscal instruments that do not have the explicit intention of modifying the behaviour of polluters and resource users (non-regularly, and possibly non-optimal or 'low'), then it is possible to produce an impressive list of economic instruments. In the OECD member countries a total of 150 economic instruments (or over 10 per country surveyed) was in use in 1987. Roughly 50% of these were charges, only about 30% were subsidies and the remainder were other types such as deposit−refund systems and trading schemes. Looking at the various economic instruments in terms of what their purpose was and how they actually performed (in both cases: either providing an incentive or raising revenue), one finds that in terms of the numbers involved, less than half of the economic instruments reviewed had a regulatory intention and over half were meant to raise revenue. Only one third effectively had a regulatory impact (Opschoor and Vos, 1989).

Generally speaking, economic instruments such as charges are likely to have a larger impact on behaviour as they differentiate more between the various options that agents have to choose between, and as the elasticities with respect to price are higher. Once charges have been perceived as potentially substantive by the agents involved, they will give rise to the formulation of expectations as to the levels of the charge over time, and adapt their behaviour accordingly; this is demonstrated by the response of Dutch entrepreneurs to anticipated water pollution charge levels in terms of their own investments in water treatment facilities.

The choice with respect to instruments appears not to be between a regulatory or an economic approach, but rather seems to be between various mixes of instruments. One rarely finds pure cases of economic instruments; typically, they are adjuncts to some regulatory scheme. Examples include: the US trading in emission credits, the Dutch water charge in connection with a permitting system, quota exchange within an overall level or bubble set by public authorities, etc.

An interesting proposal for a 'mixed' instrument is done by Cumberland (1994), namely an approach based on combining property right, incentive and regulatory zones of emission levels, so as to join the advantages of each of the associated pure instruments. See for other recent proposals of alternative instruments Costanza (1994), and in the context of ecosystems, Costanza *et al.* (1992). Costanza (1994) mentions, for instance, natural capital depletion taxes for maintaining, restoring or compensating natural capital destruction or consumption; and a precautionary polluter pays principle (4P) for dealing with pervasive and persistent uncertainties. An example of a concrete instrument in the latter context is a flexible environmental assurance bonding system, based on a deposit-refund scheme for allowing human activities to (intensively) interfere with, or exploit, ecosystems, which have to be in the original state in order for the deposit to be refunded (see Costanza and Perrings, 1990).

5.4.3.   Economic Instruments for Sustainable Development

As environmental policy moves from an effect-oriented, curative approach towards a source-oriented, precautionary approach with concern for the sustainability of the use of environmental resources, economic instruments become more important. They will emerge both as new adjuncts to regulatory approaches (e.g., at the international level: CFC trading, carbon quota, regional acidification funds), and as new instruments in their own right. They can meet the desire for more flexible, effective instruments, and be designed in such a way that they steer behaviour to a sustainable development path.

Another important reason for considering economic instruments is the fact that environmental problems increasingly manifest themselves at higher spatial levels, such as international, continental and global levels.

The international dimension has received a lot of attention recently, since it is regarded as essential for making progress in environmental policy worldwide, as already noted in the Brundtland report. This is reflected by the large number of studies on the relationship between international cooperation and agreements for environmental policy on the one hand, and foreign trade issues, cross-boundary pollution, global environmental problems, and development and poverty issues (see, e.g., Siebert *et al.*, 1980; Kruttilla, 1991; Low, 1992; Anderson and Blackhurst, 1992; Steininger, 1994; *Ecological Economics*, 1994; Barbier and Rauscher, 1994; for a recent overview, see van Beers and van den Bergh, 1995). This indicates that there is growing attention for environmental policy in open economies, which is the most common situation. Since on the international level regulatory bodies are absent or relatively powerless, the regulatory instruments' approach might be difficult to establish or lack sufficient control mechanisms. Although some of the control issues also arise in the case of economic instruments, they are in many cases more easy to realise, for instance, by international cooperation and bargaining for international distribution of gains in economic efficiency due to less environmental externalities.

Moreover, there is a need for using a decentralised approach that makes optimal use of the function of information signals that is performed by prices. More and more, prices of goods and products with a high 'environmental intensity' (i.e. high material and energetic inputs, high pollution and waste content) will have to transmit the costs of this to the buyer and the user from the very emergence of these goods in product chains, so that decision making be optimal in the true sense. This raises the issue of how to value environmental effects as an element of product costs.

One may furthermore anticipate a tendency towards harmonisation in the types of economic instruments in use between countries, and in the standards for sustainable environmental utilisation. Such standards would – if set appropriately – indirectly translate themselves into product prices reflecting environmental scarcities.

Apart from the need for market failure corrections as implicit in much of the above, there is the need to redress factual price distortions in relation to past policy decisions in other fields, such as energy, agriculture and transportation. In these areas, subsidies may (have to) be taken away, leading to alterations in the relative prices. In as much as this leads to a better reflection of relative scarcities including environmental scarcities, the WCED-intention of merging environment and economics in decision making will be realised.

It will turn out to be extremely difficult, however, to incorporate all features of 'sustainability' into economic mechanisms. To begin with, in cases of multiple use of resources, there are difficulties in establishing the appropriate carrying capacities and sustainable use standards (van der Ploeg, 1990) and of optimal costing and pricing (given the likelihood of 'joint products' and pervasive externalities). Secondly, impacts on future generations will not be easy to deal with through pricing mechanisms if only because of the effects of discounting at rates of even 3% and above, but also because uncertainties prevail with respect to future technologies and the (ir)reversibility of many changes in the environment. Thirdly, it may turn out to be extremely difficult to incorporate 'values' or 'stakes' of species and ecosystems into price mechanisms: it has not been adequately possible to value biological diversity, even if in some areas there has been progress. Hence, there are numerous grounds for expecting and even advocating non-economic instruments of the nature of regulatory instruments (and suasive instruments) to cater for socially acceptable risk-taking, concern for future generations and biological diversity.

One other area of future debate is likely to be the scope of the Polluter Pays Principle. It is a principle that may have validity as well as appeal in a setting where the levels of development of the various countries or sectors involved, are comparable. Hence, it may apply within, e.g., the EU or EFTA, or perhaps the OECD region as a whole. However, its validity and acceptability may drop as the spatial level at which the principle is to be applied extends to including nations with totally different situations in terms of development and the associated priorities for environmental protection and resource management. This is relevant now in Europe, both in the East—West context (the formerly socialist countries versus the other ones) and in the North—South context (i.e. the nordic countries versus the mediterranean ones, and more especially Europe versus the developing countries). It is to be expected that new principles e.g., based on solidarity, past accountability, cost-effectiveness or future collective interest, will have to be developed to perhaps partly replace the old adagium of: the polluter or user pays. Such new principles would also need instruments and transfer mechanisms of a financial and/or economic nature. Here, one may think of extending the notion of subsidies in the form of transfers of capital and know-how. One may think of such subsidies to originate from funds created on the basis of pollution related charges (e.g., acidification funds), or on income based international taxation (e.g., GDP-related systems), etc.

5.5. THEORY, FRAMEWORKS, METHODS AND POLICY: CONCLUSIONS

The motivation for this book emerges from the view that it is difficult to assess and evaluate the impacts of management and policy options without the support of accurate methods for dealing with complex evaluation and decision problems. The first part of this book has provided discussions of thermodynamics, alternative theoretical perspectives and integrative frameworks, and concepts and issues related to sustainability. The second part has presented suitable methods and techniques in the context of the economic−ecological theories and the sustainable development issues. Before turning to the case studies in Part Three, some general conclusions are drawn.

Because the use and integration of different methods and techniques is always taking place within the confines of a specific theoretical context, in dealing with methods one should always consider the relevant alternative perspectives first. Each of these includes − in the present setting of economic−ecological analysis − some interpretation of what is essential to the operation of the economy, of ecosystems and their interactions. The different theoretical perspectives on this can certainly inspire formal analyses of a specific environmental−economic issues. The theories may furthermore give rise to various − possibly complementary − definitions and interpretations of sustainable development.

There can also be an interaction between the application of theories on the basis of methods and techniques on the one hand, and the development of new theory on the other hand. This may be especially relevant for research aiming at analysis of policy instruments related to very specific processes and systems, because existing approaches are not always suitable for dealing with some new questions and problems. Some important examples are: management of materials−product chains aimed at efficient resource use, input substitution and recycling; the relation between economic structure and industrial metabolism; the valuation of functions and services of complex ecosystems under various management and development scenarios; the link between biodiversity, sustainability and economic instrumental values of ecosystems; the indirect uses of, and their indirect effects on, ecosystems; and the interaction between, or hierarchy of, human and ecological spatial processes on micro, local and regional levels; and the control and sustainability of open systems, such as sectors or regions.

Different frameworks of integration of scientific disciplines should be considered and re-considered as well. These allow for a particular synthesis of particular economic and ecological concepts and theories, and may not allow for certain other ones to be combined. The choice of a framework is immediately connected to a choice for a specific set of methods to be used. This is important, because the combining of analytical methods determines the type of information that will be made available. One has to decide whether this is suitable for guiding management and policy decisions towards sustainable development.

In addition to the suggestions in the previous section on the role of economic instruments in the areas of environmental policy at the local, regional, continental, or global level, some careful conclusions can be drawn. Although the theory of effluent charges and product charges has a quite long history, there are various impediments to their actual implementation. One may realise a consistent and wide-ranging implementation via systems of tax differentiation, or even ecological tax revision (ecotaxes). A second way of realising implementation of economic instruments is by full use of the market mechanism, i.e. via emissions and quota trading. This can be pursued on various levels, ranging from regional to international. The main advantage of a pollution rights' trading system on the level of national environmental policy planning is that it can allow for replacement of the commonly accepted 'fair' − i.e. on the basis of historical patterns of and relative sector contributions to emissions − distribution of environmental constraints by economic efficient allocation of pollution rights on the basis of market trading. The same holds for the international level, where 'fairness' often is interpreted quite differently by industrial (OECD) and developing countries. The distribution on sector levels may be separated from the efficient allocation. Indeed, equitable distribution is more relevant as an objective on a individual, household or income group level, and should be separated from sectors. Next, it seems that also deposit refund and enforcement incentive systems can become very effective and efficient economic instruments, especially in terms of influencing new product and process technology, materials management, recycling, and product life cycles such that materials−product chain relationships become more consistent with long-term environmental sustainability. Finally, the use of economic instruments to deal with behaviour of individuals and activities related to the local or regional scale of ecosystems is a difficult topic. Economic−ecological models on a regional scale may support the analysis of such policy instruments. However, for some relevant questions, for instance, regarding the effects of pricing instruments on recreational behaviour in natural areas and multiple use of wetlands, it is not easy to come up with simple answers.

In the third part of the book applications of some of the methods discussed in Chapters 4 and 5 are presented for five independent studies. Though these are, of course, unable to cover all of the aspects mentioned before, they are aimed to be instructive about the possible assumptions, links between theories and methods, data, methodological steps, and difficulties associated with applied economic – ecological analysis. Table 5.1 indicates which methods are applied in the various case studies in Part Three of this book.

Table 5.1. Method Application in Part Three of the Book

CHAPTER	SI	EA	MB	DM	ID	EE	EV	SA
			METHOD					
6	+		+	+	+			
7	+	+	+	+	+			
8	+			+	+	+	+	
9	+			+	+	+		
10	+				+		+	
11	+			+	+	+	+	+

Notes:

SI = Sustainability indicators
EA = Environmental accounting
MB = Materials balance
DM = Dynamic model
ID = Integrated description of economy – environment system
EE = Ecosystems explicit
EV = Evaluation (CBA/MCA)
SA = Spatial analysis

PART THREE

Application of Methods — Case Studies

6. A Multisectoral Growth Model with Materials Flows and Economic–Ecological Interactions[1]

6.1. INTRODUCTION

In this chapter we consider the design and use of a dynamic macro model which aims to provide an analytical framework for the study of the long term development of an economy in relation to its natural environment. The model may serve to assist decision makers in distinguishing between various policy strategies (or scenarios) that give rise to sustainable and unsustainable developments. Particular attention is devoted to the conceptual structure and specification of the model.

The model is designed with the aim to study the long term relationship between an economy and its natural environment. The approach is based on two main elements: (i) reciprocal interactions between on the one hand population growth, investment, allocation of inputs and outputs, technology and productivity, and on the other hand declining environmental quality, pollution and resource exhaustion; and (ii) a more realistic and consistent representation of the interdependence between various environmental effects, from extraction to emission, by using a materials balance (MB) perspective on economic processes. The model includes production functions that are consistent with MB. The model is multisectoral, including economic processes of extraction, production of commodities and investment goods, waste abatement and recycling. Environmental processes of resource regeneration and waste assimilation are linked through the economic and environmental sphere. Disaggregation leads to economic categories of investment goods, and

---

[1] An elaborate version of this chapter, including a discussion of formal expressions of materials balance production functions, is van den Bergh and Nijkamp (1994c). Results obtained with a simplified, early version of the model are presented in van den Bergh and Nijkamp (1991c). For an explanation of symbols see the Appendix at the end of this chapter.

private and public consumption, and to environmental categories of non-renewable resources, renewable resources, slowly renewable resources, and environmental pollution. The model allows for endogenous development of resource-efficient technology. Feedback mechanisms are included that take account of the effect of sustainability conditions and societal values on both technology formation and allocation of investment goods over the various economic sectors. The model is specified, calibrated and subsequently used for simulation of scenarios. Finally, some sensitivity analysis results are discussed.

What are the implications of production combined with MB for long term development? Here this question will be answered by analysing a multisectoral integrated macro model. The model describes two phenomena: (i) the material flows (and processes based upon these flows) in the economy, the natural environment and their interdependencies; and (ii) the feedback mechanisms from economy, environment and value systems to economic actions and policies. The latter occurs over a long term horizon.

The material flow is shown in Figure 6.1. It describes an economy with 6 sectors. The model has a supply orientation reflecting a long-term horizon. The model includes economic and materials balance conditions, economic activity, and production functions. These production functions satisfy materials balance conditions, as discussed in van den Bergh and Nijkamp (1994c). Economic activities include resource extraction, production, waste treatment (abatement), recycling, research and development of environmental technology, and environmental cleaning. Some of these activities are taken to be competitive for economic (financial) means, and can to some extent be stimulated by government policies.

In Figure 6.2 the economic–environmental relationships represented in the model are displayed. They include flows as well as impacts upon processes. An environmental quality indicator related to stocks of resources and pollution is used as a state variable for co-determination of the level of natural processes of regeneration and assimilation. Environmental quality is also assumed to have an impact upon the efficiency of final goods production (e.g., agriculture) and the quality of extracted renewable resources (e.g., the stock of fish). It is important to note that also changes in non-economic variables, viz. technology and population, are included.

The description of the economic activities module is based upon production and activity functions for six sectors: final goods production; investment goods production; waste treatment; recycling activity; renewable resource extraction; and non-renewable resource extraction.

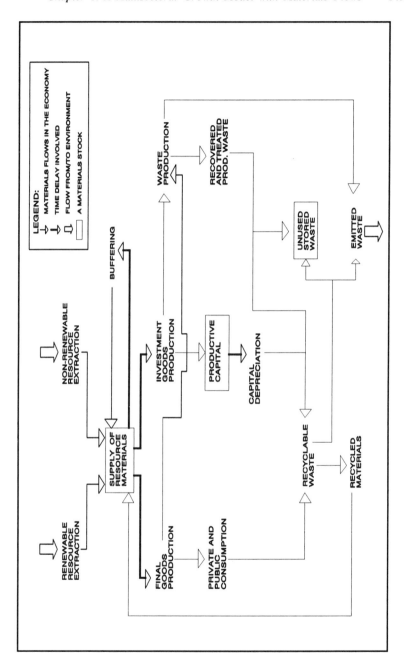

Figure 6.1. Materials flow diagram of the economy.

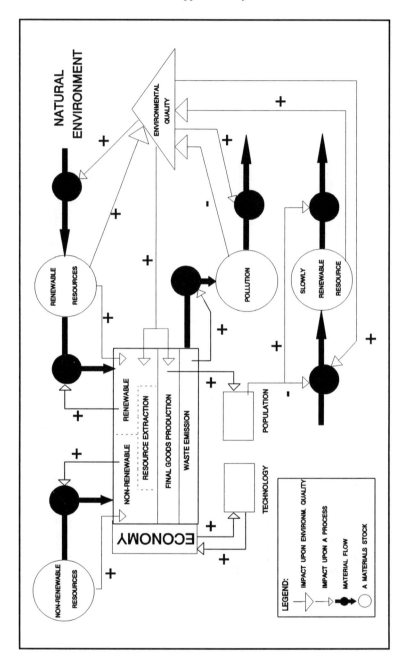

Figure 6.2. Economy−environment flows and relationships.

The functions satisfy, where necessary, materials balance conditions, and may include a mix of environmental and economic production factors, available resource materials (in inventory), environmental quality and the technological progress indicator.

6.2.   SECTORS, PRODUCTION, EQUILIBRIUM AND DYNAMICS

6.2.1.   Economic Sectors and Production Functions with Environmental Variables and Materials Balances

The first economic sector is an aggregate of all final goods producing sectors (including relevant types of agriculture). Output (Q) is produced with capital (K_Q). It requires resource inputs $c_Q(T_{rd})$ per unit of output. A higher overall environmental quality (E) positively affects the productive efficiency. The availability of resources (R_{sup}) in inventory (i.e., supply of resource materials) imposes an upper limit on the output level of production. Therefore, we have the output function as in (6.1). It is in agreement with the third type of materials balance production function (MBPF) formulation as given in van den Bergh and Nijkamp (1994c).

$$Q = MIN \left\{ F_Q(K_Q, E), \frac{R_{sup}}{c_Q(T_{rd})} \right\} \tag{6.1}$$

It is clear that output Q cannot exceed resource input and that some material loss in production is inevitable. This means that $c_Q(T_{rd}) > 1$. Technological change is assumed to generate more efficiency in terms of a lower ratio of resource input to Q, so that $dc_Q(x)/dx < 0$.

A second activity is capital goods formation (I). This may be interpreted as the production of machines and new technology. The level of output is directly related to the amount of capital in this sector (K_I). An upper limit to the output level is set by taking the ration of the supply (inventory) of resource materials (R_{sup}) less the amount required for the first (Q) production process to the per unit of output required input in this sector; thereby it is assumed that Q-production is more important than I-production for general welfare, and is therefore given priority for resource use; $c_I(T_{rd})$ is like $c_Q(T_{rd})$ made dependent on the state of technology T_{rd}. Again, (6.2) is of the third type of MBPF (van den Bergh, 1991, Section 4.3.3.; van den Bergh and Nijkamp, 1994c).

$$I = MIN \left\{ F_I(K_I), \frac{R_{sup} - c_Q(T_{rd}) * Q}{c_I(T_{rd})} \right\} \tag{6.2}$$

Next, we consider two other economic sectors that are related to environmentally beneficial activities. Both sectors use capital. One process represented in (6.3) treats production waste in such a way that not all of it is directly carried to the natural environment. The amount of waste treated (R_{wa}) is determined by the level of waste arising directly from the two 'real' production processes ($W_{Q,I}$), the amount of capital used (K_{wa}), and the state of technology (T_{rd}). The latter two affect positively the effectiveness coefficient (f_{wa}) of abatement.

$$R_{wa} = f_{wa}(T_{rd}, K_{wa}) * W_{Q,I} \tag{6.3}$$

A second process represented in (6.4) is concerned with recycling of materials. Its output R_{rec} is determined by the waste flow suitable for recycling (W_{rec}) and the state of technology, which positively affect the effectiveness coefficient (f_{rec}) of recycling.

$$R_{rec} = f_{rec}(T_{rd}, K_{rec}) * W_{rec} \tag{6.4}$$

The functions f_{wa} and f_{rec} have values between 0 and 1, so that abated (recycled) waste does not exceed production waste (waste amenable for recycling): $R_{wa} < W_Q$ ($R_{rec} < W_{rec}$); all first partial derivatives are positive. Both (6.3) and (6.4) are special cases of the last type of general MBPF as mentioned in van den Bergh and Nijkamp (1994c).

Finally, two-resource based economic activities remain to be described: renewable and non-renewable resource extraction (R_N and R_S, respectively), both using capital (K_N and K_S, respectively). The production functions, given in (6.5) and (6.6), are based upon respective stocks or resources; in the case of renewable exploitation, the environmental quality is also significant since it determines the part of the stock that is of sufficient quality (e.g., clean water, or healthy, non-toxic resources, normal size fish).

$$R_N = MIN \left\{ F_N(K_N, N, E), R_{N,perc} \right\} \tag{6.5}$$

$$R_S = MIN\{F_S(K_S, S), R_{S,perc}\} \qquad (6.6)$$

All production functions (F_Q, F_I, F_N, F_S) have positive partial derivatives. Extraction rates are limited from above by the perceived or acceptable levels of extraction ($R_{N,perc}$ and $R_{S,perc}$), which are based on a combination of ethical and ecological considerations (see Section 6.5). The production functions in (6.5) and (6.6) should not be confused with MBPF per se. $R_{N,perc}$ and $R_{S,perc}$ will in general be beneath a level of material availability as represented by actual physical stocks in the ground, since they represent perceived or acceptable levels from an ethical or value point of view (Section 6.5).

6.2.2. Economic Dynamics and Equilibrium Conditions

The economic dynamics incorporates changes in capital stocks, population, technology/knowledge, stored waste, and the inventory of resource materials. The changes in capital stocks depend on the allocation of investment (I_i, $i \in K$, $K = \{Q, I, wa, rec, N, S\}$) and the rates of depreciation ($D(K)$). The stock of capital depreciates at a rate given by $D(K)$ which is strictly monotonously increasing:

$$\frac{dK_i}{dt} = I_i - D_i(K_i), \quad i \in K \qquad (6.7)$$

The equation to describe technological progress is based on sustainable development feedback (e_e), total investment (I), governmental support for R&D (O_{rd}), and the Kaldor–Verdoorn effect (dZ/dt); δ falls in between 0 and 1 and where the two remaining coefficients are positive and increasing in e_e:

$$\frac{dT_{rd}}{dt} = \alpha(e_e) * I + \varepsilon(e_e) * \left[O_{rd} + \delta * \frac{dZ}{dt} \right] \qquad (6.8)$$

The population change is determined by the population level (*Pop*) and the level of material consumption (*C*) per capita (used as a welfare indicator):

$$\frac{dPop}{dt} = B\left[\frac{C}{Pop} \right] * Pop \qquad (6.9)$$

A stock of stored waste that cannot be reused (S_{wa}) is filled from regained production waste (a part s_1) and waste left after recycling (a part s_2; $0 < s_1, s_2 < 1$).

$$\frac{dS_{wa}}{dt} = s_1 * R_{wa} + s_2 * (W_{rec} - R_{rec}) \qquad (6.10)$$

Two state variables are introduced to represent time-delays. The inventory (buffer) of resource materials R_{sup} is introduced to allow for a time-delay between the processes of recycling and resource extraction on the one hand, and the re-use of materials in production of final goods and investment goods on the other. This inventory can be regarded as the total supply of resources (then its initial condition has to be in accordance with this interpretation). This inventory originates from four sources: renewable and non-renewable resource extraction, recycling and buffering (inventory). The latter will occur when the amount of materials needed for production is smaller than that in the stockpile.

$$\frac{dR_{sup}}{dt} = R_N + R_S + R_{rec} - \left(c_Q(T_{rd}) * Q + c_I(T_{rd}) * I\right) \qquad (6.11)$$

The choice for aggregation of renewable and non-renewable resources is to see how the use of one type develops over time relative to the use of the other. It is implicitly assumed then that the units of measurement of both R_N and R_S are such that they can be aggregated via simply adding the respective variables. This may require an additional assumption that extraction also involves some processing into a sufficient quality or concentration of required materials.

Finally, Z is an indicator for that part of total production output, the change in which has a strong impact on materials saving progress in production technology (see the equation for T_{rd}).

$$\frac{dZ}{dt} = Q + I - Z \ , \qquad Z(0) = Q(0) + I(0) \qquad (6.12)$$

The initial conditions are $K_i(0) = K_{i0}$ ($i \in K$), $T_{rd}(0) = 0$, $Pop(0) = Pop_0$, $S_w(0) = 0$, $R_{sup}(0) = R_{sup,0}$, $Z(0) = Q(0) + I(0)$, with all parameters non-negative.

Next, three economic balance conditions are required: equation (6.13) reflects the fact that production output of the final goods sector equals consumption (C) plus social R&D outlays (O_{rd}); (6.14) reflects the idea that production of capital goods equals the sum of sectoral investments (I_i); and (6.15) that total capital is the sum of sectoral capital stocks.

$$Q = C + O_{rd} \tag{6.13}$$

$$I = \sum_{i \in K} I_i \tag{6.14}$$

$$K = \sum_{i \in K} K_i \tag{6.15}$$

6.3. THE ECOLOGICAL SYSTEM

As far as the description of the ecological system is concerned, an aggregate ecological model should be consistent with a macroeconomic or regional system in terms of geographical coverage. Therefore, it should describe the essential features of a collection of various (possibly interacting) homogeneous ecological systems. Such a general model would have to be able to deal with the several functions and characteristics of ecological systems: (i) regenerative capacity, (ii) assimilation of pollution, (iii) resource supply, (iv) storage of waste materials, (v) non-material services for consumption, (vi) decreasing performance of all functions for increasing levels of pollution and/or decreasing resource stocks, and for an increasing level of other disturbances.

$$E = H(N,B,P),$$
$$dN/dt = G(N,E) - R_N,$$
$$dP/dt = -A(P,E) + W_{em},$$
$$dB/dt = \left[b_1(E) - b_2(dK/dt) - b_3(dPop/dt) \right. \tag{6.16}$$
$$\left. - b_4(R_N) - b_5(R_S) \right] * B,$$
$$dS/dt = -R_S.$$

The equations in (6.16) show a model that describes three types of environmental processes: slow and regular regeneration of resource stocks (B and N, respectively), and assimilation of pollution (P). B can be regarded as semi-renewable, i.e. falling in between a renewable and non-renewable resource (see Swallow, 1990); one may think of such categories as soil, land and water or even rain forests and similar slowly regenerating and sensitive natural systems. N may, for instance, denote biotic resources or ecosystems. The respective stocks and the overall environmental quality (E) have a non-negative relationship with the rates at which each process occurs. E is a function of N, P and B. This means that all environmental processes depend indirectly upon all three environmental stocks. A fourth environmental stock is that of non-renewable resources (S), which is assumed to have no natural environmental linkages with the other stocks or their natural processes. The exogenous impacts upon N and P are resource extraction (R_N) and waste emission (W_{em}), respectively. B is influenced by the pressure of the scale of the economy (indicated by economic capital K), the size of the population (Pop), and the intensity of extractive activities (indicated by the rates of renewable and non-renewable resource exploitation R_N and R_S). S decreases by extraction (R_S).

The initial conditions are $N(0) = N_0$, $P(0) = P_0$, $B(0) = B_0$, $S(0) = S_0$. All functions and variables are non-negative. $H(\ )$ is increasing in N and B and decreasing in P. The natural growth function satisfies $G(N_{min}, E) = G(N_{max}, E) = 0$, and for some (N, E), with $0 < N_{min} < N^* < N_{max}$, $E > 0$: $G(N^*, E) > 0$, where N_{min} is the minimum viable level of the regenerative resource and N_{max} denotes its maximum level (also referred to as carrying capacity). The natural assimilation function A is increasing in P. G and A are increasing in E. All b_i ($i = 1, 2, 3, 4, 5$) and their first derivatives are positive.

6.4. MATERIALS BALANCE CONDITIONS

Finally, the following material balance conditions apply to the flows within the economy and to the natural environment. Total waste output ($W_{Q,I}$) from 'real' production is equal to the inputs less the outputs:

$$W_{Q,I} = \left[c_Q(T_{rd}) - 1 \right] * Q + \left[c_I(T_{rd}) - 1 \right] * I \qquad (6.17)$$

This 'dirty' waste is treated first (producing R_{wa} in equation (6.3)) before it goes to one of three categories (see Figure 6.3, namely unused stored waste, waste amenable for recycling, or emitted waste, as reflected by equations (6.10), (6.19) and (6.22), respectively.

The indicator of the demand for new resources is based on the amounts needed as inputs to production of Q and I less the recycled amounts from the present period:

$$R_{new} = c_Q(T_{rd}) * F_Q(K_Q, E) + c_I(T_{rd}) * F_I(K_I) - R_{rec} \qquad (6.18)$$

Waste amenable for recycling purposes is the sum of private and public consumption, discarded capital and a part of treated production waste:

$$W_{rec} = Q + \sum_{i \in K} D_i(K_i) + (1 - s_1) * R_{wa} \qquad (6.19)$$

The result W_{rec} goes into the recycling process (equation (6.4)). As is made clear in equations (6.10) and (6.20), the expression 'amenable for recycling purposes' indicates that only part of W_{rec} will be recycled (i.e., recycling is stricly less than 100%), and the remaining part ends up as waste that is being stored or emitted.

Emission of waste to natural mediums (W_{em}) thus equals the sum of non-treated production waste and the part of waste remaining after recycling that is not stored into S_{wa}:

$$W_{em} = (W_{Q,I} - R_{wa}) + (1 - s_2) * (W_{rec} - R_{rec}) \qquad (6.20)$$

6.5. SUSTAINABLE DEVELOPMENT FEEDBACK

Sustainable development feedback can be regarded as a process of adjustment to meet or approximate sustainable development conditions (see Section 3.2.1). Such conditions reflect goals associated with intergenerational equity and the maintenance of natural environmental qualities and quantities. We make a distinction between two types of conditions. First, constraints may be set on the level of welfare (for a whole generation or per capita), where the choice is to require that welfare: (i) exceeds a given subsistence level; and (ii) follows a non-decreasing time path. A second type is formed by constraints on stocks or flows (interchangeable) in and between economic and environmental systems. The notion of stock constancy may serve as an illustration of sustainable development conditions of the latter type.

The completed model allows for feedback from environmental quality, overall resource scarcity, unsustainable renewable resource exploitation, and unsustainable waste emission pollution to decisions regarding investment activities and technology. Conditions based on regeneration and assimilation on the one hand, and concern for future generations and natural environment on the other, are central in the feedback mechanism. They determine the acceptable or aspired extraction and emission levels.

In the model this proceeds as follows. At the core are sustainable development (flow) conditions that apply to the flows of resources and waste of the type mentioned above. These are transformed, via behaviourial or social control parameters, into variables that indicate the perceived levels. This involves an ethical choice by society or decision makers with regard to the degree of concern for the well-being of future generations. Market mechanisms (prices) and social controls (regulations and price corrections) are implicitly taken into account. They provide incentives that have an effect on the model outcome via the reaction of investment allocation and technological progress. For instance, a strong incentive may result from scarcity of resources through increasing prices. Low regeneration or assimilation rates, or increasing (decreasing) stocks of pollution (renewable resources), may induce social actions. These may take the form of controlling investment through land use policies, subsidies on environmentally beneficial investments, or artificial higher prices for resource materials. They may also stimulate certain technological changes by subsidies or time paths for required levels of resource use or waste generation.

Based on social value considerations with respect to future generations and the relationship with nature, as well as ecological considerations with regard to regeneration and assimilation, we can devise the following three indicators: acceptable renewable ($R_{N, perc}$), non-renewable ($R_{S, perc}$), and total (R_{perc}) resource extraction:

$$R_{N,perc} = MAX\{0, d * p_N * N + (1-d) * G(N,E)\} \qquad (6.21)$$

The dummy variable d may reflect an objective of sustainable use ($d=0$) or a less strict objective ($d=1$), which requires an additional parameter for intergenerational concern, p_N (falling between 0 and 1); the latter shows high degrees of moral concern for future generations by taking low values. A second interpretation of this parameter is variable degrees of caution (prudence or risk-aversion) in the face of high uncertainty.

$$R_{S,perc} = p_S * S \qquad (6.22)$$

The parameter p_S is similar to p_N for non-renewable resources. Therefore, d, p_N and p_S reflect value stances.

$$R_{perc} = R_{N,perc} + R_{S,perc} \qquad (6.23)$$

Thus, total perceived resource availability is simply the sum over the two sources. Notice that this is a sum of *perceived* and not real quantities.

A variable R_{short} indicates the scarcity of resources by taking the ratio of R_{perc} and the required extraction of resources (R_{new}, see equation (6.18)). A value higher than one means that there is no reason for an sudden strong economic reaction.

$$R_{short} = MIN\left\{1, R_{perc}/R_{new}\right\} \qquad (6.24)$$

Other specifications may serve the same purpose, but (6.24) has the advantage of generating a dimensionless number.

Similar to the approach for resource feedbacks, one can also take a ratio of waste assimilation $A(P, E)$ and waste emission to obtain an indication of the degree of unsustainability of waste emission (too much waste emission, indicated by W_{too})[2]:

$$W_{too} = MIN\left\{1, A(P,E)/W_{em}\right\} \qquad (6.25)$$

Since all three variables R_{short} and W_{too} have values ranging from zero to one, the following functional structure ensures a range similar to that of E for the ecological effect variable e_e that appears in the model of endogenous technological progress in (6.8) and later in the investment (feedback) decision process (equations in (6.27) in Section 6.6.2).

$$e_e = R_{short} * W_{too} * E \qquad (6.26)$$

Based upon the indicator e_e we can include a feedback from the environmental state and the ethical stance to economic actions or decisions. This means that, in addition to feedback to production technology (equation (6.10)), investment rules can be stated that

---

[2] Sustainable waste emission is used analogously to sustainable resource use in a strict sense (applied to renewable resources): the controlled flow of waste emission is such that the stock of pollution remains at the same level, or, in other words, such that the assimilative capacity is not exceeded. Alternatively, one may define it as avoiding a decrease in the stock of renewable resources, since it is linked to the assimilative capacity. In fact, sustainable management could be defined as a choice of combinations of resource extraction (use) and residuals emission, such that the resource size – and thus the assimilative capacity – is not reduced.

incorporate the relevant indicator. This will be done in the context of specific scenarios in Section 6.6.2.

6.6. SPECIFICATION, CALIBRATION, SCENARIO AND SENSITIVITY ANALYSIS

6.6.1. Specification and Calibration

Calibration was performed in order to satisfy conditions on initial values that reflect several aspects of supply−demand balance and environmental sustainability, so that a stationary or stable pattern is accomplished during an certain period of time. These conditions van be found in van den Bergh and Nijkamp (1994c, Appendix B). The calibration also aimed at producing a base case model that represents a rather pessimistic opinion about the ultimate state of the economic system far in the future, namely one that collapses. This is done for the sake of comparative analysis of scenarios, i.e. tracing the differential effects of certain additional developments or policies as compared to the base case. Such a choice does certainly not mean to imply that a base case will give rise to a collapsing system in the very long run. Such a prediction cannot be provided with any appropriate degree of accuracy. Accordingly, the present model is not aiming at solving predictive issues.

The aggregation level of the model makes it difficult to base functional forms and parameter values on empirical data with straightforward interpretations. Estimated values for parameters are partly chosen in a realistic range. Some of these represent fractions, which are logically constrained. Others are based on, for instance, notions of maximum efficiency (such as in the case of recycling). The motivation for such choices are mentioned hereafter. Other variables have a long run physical interpretation, so that their units of measurement are to be interpreted accordingly. Some values are set fixed over all scenarios, after calibrating to meet the above mentioned goals. Variations were allowed in other variables (controls) on the basis of their interpretation, policy relevance, strategic value, or because of model sensitivity. The model base case and the various scenarios are thus hoped to represent a realistic setting, which may be a country with an economy that is to a large extent based on natural resources and environmental conditions within its national boundaries.

The specifications and parameter choices result from consistency requirements and minimal functional characteristics, realistic ranges for some important, uncertain, policy or behavioural parameters (possibly changing over time). All functions and variables are non-negative. For more details on assumptions, data and specifications the reader is referred to van den Bergh and Nijkamp (1994c).

6.6.2.   Scenario Analysis

Scenario analysis serves two purposes. First, it shows the type of patterns that can be generated by the model. Second, certain types of strategies and exogenous events and processes can be illustrated by it. The sensitivity analysis is restricted here to changes in certain initial environmental stocks, as these may have a large impact upon the system.

Table 6.1   Scenarios for Analysis.

SCENARIOS	CONTROL			VARIABLES		
	K_I	N	P	S	d	inv
0. Base Case	3.6	15,000	100	3000	1	0
1. No Ethical Concern			599		0	
2. Low Level of Environmental Quality		10,000	599		0	
3. Low Level of Nonrenewables				1000	0	
4. Low Quality and Ethical Concern		10,000				
5. Moderate Growth	5				0	
6. Strong Growth	7				0	
7. Extreme Growth	10				0	
8. Sustainability and Ethical Concern						1
9. Extreme Growth, Sustainability and Ethical Concern	10					1
10. Extreme Growth and Sustainability	10				0	1

Notes
An empty cell indicates that the same value for the control variable applies as in the base case scenario; K_I, N, P, S, d and *inv* stand for initial stocks of capital in the investment sector, initial stocks of natural resources, pollution and non-renewable resources, and two dummy variables for the presence or absence of ethical concern and the feedback to investment allocation, respectively.

Table 6.1 lists 11 scenarios under which model simulations were performed. The results of these in terms of generated time patterns for certain indicators are shown in Figures 6.3 to 6.10. Table 6.1 indicates which control variables in scenarios 1–10 differ from the Base Case scenario 0. These variables were choosen in order to take the value system, environmental quality, non-renewable resources, and the pace of growth into account. The 'Base Case' scenario 0 represents a stationary economy (no capital stock changes) with a balance of the demand for and supply of investment goods, maximum environmental quality, a balance of demand for and supply of resource materials, and maximum ethical concerns for future generations. Each of the other scenarios deviates from this base case scenario in at least one of these respects. Scenario 1, 'No Ethical Concern', differs from the Base Case by including a minimum of ethical concern, as reflected by the dummy d (see equation (6.21)). In the scenarios 2, 'Low Level of Environment Quality', and 4, 'Low Quality and Ethical Concern', the environmental quality variable E is initially equal to 0.5 as a result of the chosen initial – lower than in the base case – stock values for renewable resources and pollution. The scenarios 5, 6 and 7, 'Moderate Growth', 'Strong Growth' and 'Extreme Growth', represent moderate, strong and very strong ex ante growth schemes, based on a choice of the initial capacity for growth, given by the stock of capital in the investment sector. Scenarios 8 to 10, 'Sustainability and Ethical Concern', 'Extreme Growth, Sustainability and Ethical Concern', and 'Extreme Growth and Sustainability', try to differentiate the effects of extreme growth, and ethical concern, given the active sustainability feedback to investment decisions. This means that investment is re-allocated from final output to abatement and recycling when the indicator e_e (taking values between or equal to 0 and 1) is below its maximum. The correction terms that are applied respectively to investment in final goods production, waste abatement, and recycling are given in (6.27).

$$correction \ I_Q = cor_{I_Q} = -inv * part_Q * (1 - e_e) * I_Q$$
$$correction \ I_{wa} = part_{wa} * cor_{I_Q}$$
$$correction \ I_{rec} = part_{rec} * cor_{I_Q} \tag{6.27}$$
$$part_{wa} + part_{rec} = 1$$

The parameter values chosen are as follows: $part_{IQ} = part_{Iwa} = 0.5$; the pattern of Q was similar when $part_{Iwa}$ was changed in 0 or 1. The dummy inv denotes whether or not the feedback to the investment allocation is working (1 and 0, respectively). In scenario 'Sustainability and Ethical Concern' the initial allocation and level of investment are based on the assumption of a stationary state. In scenario 9 strong growth is combined with endogenous investment allocation. Scenario 10 differs from 9 by suppressing strong ethical concern, so that reactions in both investment allocation and technological progress will be less than under scenario 9.

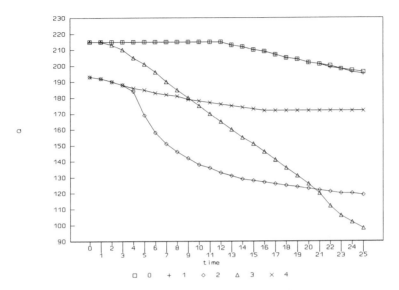

Figure 6.3. Final goods production for scenarios 0–4.

Since environmental quality is higher for scenarios 0, 1 and 3 than for scenarios 2 and 4, the initial production output is also higher (see Figure 6.3). For scenarios 2 and 3, environmental quality is the single cause of decreases in output. For the other three scenarios resource scarcity is an additional cause, as it leads to under-investment and decreasing stocks of capital over time (see Figure 6.4). However, the curve for scenario 4 in Figure 6.3 shows that more concern for future generations and natural environment gives rise to a slowing down of the decline in output. Notice that the difference between scenarios 0 and 1 is negligible, due to the fact that a stronger ethical concern (as in the Base Case scenario 0) does not give rise to impacts on (tempered) growth as long as the system behaves in a sustainable pattern over the time period considered. However, when a non-stable pattern is followed, the differential outcomes of scenarios 2 and 4, which is due to the same difference in control settings, is not negligible.

The pace of technological progress is apparently influenced by 3 factors: investment, environmental effects, and ethical concerns. With specific attention (or ethical concern) for future and environment, and

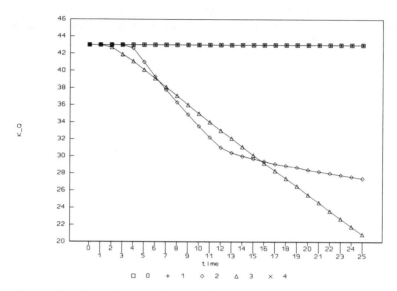

Figure 6.4. Capital in the final production sector for scenarios 0−4.

with an non-optimal environmental quality, technological progress is seen to be highest in scenario 4 (see Figure 6.5).

In scenario 4 two out of three factors are active. Scenario 2 shows also a high technological progress, because the system described by it suffers from very low environmental quality (one factor). Scenarios 0 and 1 have an equal pace of technological progress as a result of equal capital investment (both initially stationary state paths). Scenario 3 shows the slowest technological progress, partly since the environmental effects are missing. To observe this completely, one should compare the environmental quality for each scenario in Figure 6.6. This may be interpreted as few non-renewable resources (e.g., fossil energy resources) giving rise to output decline and neutral or propitious environmental effects.

Supply patterns of resource materials (Figure 6.7) differ widely because of the following factors: renewable resource stock, non-renewable resource stock, extraction and recycling capital, technological progress affecting extraction and recycling efficiency of capital. Concern for future generations allows the supply of materials for the present choice of initial natural resource stocks to keep increasing (scenarios 1 and 4). A low environmental quality causes materials supply to be initially lower

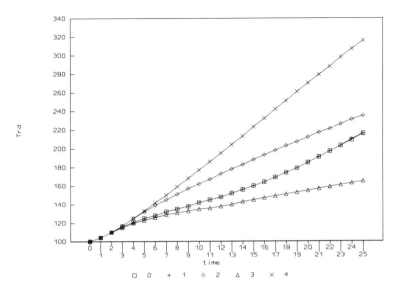

Figure 6.5. Technological progress for scenarios 0−4.

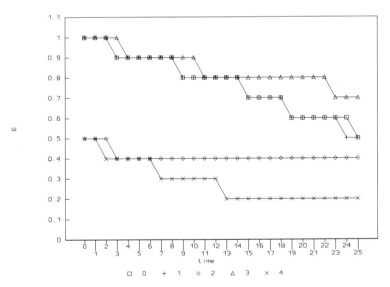

Figure 6.6. Environmental quality for scenarios 0−4.

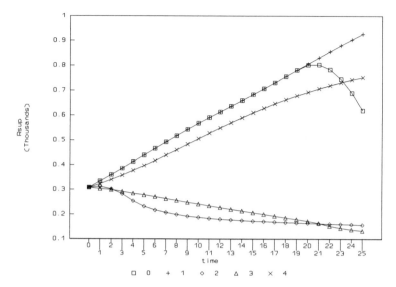

Figure 6.7. Total supply of natural resource materials for
scenarios 0−4.

for scenario 2 than for 3, but at a later stage this relationship inverts. This change results from a favourable development of capital and technology.

In Figure 6.8 different growth patterns are shown. Here, one can compare long term effects of variation in the initial capacity for growth on output. Only 'Moderate Growth' seems sustainable over the time period shown. Strong growth leads to a quickly decreasing environmental quality, and a collapse in output. The size of the fall in output levels is comparable for 'Strong Growth' and 'Extreme Growth'. As a consequence, it seems not to matter (relatively) how fast one grows, since the collapse will be relatively hard. However, the output level under 'Strong Growth' is catching up with that under 'Extreme Growth' at the end of the period shown (the environmental quality levels are also equal).

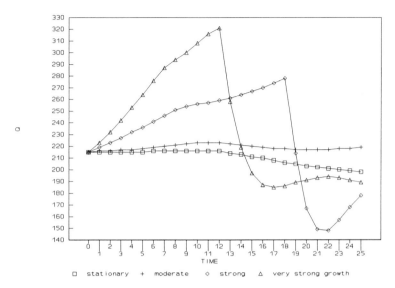

Figure 6.8. Final goods production for scenarios 0, 5, 6 and 7.

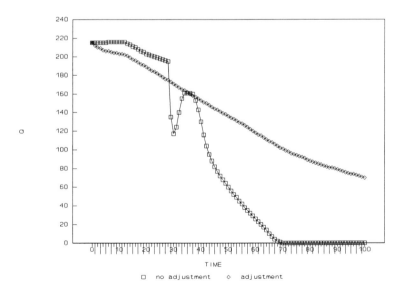

*Figure 6.9. Final goods production for scenarios 8 (adjustment)
and 0 (no adjustment).*

Figures 6.9 and 6.10 show the results in terms of final goods output of various scenarios. We have taken a time horizon of 100 years since we want to investigate the very long term effects of a completely different development of the sectoral structure. Here the investment allocation is endogenously influenced by the state of the environment and the ethical concern, which we referred to in Section 6.5 as sustainable development feedback (according to the equations in (6.27)). From Figure 6.9 it is clear that this reaction (called 'adjustment') has a positive effect on output in the long run, as compared without such a reaction. Collapses followed by growth are evaded, i.e. patterns are smoothed out. Initially the output decreases faster under the investment allocation reaction, but from time 40 on output is higher. The collapse followed by recovery and a second, catastrophic collapse are explained by the fact that a collapse of the economy allows for decreasing environmental pressure and new economic opportunities for growth. However, the growth path is so steep, because of the relatively large supply of investment goods, that environmental pressure increases along with it. This causes the final collapse.

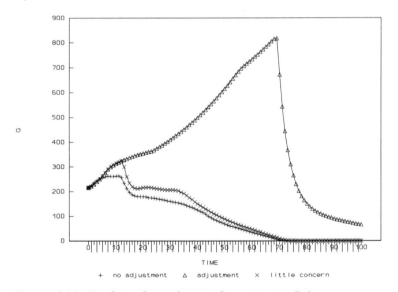

Figure 6.10. Final goods production for scenarios 7 (no adjustment), 9 (adjustment) and 10 (little concern).

In Figure 6.10 patterns can be compared between 'Extreme Growth' (without adjustment of investment allocation), 'Extreme Growth,

Sustainability and Ethical Concern' (with investment reaction and ethical concern) and 'Extreme Growth and Sustainability' (minimum ethical concern for future generations and/or natural environment). It is clear that without much ethical concern the reaction is too weak for output to stay on a growth pattern. When adjustment of investment allocation is based on the strong notion of ethical concern, the growth pattern can be maintained for a very long period of time. Finally, a sharp fall in output results, caused by both the negative impact on the environment of maintained growth and the investment reaction diverting investment from final goods production to waste abatement and recycling sectors. The pattern finally seems to stabilise on a positive lower level. The conclusion is that the sectoral structure has a significant long run impact on the output of final goods.

6.6.3. Sensitivity Analysis

Finally, also sensitivity analysis was performed to investigate the model reactions to changes in certain intitial conditions. Especially the natural renewable resources N and pollution P are open to different interpretations, and therefore their levels were varied. The results show that patterns depend strongly on initial values of these variables, and that patterns of collapse are usually followed by recovery, though at a lower level than the initial one. This can be explained by the fact that a collapse of output may go along with a decrease of environmental pressure from both less resource use and less waste residuals being generated. This depends first of all on the magnitude of a fall in environmental quality and resource scarcity that causes an economic breakdown. Furthermore, whether recovery can occur, especially at a fast speed, depends also on certain characteristics of the economic system that determine its recovery capacity, such as technological progress, and capacities of abatement and recycling activities relative to production capacities. See for more details on the sensitivity analysis van den Bergh and Nijkamp (1994c). A general conclusion is that the two-way economic-environmental interactions cause interesting feedback loops. One cannot simply make the general statement that a better initial environmental state will lead to better economic performance over a certain period of time. One has to realise that a better environment may give incentives for high growth and (ex post) undesirable or wrong directions of technological progress.

6.7.   CONCLUSIONS

The approach discussed in this chapter extends upon growth theory, materials balance accounting, and integrated economic–ecological modelling by combining complex interactions within both the economy and the environment. It is clear from the scenario analysis results that interesting and non-trivial insights can be obtained. The model can be regarded as helpful in our understanding (i.e., deduction) of how economy and environment interact in the long run, when material and physical relationships, and behavioural feedbacks are regarded. However, the important interpretations of the results should not be that within a known period of time the system will break down. More important are the types of patterns, economic reactions, and intermediate dynamics of collapse and recovery. Still, the results lead to an important observation, namely that permanent decreases in environmental quality or environmental stocks seem to make it very difficult to sustain a positive trend or even a constant level of economic performance. One may even draw the conclusion that cautious behaviour does not necessarily lead to worse performance in the long run, but may certainly protect against adverse long term developments. The model is very sensitive to changes in initial environmental and economic stocks, while patterns often tend to return to stable levels, even though possibly preceded by strong growth and collapse patterns. This is a clear non-linear characteristic of the model, which is tempered mostly by internal consistency provided by materials balance.

The inclusion of a materials flow and materials balance in dynamic models with non-linear processes has shown to be able to provide a realistic and helpful tool for investigating long term relationships between economy and natural environment. Application of this approach is limited by on the one hand data limitations, and on the other hand the problem of aggregation of physical information. One should either choose experimental models like the present one, or adopt a more specific disaggregated and often partial approach. The resulting model system provides a direction for further model-oriented research for long term environmental policy and scenario analysis.

APPENDIX: LIST OF SYMBOLS

The set $K = \{Q, I, wa, rec, N, S\}$ denotes the 6 economic sectors

Stock variables:

B	=	a slowly renewable resource (soil, land, water)
K	=	total economic capital
K_Q	=	productive sector capital
K_I	=	investment sector capital
K_{wa}	=	waste abatement/treatment capital
K_{rec}	=	recycling capital
K_N	=	renewable resource extraction capital
K_S	=	non-renewable resource extraction capital
N	=	the stock of renewable resources
P	=	stock of pollution in natural mediums or organisms
Pop	=	human population level
R_{sup}	=	inventory (supply) of natural resource materials
S	=	the stock of non-renewable resources
S_{wa}	=	the stock of useless, stored waste
T_{rd}	=	progress indicator of environmental technology
Z	=	total 'real' output delayed

Flow variables:

C	=	consumption
E	=	indicator for overall environmental quality
I	=	total investment in replacement and new capital
I_i	=	investment in sector i ($i \in K$)
O_{rd}	=	social investment in research and development
Q	=	output of final goods sector
R_{dem}	=	total productive and consumptive demand for resources
R_N	=	renewable resource extraction
$R_{N,perc}$	=	subjective/perceived availability (rate) of renewable resources
R_{new}	=	required extraction of resources
R_{perc}	=	subjective/perceived availability (rate) of all resources
R_S	=	non-renewable resource extraction
$R_{S,perc}$	=	subjective/perceived availability (rate) of non-renewable resources
R_{short}	=	indicator for insufficiency of perceived resource supply
R_{rec}	=	recycled resource materials
R_{short}	=	perceived shortage of resource supply to demand

R_{wa}	=	abated/treated waste
e_e	=	ecological effect indicator for technical progress
W_{em}	=	emitted waste
$W_{Q,I}$	=	gross waste from final and investment goods sectors
W_{rec}	=	waste amenable for recycling
W_{too}	=	indicator for unsustainability of waste emission

Functions:

A	=	assimilation function
B	=	population growth rate
b_i	=	regeneration and damage functions of slowly renewable resources ($i = 1, .., 5$)
c_Q	=	ratio of resource input to material output in final goods sector
c_I	=	ratio of resource input to material output in investment goods sector
D_i	=	discarded capital ($i \in K$)
F_Q	=	unrestricted production function final goods sector
F_I	=	unrestricted production function investment goods sector
F_N	=	unrestricted production function of renewable resource extraction sector
F_S	=	unrestricted production function of non-renewable resource extraction sector
f_{wa}	=	part of production waste that is abated/treated
f_{rec}	=	part of waste amenable for recycling that is recycled
G	=	regeneration function of renewable resource capacity
H	=	environmental quality function
α	=	general investment effect on technology
ϵ	=	effect of social R&D and production growth on technology

Parameters:

d	=	dummy for linking resource availability to stock or sustainable flow
p_N	=	fraction of stock of renewables regarded as available for use now

p_S = fraction of stock of non-renewables regarded as available for use now

s_1 = fraction of treated waste ending up in unused stored waste

s_2 = fraction of recycled waste ending up in unused stored waste

E_{crit} = environmental quality threshold for impacts on environmental and economic processes

a_Q = environmental effect parameter in commodity production

b_Q, c_Q = parameters of function $c_Q(\ )$

b_I, c_I = parameters of function $c_I(\ )$

k_Q, k_I = capital parameter in functions $F_Q(\ )$ and $F_I(\ )$

$a_{wa}, b_{wa},$
c_{wa} = parameters of waste treatment function

$a_{rec}, b_{rec},$
c_{rec} = parameters of recycling function

$a_N, \alpha_N,$
β_N = parameters of function $F_N(\ )$

$a_S, \alpha_S,$
β_S = parameters of function $F_S(\ )$

δ_i = depreciation of capital

δ = production increase parameter in technology formation equation

α, ϵ = parameters in functions $\alpha(\ )$ and $\epsilon(\ )$

$N_{crit}, B_{crit},$
P_{crit} = parameters of environmental quality function $H(\ )$

r, C_N = intrinsic growth and carrying capacity parameters in regeneration function $G(\ )$

a_P, b_P = parameters in assimilation function $M(\ )$

a_B = param. in population growth function $B(\ )$.

7. Environmental Accounting, Materials Balances and Sustainability Indicators — Cadmium Accumulation in Soil[1]

7.1. INTRODUCTION

The role of environmental accounts and their interaction with dynamic materials balances and indicators of sustainable development are the subject of this case study. The accumulation of cadmium in Dutch soil is used as a case study to demonstrate both the development of environmental accounts, a dynamic materials balance, environmental indicators and a sustainability indicator, and their interactions. This cadmium issue was selected largely because of the availability of data and the existence of materials balances for a number of years (Feenstra, 1975, for 1975; van Vliet en Feenstra, 1982, for 1980; van der Voet *et al.*, 1989, for 1985). Note that 'sustainability' issues with regards to cadmium's being a nonrenewable natural resource, its contamination of groundwater, or its bioaccumulation in ecosystems fall outside the context taken for sustainability in this study. Other features behind the selection of cadmium include: firstly, it is produced in the smelting of zinc, and so constraints on the production of primary cadmium require corresponding constraints on the production of primary zinc; secondly, the absence of (significant) domestic sources of cadmium; and thirdly, cadmium is accumulating in Dutch soil to such an extent that detailed standards are being set for agricultural uses (Stoop and Rennen, 1990).

The aim of this case study may be broadly stated as: demonstrating interrelationships, and even synergism, among dynamic materials balances,

[1] This chapter has been written by Alison Gilbert. It is based on a research project commissioned by the Dutch National Institute for Public Health and Environmental Hygiene (RIVM). The author wishes to acknowledge and to thank Jan Feenstra for his cooperation in the development of the simulation model and indicators.

environmental accounts, and indicators for sustainable development. Existing materials balances for cadmium comprise a form of Environmental Accounting (EA). They are also the primary data source for the development of the dynamic materials balance and the indicators. Various approaches to EA, in particular satellite accounts as proposed de Boo *et al.* (1991), are expected to incorporate data from such balances. The environmental accounts presented at the end of this chapter not only present these balances, but also consolidate the data from the materials balances into a limited set of variables which provide the basis for three indicators; and interact with the dynamic materials balance to generate estimates of both future accounts and future indicators, both of which provide information on development trajectories.

Central to this case study is the construction of a dynamic materials balance. Its purpose was to investigate the extent to which environmental quality and sustainability functions could be combined, key variables identified and, subsequently, sustainability indicators developed. Dynamic material balances may be seen as a combination of materials balances and simulation modelling. Materials balances, as discussed in Part I, are a form of environmental accounting. However, their static or 'snap shot' nature leads to a greater focus on flows than on stocks, with the result that issues of accumulation tend not to receive sufficient emphasis. A dynamic materials balance provides a means for documenting both cadmium flows and subsequent changes in stocks. The importance of cadmium's accumulation in various stocks is indicated by:

(i) Almost one-third of cadmium entering economic activities is destined for products which remain in economic use for a period of years before entering waste streams (e.g. rechargeable nickel-cadmium batteries);

(ii) the vast majority of cadmium in waste streams (about 80%) is disposed of and accumulates in landfills and waste storage facilities;

(iii) cadmium is accumulating in the environment, not only soil but also in aquatic sediments and food webs.

Dutch initiatives into the development of indicators of sustainability (reported in Kuik and Verbruggen, 1991) recommended the development of three types of highly aggregated indicators (Opschoor and Reijnders, 1991):

(a) *Pressure indicators*, showing the development over time of, e.g., the pollutant burden being placed on the environment by man's activities;

(b) *impact indicators*, showing the development over time of environmental quality levels and/or the impact of changing environmental quality; and,

(c) *sustainability indicators*, expressing the distance of a given situtation from a desired, 'sustainable' one and requiring the specification of criteria for that sustainability.

Gilbert and Feenstra (1992, 1994) report the development of a dynamics materials balance and indicators for the issue of cadmium's accumulation in Dutch soil. This case study adds to this work by including environmental accounting. The structure of the chapter is as follows. Section 7.2 provides the 'sustainability' context for cadmium's dispersion, by describing the movement of cadmium through the Dutch economy. Analysis for sustainable development makes use of three techniques which are discussed in Sections 7.3 – 7.5: Section 7.3 briefly describes the dynamic balance and its output; Section 7.4 discusses the indicators for cadmium dispersion, focusing on the sustainability indicator; and Section 7.5 presents the environmental accounts. Section 7.6 discusses interactions among the accounts, the dynamic materials balance and the indicators.

7.2. 'SUSTAINABILITY' AND CADMIUM IN THE DUTCH ECONOMY

7.2.1. Introduction

Materials balances for cadmium's movement through the Dutch economy are available for 1975 (Feenstra, 1975), 1980 (van Vliet and Feenstra, 1982) and 1985 (van der Voet *et al.*,1989); a balance for 1990 is currently under construction by the Dutch Central Bureau of Statistics. This section provides a general description of cadmium flows which are considered in three stages: firstly, allocation of incoming cadmium across economic activities; secondly, generation and disposal of wastes containing cadmium; and thirdly, movement of cadmium into the environment.

7.2.2. Allocation of Imported Cadmium

Cadmium enters the economy in three general forms: zinc ores; products which expressly containing cadmium (e.g. certain pigments, cadmium compounds, Ni-Cd batteries); and products which are imported for purposes other than their cadmium content (e.g. coal, phosphate fertilizers, zinc and zinc compounds). Some cadmium entering the Dutch economy is of domestic origin, primarily cadmium in natural gas. However, this is an extremely small source of cadmium, and so cadmium can be considered to derive only from imports.

Imported cadmium is allocated across five main streams (see Figure 7.1): exports, batteries, accumulators, structures and other economic activities. Exports include cadmium in zinc ores, remnants from zinc smelting which are processed further elsewhere, pigments, stabilizors, and other products including phosphates, zinc and zinc compounds.

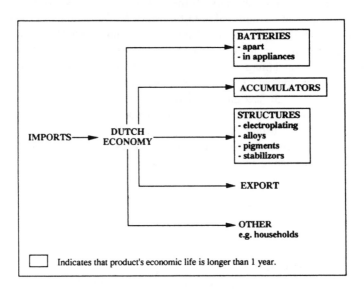

Figure 7.1. Simplified model of cadmium flowing through the Dutch economy.

Cadmium used by 'other' economic activities enter waste streams during the same time period. This stream comprises the following economic activities:

(i)   Electricity generation (cadmium in fossil fuels);
(ii) fertilizer production (cadmium in phosphate ores);
(iii) agriculture (cadmium in phosphate fertilizers);
(iv) households and industry (cadmium in final products such as plastic bottle caps);
(v)   manufacturing industry (zinc smelting as well as industries using various cadmium compounds).

Batteries (Ni-Cd batteries only), accumulators and structures are presented in Figure 7.1 as stocks and comprise final products which remain in use longer than the time period of the material balance (i.e. one year). The lifetimes of the various products within these three general groups varies but are of the order of ten years. Batteries may be available separately to consumers, or may be incorporated in various appliances. Structures comprise four product groups which are imported directly or which are domestically manufactured from imported cadmium – alloys, electro-plated products, stabilizors and pigments. Examples of final products include window frames and other building materials, cars, appliances, etc. Structures may also be defined to include the reuse in civil engineering works of flyash from incinerators. Flyash contains a number of heavy metals including cadmium. All of these long-lived products lead to cadmium in waste streams displaced in time from its entry into the economy.

7.2.3. Waste Generation and Disposal

Waste generation and disposal is summarized by Figure 7.2. Wastes containing cadmium are generated by most economic activities. Disposal means comprise:

(i) Incineration and landfill, used primarily for the disposal of municipal rubbish and demolition wastes;
(ii) 'safe storage', by which wastes are accumulated and contained to prevent their entering the environment;
(iii) direct emission into the environment, including the use of cadmium-contaminated fertilizers by agriculture;
(iv) sewerage reticulation;
(v) export.

Of the various waste disposal means, landfill and storage lead to the accumulation of waste cadmium but with little likelihood of immediate loss to the environment. Disposal via incineration, direct emission and sewerage systems leads to immediate environmental loads.

Battery collection programs were instituted in the mid-1980s and tend to target batteries bought separately by consumers. It is uncertain to what degree batteries in appliances can and will enter such programs. Consumers may not know of their presence in appliances and may not remove them for separate disposal. Conversely, commercial users of such appliances may make bulk use of collection programs. Batteries which are not collected ultimately enter municipal refuse.

Municipal refuse, primarily from households, comprises other cadmium-containing wastes apart from batteries, such as plastic bottle caps (Consumentengids, 1990, 1992). These wastes are disposed of via incineration and landfill. Larger wastes such as demolition wastes and large appliances containing batteries are collected separately by municipalities and disposed of in landfills. Scrap metal is removed from waste to be incinerated for recycling by the iron and steel industries, and leads to cadmium emissions to the air; flyash and slag from incinerators may either be stored on-site or reused in, e.g., concrete and the construction of roads.

Manufacturing industries, including those involved in electro-plating and the manufacture of alloys, pigments and stabilizors, generate cadmium-containing wastes which are disposed of via direct emission, on-site storage, and sewerage reticulation systems. Used accumulators are exported.

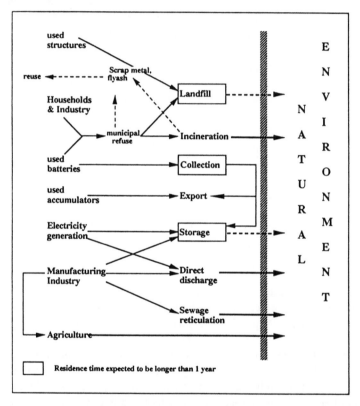

Figure 7.2. Allocation of cadmium products and cadmium-containing wastes.

7.2.4. Accumulation in the Environment

Wastes which do not accumulate in landfills and storage sites are shown in Figures 7.2 and 7.3 to flow into the environment. The focus of Figure 7.3 is on the movements of cadmium into and between the various environmental media, leading to cadmium's accumulation. Biological processes involved in these and other transformations of cadmium are not represented. Direct emissions are made to three environmental media: air, water, and soil. Transboundary movement of air- and water-borne cadmium (the latter via the Rhine, Meuse, Scheldt and Dommel Rivers) also affect cadmium levels in the Dutch environment. Cadmium in the air eventually deposits, and cadmium in surface waters eventually sediments, leading to accumulation. Losses from the soil are indicated in the figure, viz. leaching with subsequent accumulation in groundwater, runoff into surface water systems, and uptake by crops. Cadmium is unlike most heavy metals in that it can be taken up by plants (de Voogt *et al.*, 1980; Rozema *et al.*, 1990; de Knecht *et al.*, 1992; Posthuma *et al.*, 1992), providing for a return flow back to economies as a contaminant in agricultural products. Dredging, primarily in Rotterdam Harbour, removes cadmium-contaminated sediments from the environment into special storage facilities.

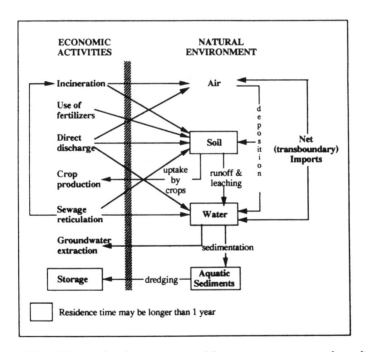

Figure 7.3. Flows of cadmium into and between environmental media.

7.2.5. The Sustainability Context
As a result of cadmium's use by the Dutch economy, cadmium is accumulating in waste stocks and in environmental media (notably soil and aquatic sediments). Cadmium in waste stocks constitutes a 'chemical time

bomb' (IIASA/FEMA, 1990) and poses a risk of future environmental contamination. For example, DHV Raadgevend Ingenieursbureau BV (1990) has reported leakage of cadmium into local groundwater from tailings ponds at the zinc smelter in Budel, the Netherlands. In general, the limited mobility of cadmium in many wastes makes leakage a relatively unlikely and localized effect (van Herwijnen *et al.*, 1989).

Concern with cadmium's increased presence in the environment lies with its health effects on humans and its bioaccumulation in ecosystems, both of which imply unsustainable development. Bioaccumulation begins with cadmium's uptake by plants and microorganisms, a process which is stimulated by various factors such as pH — Dutch soils are exposed to the acid depositions. Accumulation factors (the quotient of concentration in an organsim and the concentration in the environment) of up to 20,000 in plants and 10^6 in animals have been found in aquatic organisms. In the Jintsu area in Japan where the Itai-Itai disease (the cadmium equivalent of Minimata disease) occurred, the consumed rice contained $0.45-4$ ppm cadmium, whereas the soil contained $2-3$ ppb and concentrations in the Jintsu River downstream from the source mine were 0.009 ppm (de Voogt *et al.*, 1980; Copius Peereboom and Copius Peereboom-Stegeman, 1981).

7.3. A DYNAMIC MATERIALS BALANCE FOR CADMIUM

The dynamic materials balance constructed by Gilbert and Feenstra (1992) does not incorporate all of the above flows as this was considered unnecessary detail given the model's purpose. The model aggregated and exogenized the vast majority of flows, but provided detail in those areas being targeted by policy, viz:

(i)   import, use and disposal of Ni-Cd batteries;
(ii) use of cadmium in four product groups within 'structures' and disposal of subsequent wastes;
(iii) the development of capacity for collection and recycling of cadmium.

This selection reflects early recognition of the delay between cadmium's import and its entering waste streams (van Vliet and Feenstra, 1982) and the potential role of collection and recycling policies in diverting waste streams and reducing environmental loads. The environmental part of the model considers only cadmium accumulation in soil (cf accumulation in aquatic sediments and groundwater), and the mobility of cadmium in soils and groundwater is represented in a very limited and aggregated way.

The dynamic materials balance comprises four modules: (1) import, use and disposal of Ni-Cd batteries; (2) import, use and disposal of structures and non-battery household products containing cadmium; (3) waste disposal primarily via incineration and landfills; and 4) addition to and losses from agricultural soil and soil under natural vegetation. Three scenarios were developed. The base scenario holds exogenously determined variables constant at their 1985 value after 1985; only policies effected before this time are reflected. The moderate policy scenario includes measures developed and implemented in the late 1980s. This includes reductions in cadmium use in structures, collection and recycling programs, and reductions in cadmium release by direct emission, fertilizer use and sewage disposal.[2] The strict policy scenario includes measures proposed in the latest statement of cadmium policy (Minister van VROM, 1991). It is a stricter version of the moderate policy scenario. One major area of distinction between these two policy scenarios is the success of battery collection programs. The moderate policy scenario achieves, at best, 60% collection of apart batteries and batteries in small (household) appliances; the strict policy scenario achieves 100% collection of all batteries. The latter is extremely ambitious. Further details on the three scenarios are provided in Gilbert and Feenstra (1992). Model equations and output are presented in Gilbert and Feenstra (1992) and Gilbert (1996).

7.4. AN INDICATOR OF SUSTAINABILITY

Pressure, impact and sustainability indicators for cadmium accumulation in soil were proposed in Gilbert and Feenstra (1992); a fourth indicator, relating the sustainability indicator to domestic policy was also proposed. The following summarizes this discussion but emphasizes the sustainability indicator. Two themes were common to the construction of the pressure and impact indicators: capturing as much as possible of the cause–effect chain in which cadmium disperses; and inclusion of policy variable for assessment of their effectiveness. Variables used in construction of the pressure and impact indicators were classified according to whether they were a cause of cadmium dispersion (essentially use of cadmium by the economy), whether they reflected policy, whether they consituted a burden or pressure on the environment, or whether they reflected the effect or impact of that pressure:

(i) Total import of batteries (cause);

---

[2] Flows of cadmium from sewage disposal have been overestimated (CBS, 1992).

(ii)   total use of cadmium-containing products within the category structures (cause and policy);
(iii) collection of batteries (policy);
(iv)   atmospheric deposition of cadmium on land (pressure);
(v)   disposal of cadmium in landfills (pressure);
(vi)   accumulation of cadmium in soil (impact);
(vii) accumulation of cadmium in landfills (impact).

No sustainability context has yet been proposed for the accumulation of cadmium in waste stocks such as landfills, and so no sustainability indicator for this issue has been developed. For cadmium accumulation in soil, the proposed sustainability indicator comprises the pressure and impact variables, modified to reflect a 'sustainability' context. This context was initiated by Minister van Volkshuisvesting, Ruimtelijke Ordening en Milieubeheer (1991), in which the following was deduced as a criterion for sustainable development:

• Additions of cadmium to the soil must be balanced by losses. This criterion relates to the pressure on soils. On its own, it is inadequate and a second criterion was proposed by Gilbert and Feenstra (1992).
• Cadmium content of the soil must be less than a soil quality standard. This reflects the impact of cadmium's release to the environment on soil. Both criteria must be satisfied for sustainable development, with respect to the accumulation of cadmium in soil, to be indicated.

With regards to the second criterion, a nationally aggregated standard of 0.8 mg Cd/kg dry weight of soil has been proposed by Gilbert and Feenstra. It was derived by aggregating standards for the variety of soil types and uses presented in Stoop and Rennen (1990), comparing with standards for soils under natural cover (there is discussion as to whether these standards are too strict), and guaranteeing the multifunctionality of soil uses.

Construction of the proposed Sustainability Indicator requires three steps. The first specifies the pressure which cadmium places on the soil:

$$ND_t = -(A_t - L_t) \qquad\qquad (7.1)$$

where

ND_t = net deficit in tonnes cadmium per year
A_t = total additions (deposition, fertilizers, sewage sludge) net of runoff
L_t = losses from the soil (leaching and uptake by crops).

It leads to the following correspondence to the first sustainability criterion:

$-ive$ $+ive$

----------------------------->   0   <---------------------------

unsustainable   *sustainable*   *better than sustainable*

The second step specifies the impact of cadmium release and compares the stock of cadmium in the soil with the (sustainability) standard. The result is an index of soil quality with the same behaviour as that for net deficit. This is achieved with the following equation:

$$SQI = \left[\frac{S_t}{S_{st}} - 1 \right] \qquad (7.2)$$

where

SQI = soil quality index reflecting the soil's cadmium content
S_t = the volume (stock) of cadmium in the soil at time t
S_{st} = the standard stock for cadmium.

When the stock at time t equals the reference stock, implying correspondence with the second sustainability criterion, the value of this index is 0. At stock values greater than the reference, the index is negative suggesting contaminated soils and unsustainability; at values less than the reference, it is positive suggesting conditions cleaner than sustainability.

The result of these two steps is two values, net deficit and soil quality index, each of which has the behaviour set as described above. A coordinate approach, in which the two values are used to specify a point on a graph, is proposed for the indicator's presentation. This is shown in Figure 7.4 where the range of coordinates derived from these two criteria and their implications for sustainability are summarized. The soil quality index is on the vertical axis, being dependent on the net deficit (horizontal axis).

One advantage of such an approach is the way in which time series can be presented. Figure 7.5 presents the output of the three scenarios from the dynamic materials balance as trajectories. All three paths, with the exception of the coordinate for 2020 from the base scenario, are located in the 'trend towards unsustainable' quadrant. The two policy scenarios shift the trajectory towards the vertical axis and slow down the rate of soil quality deterioration but additional policies will eventually be needed to prevent the soil quality standard from being exceeded. There is less urgency for these additional measures if strict policy measures are undertaken.

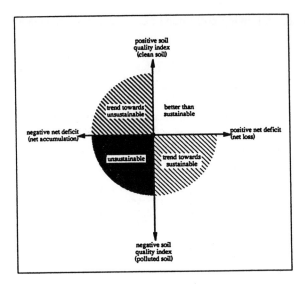

Figure 7.4. *Presentation of the two values comprising the sustainability indicator.*

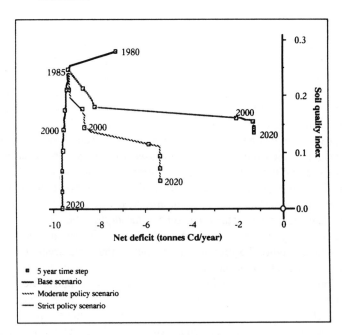

Figure 7.5. *Output from the dynamic materials balance as a time series of sustainability coordinates.*

However, these measures are perhaps unnecessarily strict, and therefore costly to industry, since it is arguable that there is time for additional policies with the moderate policy scenario.

Figure 7.6 displays the fourth approach to indicators with the assessment of domestic policy and its role in achieving sustainable development. The top part of the figure reproduces Figure 7.5 with the trajectories from the three scenarios. The bottom part of the figure excludes transboundary pollution from the calculation of net deficit (it is not excluded from the calculation of the soil quality index). The role of transboundary pollution

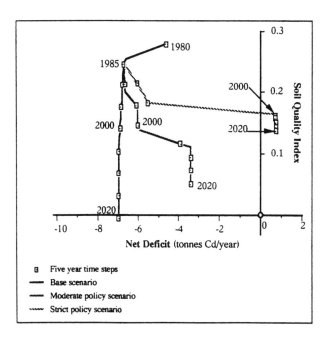

Figure 7.6.   Domestic policy assessment with the sustainability indicator.

in adding to cadmium's pressure on the Dutch environment was outlined in Section 7.3. When this contribution is excluded, net deficit in the strict policy scenario becomes positive by 2000. This figure reinforces the tentative assessment of the strict policy scenario above – that it is too strict and therefore too costly to domestic industry. This figure raises a more general issue, that of the role of domestic policy when much of the problem derives from outside the realm of influence of this policy.

7.5. THE ENVIRONMENTAL ACCOUNTS

7.5.1. Introduction

The methodologies proposed by United Nations (1993) and de Boo *et al.* (1991) should result in environmental accounts which contain the basic data for the construction of materials balances. Time series of these accounts should offer sufficient information for the subsequent development of detailed dynamic materials balances. The accounts presented later in this section differ in that the data are consolidated for the purpose of generating the basic elements of the four indicators discussed in Section 4. Parallels can be drawn with the Consolidated Income and Product Account of the SNA and its antecedents (see Section 4.3) in which the basic measures of production are generated and presented. The following section provides the mathematical basis for a complete set of environmental accounts from the perspective of cadmium dispersion.

7.5.2. Mathematical Framework for Cadmium Accounting

Construction of environmental accounts requires identification of the various stocks of cadmium and specification of the activities/sectors which are responsible for the flows. Sections 7.2 and 7.3 suggest:

(i)   Three types of cadmium stocks − economic, waste and environmental;
(ii) economic sectors be identified on the basis of use of cadmium-containing commodities and the generation of cadmium-containing wastes;
(iii) specification waste disposal sectors based on an activity-oriented approach;
(iv) specification of environmental sectors on the basis of the activities moving cadmium in the environment.

Classifications and definitions
Economic stocks comprise cadmium-containing commodities in use in the economy. The dynamic materials balance above focuses on batteries and structures, the former are disaggregated into apart batteries and batteries in appliances and the latter into electro-plated products, alloys, long- and short-lived pigments, stabilizors, and other household products, as economic stocks; accumulators and civil engineering works which use flyash could also be included. Waste stocks comprise stockpiled wastes which are constrained or even prevented from releasing their cadmium into the environment. The dynamic materials balance focuses on collected batteries and landfill as waste stocks, although 'safe' storage for example of dredge

spoil and solid industrial waste, would also comprise waste stocks. Environmental stocks comrpise cadmium accumulated in environmental components. The dynamic materials balance focuses on soil, but aquatic sediments, groundwater and species could also comprise relevant environmental stocks.

Ni-Cd batteries, plastics containing cadmium pigments and stabilizors, concrete containing flyash are all final products used by many economic activities. Cadmium-containing flows from economic sectors are generated as a result of the disposal of these commodities, as well as by various manufacturing (e.g. zinc smelting, fertilizer production, iron and steel) and agricultural activities. For the issue of cadmium dispersion, economic sectors are more usefully classified on these bases than on more conventional criteria. The dynamic materials balance focuses on activities using batteries and structures, fertilizer use by agriculture, direct emissions by industry, and sewage sludge disposal by waste authorities as economic sectors. Additional economic sectors could include civil engineering works, which reuse flyash, and solar power generation using cadmium-containing photovoltaic cells − these are expected to come into use towards the end of the century.

Different commodities are disposed of differently. Specification of waste sectors on the basis of disposal activities is necessary for assessment of cadmium dispersion, and reinforces the need for a commodity-oriented basis to specification of economic sectors. The dynamic materials balance focuses on battery collection, disposal in landfill, recycling and incineration as waste sectors, although disposal in 'safe' storage and export could also be included.

Environmental sectors are activities responsible for cadmium's movement in the environment. The dynamic materials balance refers to three types of activities within the air and soil media: the receiving of cadmium, from both waste sectors and from other media; the transferring of cadmium to other media; and the accumulation of cadmium within soil. Surface and groundwater and their interactions with soil and air, as well as bioaccumulation or biomagnification of cadmium in ecosystems would also contribute to this list of environmental sectors.

General structure of cadmium balance sheets
The general form of a balance sheet in economic accounting documents stocks and flows within an activity in monetary units. Stock balances as used in natural resource accounting (see Section 4.3.2) tend to focus on one particular stock and document changes in physical units. In both cases the equation is the same, viz.:

$$S_0 + \sum_{i=1}^{n} A_i = \sum_{j=1}^{m} C_j + S_1 \tag{7.3}$$

or

$$\sum_{i=1}^{n} A_i - \sum_{j=1}^{m} C_j = \Delta S \tag{7.4}$$

where

S_0, S_1 = stock at beginning and end of time period, respectively;
ΔS = change in stock over the time period, or $S_1 - S_0$;
A_i = contribution to stock from activity/sector i;
C_j = subtraction from stock of activity/sector j;
n, m = total number of activities/sectors involved in contributing or subtracting from stock, respectively.

However, the accounting problem with regards to cadmium's dispersion can be more simply stated as: during any specified time period, net import of cadmium equals net addition to stocks. Mathematically, this may be expressed, for a given time period, as:

$$I_e + I_w + I_n = \sum_{i=1}^{p} \Delta E_i + \sum_{j=1}^{q} \Delta W_j + \sum_{k=1}^{r} \Delta N_k \tag{7.5}$$

where

I = net import to economic (e), waste (w) and environmental (n) sectors during an unspecified time period;
ΔE_i = net change in economic stock i during the same time period;
ΔW_j = net change in waste stock j during the same time period;
ΔN_k = net change in environmental stock k during the same time period; and,
p, q, r = the total number of economic, waste and environmental stocks respectively.

Each of these stock changes can be reformulated in terms of equation 7.4, and absolute levels of stocks documented in the accounts.

Disaggregation of this equation leads to the following set of equations for any given time period:

$$L + R + I_e = \sum_{i=1}^{p} \Delta E_i + W + A \qquad (7.6)$$

$$B + W + I_w = \sum_{j=1}^{q} \Delta W_j + D + R \qquad (7.7)$$

$$A + D + I_n = \sum_{k=1}^{r} \Delta N_k + L + B \qquad (7.8)$$

where

L = total uptake of cadmium from the soil and returned to the economy in agricultural products;

R = total volume of cadmium in recycled or reused waste products;

W = total volume of cadmium-containing waste produced by the economy;

A = total volume of cadmium in fertilizers applied to the land by the agriculture sector;

B = total volume of cadmium removed from the environment and storaged in waste stocks; and,

D = total volume of cadmium released into the environment.

Both W and D can be further specified:

$$W = \sum_{i=1}^{p} \omega_i E_i + w_e \qquad (7.9)$$

$$D = \sum_{j=1}^{q} \lambda_j W_j + d_w + d_e \qquad (7.10)$$

where

$\omega_i E_i$ = wastes (subtractions) from economic stock i;

w_e = other sources of wastes from economic sectors;

$\lambda_j W_j$ = leakages (subtractions) from waste stock j into the environment;

d_w = discharges to the environment from waste sectors; and,

d_e = direct discharges to the environment from economic sectors.

Cadmium's pressure on the environment during a given time period comprises two parts: flows to waste stocks as these are potential chemical time bombs, and flows into the environment. These two components may be mathematically expressed as:

$$P_w = \sum_{j=1}^{q} \Delta W_j = N + W + I_w - D - R \qquad (7.11)$$

and

$$P_n = A + D + I_n \qquad (7.12)$$

where

P_w, P_n = pressure of cadmium via flows to waste stock and into the environment respectively.

Both equations represent total or gross pressure, but there are slight differences in approach. Pressure via flows to waste stocks is net of return flows to the economy (R) and of discharges to the environment (D). Neither of these flows ever contribute to waste stocks and so their exclusion from the measurement of pressure is legitimate. This contrasts with environmental stocks where flows out of environmental stocks, either to waste stocks (B) or to back into the economy (L), are not subtracted. These flows comprise cadmium which has contributed to environmental stocks, either in previous time periods or in the current one. For the same reason, discharges from waste stocks, $\omega_j W_j$, should also be excluded from the calculation of P_w. However, limited mobility of cadmium in these stocks (see Section 7.2) means that the volumes involved are relatively small.

A context for sustainability exists for the accumulation of cadmium in soil (see Section 7.4), viz, during any time period:

$$\Delta N_s \leq 0 \qquad (7.13)$$

where N_s refers to soil. This can be extended to all environmental stocks in one of two ways:

$$\Delta N_k \leq 0 \quad \vee \quad \sum \Delta N_k \leq 0 \qquad (7.14)$$

The former criterion would permit no accumulation in any environmental component, while the latter would permit accumulation in some so long as it was balanced by losses in others. For waste stocks, the issue is not so much reducing the change in stock to zero, but reducing the risk of environmental discharge to zero.

The impact of these pressures is cadmium's accumulation in the environment, either in waste stocks or in environmental components. The absolute volume of cadmium in a stock is required, rather than the change over a measurement time period, and reflects the sum of changes over all preceeding time periods. This requires an estimate of a stock at some earlier, specified time, and documentation of subsequent changes. This may not always be possible. An alternative is to set the stock volume at zero for a base year after which the changes are known. The dynamic materials balance adopted this approach for landfill stocks which were set at zero in the base year. Calculation of the impact uses a basic equation:

$$S_T = S_0 + \sum_{t=1}^{T} \Delta S_t \qquad (7.15)$$

where

S_T = the total volume of cadmium present in stock S at time T;
S_0 = the total volume of cadmium in the base year or year of estimation/measurement; and,
ΔS_t = the change in stock during time period t, or $S_t - S_{t-1}$ and derived from a time series of equations (7.7) or (7.8) depending on the type of stock.

The sustainability context with regards to environmental stocks of cadmium has been discussed in the previous section and requires the specification of maximum levels or standards for categories of environmental media and for indicator species (e.g. the blue mussel, *Mytilus edulis*). This suggests the used of an index to compare actual values with the standard, such as the Soil Quality Index (SQI) of equation 7.2. The sustainability criterion is then given by:

$$SQI \le 0 \qquad (7.16)$$

Assuming that the data are available, such an accounting system offers consistency in the tracing of cadmium in both the economy and the environment. It would permit the construction of input–output tables for economic, waste and environmental sectors, and even the construction of a mixed unit input–output model. The latter offers opportunities for more explicit economic links. However, data in the available materials balances are neither detailed nor consistent enough to permit this. The larger or dominant flows of cadmium are generally available, and so a partial set of accounts are possible. It is expected that data availability and consistency will improve, particularly with the construction of satellite accounts and updated cadmium balances by the Central Bureau of Statistics.

7.5.3. Consolidated and Sustainability Accounts

The accounts below provide a sample of what is currently possible for cadmium accounts. Limitations to the available data and their interpretation are indicated by the balances not balancing. Table 7.1 presents equation (7.5) for 1980 and 1985 and is termed the Consolidated Dispersion Account. It aggregates, in one account, the sources and destinations of cadmium. Tables 7.2−7.4 present equations (7.6) to (7.8) for 1980 and 1985, and are termed, respectively, the Consolidated Economic, Waste and Environment Accounts. The data are based on the 1980 and 1985 balances and on earlier versions of the dynamic materials balance reported in Gilbert and Feenstra (1991).

Table 7.1. Consolidated Dispersion
Account for Cadmium
(Tonnes), 1980 and 1985

	1980	**1985**
NET IMPORTS, *I*	**44.3**	**285.7**
Economic, I_e	429.3	394.5
Waste, I_w	−119.2	−132.1
Environment, I_n	72.2	23.3
STOCK CHANGE, Δ*S*	**440.6**	**266.9**
Economic, Δ*E*	72.7	−47.2
Waste, Δ*E*	288.9	275.3
Environment, Δ*N*	79.0	38.8
Unaccounted for	**4.7**	**18.8**

Table 7.5 illustrates a sustainability account which also includes the pressure and impact variables associated with cadmium's accumulation in soil. The data are derived from the 1980 and 1985 materials balances as used in the dynamic materials balance briefly described above. The basic structure of the accounts follows a stock balance for soil, such as is described by equation (7.3). The equations which are also incorporated in this account are:

1. Cadmium's pressure — equation (7.12) — on soil;
2. Cadmium's impact — equation (7.15) — on soil;
3. Sustainability criteria — equations (7.1) and (7.13), (7.2) and (7.16).

Table 7.2. Consolidated Economic Account for Cadmium (Tonnes), 1980 and 1985.

	1980	1985
FLOWS INTO ECONOMY	**499.8**	**402.4**
Net economic imports, I_e	492.3	394.5
- batteries	32.0	44.0
- structures	176.0	45.6
- accumulators	78.0	78.0
- other	206.3	226.9
Uptake by agricultural products, L	2.3	2.3
- crops	2.0	2.0
- livestock products	0.3	0.3
Reused products	5.2	5.6
- flyash	2.6	2.8
- scrap metal	2.6	2.8
ALLOCATION OF INPUTS	**503.6**	**408.0**
Change to economic stocks, ΔE	72.2	−47.2
- batteries	24.0	24.0
- structures	43.5	−76.7
- accumulators	0.0	0.0
- reused products	5.2	5.6
Agricultural use, A	5.5	7.6
Total waste generation, W	425.4	447.6
- batteries	8.0	20.0
- structures	122.3	132.5
- accumulators	78.0	78.0
- other	185.3	217.1
Unaccounted for	**−3.8**	**−5.7**

Table 7.3. Consolidated Waste Account for Cadmium
(Tonnes), 1980 and 1985

	1980	1985
TOTAL WASTES	**328.2**	**330.0**
Net waste imports, I_w	−119.2	−132.1
Environment, N	22.0	14.5
Waste generation, W	425.4	447.6
- batteries	8.0	20.0
- structures	122.3	132.5
- accumulators	78.0	78.0
- other	185.3	217.1
DISPOSAL OF WASTES	**319.2**	**306.2**
Change to waste stocks, ΔW	289.9	276.6
Discharge to environment, D	24.1	24.1
- air	4.6	4.5
- water	17.1	18.6
- soil	2.4	1.0
Recycling, R	5.2	5.6
- scrap metal	2.6	2.8
- flyash	2.6	2.8
Unaccounted for	**9.0**	**23.8**

Table 7.4. Consolidated Environment Account for Cadmium
(Tonnes), 1980 and 1985

	1980	1985
FLOWS TO ENVIRONMENT	**101.86**	**54.95**
Net imports of pollution, I_n	72.2	23.3
- air	3.03	3.4
- surface water	113.2	19.9
- sediment	−44.0	0.0
Agricultural Use, A	5.5	7.6
Discharge to environment, D	24.1	24.1
- air	4.6	4.5
- water	17.1	18.6
- soil	2.4	1.0
DISTRIBUTION IN ENVIRONMENT	**103.31**	**55.55**
Environmental stock change, ΔN	79.0	38.8
- soil	13.6	13.8
- aquatic sediments	65.4	25.0
From environment, N	22.0	14.5
Recycling, R	2.3	2.3
- crops	2.0	2.0
- livestock products	0.3	0.3
Unaccounted for	**−1.45**	**−0.6**

Table 7.5. Sustainability Account for Soil (Tonnes Cd), 1980 and 1985

	TOTAL SOIL		Agricultural soil		Soil under natural cover	
	1980	1985	1980	1985	1980	1985
S_0	1013.9	1059.4	656.0	693.7	357.8	365.7
Additions, P_{soil}[1]	11.0	12.7	9.3	11.1	1.8	1.5
(domestic sources)	(9.5)	(11.3)	(8.2)	(9.1)	(1.1)	(0.9)
- sewerage sludge	1.2	0.7	0.5	0.3	0.6	0.4
- fertilizer	5.5	7.6	5.5	7.6	0.0	0.0
- deposition	4.4	4.3	3.3	3.2	1.1	1.1
(domestic sources)	(2.8)	(2.7)	(1.2)	(1.2)	(0.54)	(0.52)
Total losses	2.60	2.70	2.60	2.60	0.10	0.10
- runoff	0.11	0.13	0.09	0.11	0.02	0.02
- leaching	0.23	0.26	0.20	0.22	0.03	0.04
- uptake	2.30	0.00	2.30	2.30	0.00	0.00
S_1, $Impact_{soil}$[2]	1022.3	1069.4	662.7	702.3	359.6	367.1

Sustainability criteria:

(1) Net deficit, ND[3]	−8.4	−10.0				
Net deficit ≥ 0[4]	**NO**	**NO**				
			$\Longrightarrow$	**Trend towards**		
(2) SQI[5]	0.280	0.247		**unsustainability**		
or **SQI ≥ 0[6]**	**YES**	**YES**				

Notes:
1. As per equation (7.12).
2. As per equation (7.15).
3. As per equation (7.1).
4. As per equation (7.13).
5. Based on a soil concentration of 0.8 mg Cd/kg dry weight and equation (7.2).
6. As per equation (7.16).

Table 7.6. Sustainability Accounts, Per Scenario, for Cadmium Accumulation in the Soil (Tonnes)

	1980	1990	2000	2010	2020
Base scenario					
S_0	1013.9	1109.6	1210.8	1313.2	1416.0
Additions, P_s	11.0	12.8	12.9	13.0	13.0
- sewage sludge	1.1	0.7	0.7	0.7	0.7
- fertilizer	5.5	7.6	7.6	7.6	7.6
- deposition	4.4	4.5	4.6	4.7	4.7
Losses	2.6	2.7	2.7	2.8	2.8
- runoff	0.11	0.13	0.13	0.13	0.13
- leaching	0.24	0.26	0.29	0.32	0.35
- uptake	2.3	2.3	2.3	2.3	2.3
S_1	1022.3	1119.6	1221.0	1323.5	1426.2
(1) Net Deficit	−8.4	−10.1	−10.2	−10.3	−10.3
Net deficit ≥ 0	NO	NO	NO	NO	NO
(2) SQI	0.28	0.21	0.14	0.07	−0.01
SQI ≥ 0	YES	YES	YES	YES	YES
Moderate policy scenario					
S_0	1013.9	1109.3	1204.9	1267.8	1337.0
Additions, P_s	11.0	12.6	12.0	8.7	8.7
- sewage sludge	1.1	0.7	0.7	0.7	0.7
- fertilizer	5.5	7.6	7.6	5.0	5.0
- deposition	4.4	4.3	3.7	3.0	3.0
Losses	2.6	2.7	2.7	2.7	2.7
- runoff	0.11	0.13	0.12	0.09	0.09
- leaching	0.24	0.26	0.29	0.31	0.33
- uptake	2.3	2.3	2.3	2.3	2.3
S_1	1022.3	1119.2	1214.2	1282.8	1343.0
(1) Net Deficit	−8.4	−9.9	−9.3	−6.0	−6.0
Net deficit ≥ 0	NO	NO	NO	NO	NO
(2) SQI	0.28	0.21	0.14	0.09	0.05
SQI ≥ 0	YES	YES	YES	YES	YES
Strict policy scenario					
S_0	1012.4	1106.6	1179.3	1198.4	1215.6
Additions, P_s	11.0	12.0	5.1	4.3	4.4
- sewage sludge	1.1	0.7	0.5	0.5	0.5
- fertilizer	5.5	7.6	1.6	1.6	1.6
- deposition	4.4	3.7	3.1	2.3	2.3
Losses	2.6	2.7	2.6	2.6	2.6
- runoff	0.11	0.12	0.05	0.04	0.04
- leaching	0.24	0.26	0.28	0.29	0.29
- uptake	2.3	2.3	2.3	2.3	2.3
S_1	1020.8	1116.0	1181.7	1200.1	1217.3
(1) Net Deficit	−8.4	−9.3	−2.5	−1.7	−1.7
Net deficit ≥ 0	NO	NO	NO	NO	NO
(2) SQI	0.28	0.21	0.16	0.15	0.14
SQI ≥ 0	YES	YES	YES	YES	YES

7.6. INTERACTIONS AMONG ACCOUNTS, INDICATORS AND MODEL

Interactions among environmental accounts, dynamic materials balances and indicators, on the basis of the discussion in Section 7.5 can be summarized as follows:

(i)   The materials balances incorporated in the resource accounts provide the basic data for construction of the dynamic materials balance;

(ii) the dynamic balance requires more data than are provided by the balances, in particular initial stock levels and the rates of change of variables, and so pose additional questions, some of which serve to identify data constraints, oversights and/or inconsistencies in the balances;

(iii) these constraints, oversights and/or inconsistencies should be apparent from construction of accounts along the formal lines outlined above, providing incentives and specifics for further data collection and future construction of resource accounts;

(iv) while selection of key variables for inclusion in the indicators can occur without a dynamic materials balance, such a model permits a more rigorous assessment of the system's behaviour and so provides a more analytical basis for selection;

(v)   the indicators can be constructed with data from the materials balances or the environmental accounts; and,

(vi) the power of the indicators is enhanced when combined with the dynamic materials balance which expressly includes policy variables, providing a means of assessing alternative policy scenarios and of offering implications for further policy development.

The following elaborates on the last point by including the environmental accounts. Table 7.6 presents the output from the dynamic materials balance in the form of projected sustainability accounts. These accounts, one for each scenario, present the basic variables used in the four indicators discussed in the previous section. The indicators make use of diagrammatic forms so that states and trends are easy to recognize. The accounts provide the data essential to these forms, as well as the essential components of these data. For example, the strong influence of fertilizer use and of transboundary pollution in both the pressure and sustainability indicators is to be seen in these accounts, but not necessarily from the indicators themselves.

8. Sustainable Multiple Use Management and Values of Dutch Forests[1]

8.1. FORESTS: MULTIPLE USE, STRESS, ECONOMICS AND POLICY

The forests in the Netherlands serve various interests and are under various types of stress. Three major interests are distinguished. First, timber production, which has been the major driving force for the reforestation of heathland in the early decades of the 20th century, and as a consequence is the dominant factor in the present structure of the forests in the country. Demand for wood has increased at high rates in the last few decades, so that the yearly timber output still only accounts for about 8% of the national demand. The second form of use is outdoor recreation. A walk through the local forest is the nation's first ranking outdoor recreation activity. With only 7% of the terrestrial surface covered by forest ecosystems, the stress on the systems from recreational visits is considerable and increasing. The third major interest is nature conservation. Conservation interests are reshaping the forest landscape as they are becoming increasingly stronger as a factor in forest development policy. Each of these forest uses involves quite a different management approach, which makes multiple use management a complicated issue.

Next to natural stress factors, three major types of anthropogenic stress are distinguished. Firstly, acidification. Over the last few decades the forests in the Netherlands, like those in other parts of Western and Central Europe and the Northeastern United States have been exposed to airborne acid depositions peaking at about 9000 mol/ha/year. The second stress factor is eutrophication. Nitrogen oxides and ammonium constitute a major part of the acidifying deposition. The nutrient enrichment affects

---

[1] This chapter was written by L.C. Braat, based on dissertation research. See for more details on the study Braat (1992).

tree growth and changes the understorey vegetation and soilsystems. And thirdly a large part of the forest area experiences increasingly lower groundwater tables which results in lower soil moisture values and increased mineralisation. This is referred to as desiccation. In short, the ecological sustainability is at risk.

Development and management costs of multiple use forests in particular are high and timber sales do not cover the costs. In addition, timber prices on the world market are low and have been decreasing in the last decade, so the financial sustainability of forest operations is at risk as well. Multiple use forests produce a greater range of non-monetary economic values than mono-species stands, which is relevant both at the national level where funding from other sources may be considered and at the local level where the sustainability of multiple use values may be a reason for allocation of government funds.

In 1984, the State Forestry Service of the Netherlands launched its first integrated National Forest Development Plan (*nfdp*) with a target date set at the year 2050. It is a comprehensive attempt to generate a strategy which maximises, over time, the overall value of forest ecosystems to the public and the economy. The plan has been developed around the following three major policy objectives:

(1) With respect to the social and economic functions: sustainable multiple use, i.e. a combination of timber production, outdoor recreation and nature conservation;
(2) with respect to growth and development conditions: ecological sustainability;
(3) with respect to the economics of forestry: financial sustainability.

In light of the present growth of conflicting demands for forest functions and considering the environmental conditions and the current cost−revenue ratios in forestry, the objectives may be considered ambitious.

8.2. THE CASE STUDY LAYOUT

The remainder of this chapter presents the case study of multiple use forestry under stress. A summary overview is given of an integrated economic−ecological decision support system which consists of a simulation model combined with an evaluation model to comparatively evaluate forest management strategies with respect to their ecological and economic sustainability and the values of forest ecosystems to different users. A full discussion and documentation of the model is available in Braat (1992). The decision support system presented here includes:

(1) *Indicators* of forest performance and value to owner, managers, specific users and the general public;
(2) *simulation models*, which incorporate the indicators, and which are run with scenarios;
(3) *management scenarios* to explore alternative forest futures;
(4) *evaluation models* to compare simulation results of different scenarios and with target and reference values.

In Section 8.3 the conceptual basis of the decision support system is discussed. The operational version of the simulation model is summarised in Section 8.4. Model tests are discussed in Section 8.5. Scenarios and simulation results are presented in Section 8.6. Evaluations of the scenarios are included in Section 8.7. The last section summarises the conclusions of the study.

8.3. MODELS FOR FOREST MANAGEMENT

To introduce the uninitiated reader to the issues in forest management, a conceptual model of forest management is shown in Figure 8.1. The following components are distinguished. The forest ecosystem is the physical object which is monitored and manipulated by the forest managers. Management activities include site protection, preparation and planting, thinning and harvest, zoning the forest and development of recreation facilities.

Furthermore, managers gather data about the state of the forest ecosystem, disperse information about the forest and control hunting permits, groundwater pumping rights and grazing of forest lands. Money is received for timber, water and various services, and is paid for goods and services, labour, fuels and electricity. In addition, the forest manager receives subsidies from the (Dutch) government.

The forest ecosystem grows and develops on the basis of natural energies (sunlight, wind, rain, inflowing groundwater, rock and sediments, and air pollutants), fuel based energy (e.g. mechanical planting and harvesting) and human actions (management and recreational). In the processes the various forms of energy are transformed. Some is embodied in the forest structure and some energy is dissipated as heat and leaves the system (see for details of energy flow in ecological and economic systems Odum, 1971, 1983). Three major users

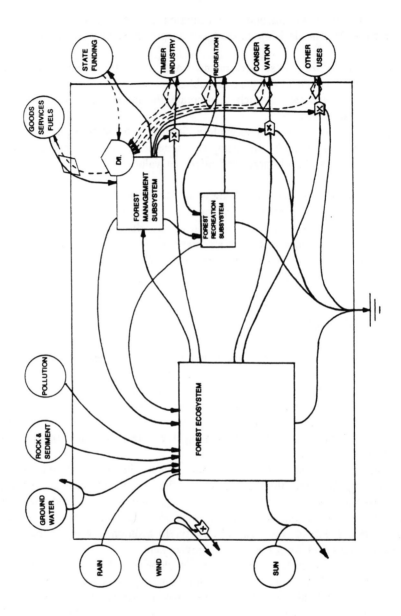

Figure 8.1.   A Conceptual Model of Forest Management.

Source: Braat (1992).

are recognised in the diagram, the timber industry, recreational visitors, and people with nature conservation interests. These users obtain timber, information about the forest and opportunities to recreate. Other forms of use are aggregated in a fourth class.

Sustainability in forest management is linked to three different aspects of the forest management operation:

(i) Sustainability of multiple use: maintain values for each of the users;
(ii) ecological sustainability: for trees, maintain average normal volume growth; and for low vegetations, a continuous small share of area by pioneer grasses such as Molinia and Deschampsia;
(iii) financial economic sustainability: a continued achievement of a non-negative income of the forest operation.

In multiple use management the manager faces the task of selecting the strategy that maximises the value of the forest to the different users. This is problematic for a number of reasons, one of them being that there are different views of what value is and how it should be measured. A major difference regards the view of the source of value. In the objective view, represented by classical theories and the emergy theory (Odum, 1987), value is equated to the effort it takes to produce a commodity. This is called the supply side view. Effort assessments may be monetary, in which case the monetary value is estimated of payments for the human energy effort (labour) associated with and required for production of a good or service. Alternatively, one may assess efforts in terms of energy, i.e. reflecting the total energy cost of producing a good or service. In the subjective view, values are what people think something is worth, most often in a relative, comparative sense, or what they are prepared to pay for something. In determining the value, the expected utility of a good or service is the predominant factor. This is referred to as the demand side or consumer preference view, which is at the basis of the neoclassical economic theory.

In this chapter, valuations based on the consumer preference view are presented. The value to the users is measured by the numerical values of performance indicators, i.e. forest features which are positively valued by the respective users. The aggregate user value indicators in the simulation model are: harvested timber, recreational attractiveness, cohort–habitat diversity and naturalness.

Most forest models consider the forest as an economic resource and ignore ecological dynamics, or represent the forest as an ecosystem which may or may not produce social and economic benefits, and consequently ignore economic aspects. Relatively few models address multiple use forestry and most of those are theoretical. Empirical studies with numerical examples are scarce. Impacts of anthropogenic environmental stress have been studied extensively in the last decade, but most models concentrate on physiological impacts in the forest and ignore interactions with parasites, climate and management. In view of this situation, a simulation model has been synthesised from a number of different approaches, each relevant to a particular aspect of the issue of sustainable multiple use forestry under stress.

8.4. THE OPERATIONAL MULTIPLE USE FOREST MODEL

The Smilde—Appelscha forest in the northeastern part of the Netherlands was selected for the case study. Most of the 3600 hectares of the forest are covered with monocultures of conifers exotic to the Netherlands and planted for timber. Recreational facilities are well developed. There are however hardly any naturally regenerating indigenous forest ecosystems, one relatively large drift sand area and several small patches with heathland and fen communities. The system as a whole is exposed to considerable airborne acid and nitrogen depositions and its groundwater table is substantially lower than a few decades ago. With respect to its financial state, the forest is currently operated with a deficit and is subsidised by the State.

The operational version of the conceptual forest model, based on data from the Smilde—Appelscha forest system has been implemented as a dynamic simulation model in a Lotus 123™ electronic spreadsheet. It is partly simplified, and partly more detailed when compared to the conceptual model presented above (see the diagram in Figure 8.2 and the appendices in Braat, 1992, for full documentation).

The model contains growth and development specifications for 11 tree species and for low vegetation communities such as heathland, drift sand, grassland and fens. The basic dynamic unit in the model is the species—cohort. Such a unit contains all the trees in the forest (wherever they may be located) which belong to a particular species and which have germinated (or were planted) in the same 10 year period of time. The low vegetation types each constitute a single cohort.

A selection of indicators is used in the model to reflect the forest performance with respect to the NFDP objectives and the values to users:

Indicator 1:   Evenness, calculated as a function of tree species diversity and the number of species.

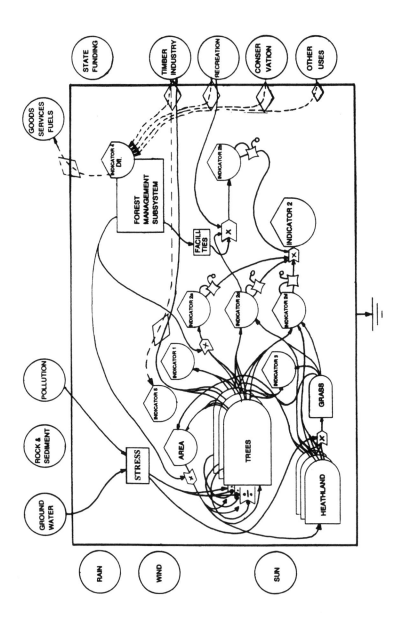

Figure 8.2. A Diagram of the Operational Case Study Model.

Source: **Braat** (1992).

Indicator 2: Sustainable multiple use, defined in the model as a combination of sustained production of timber (2a), recreational attractiveness (2b), cohort−habitat diversity (2c) and naturalness (2d). If any one of the 4 component indicators falls below a minimum acceptable level, the overall sustainability indicator produces the numerical value 0, which indicates that the management objective is not achieved.

Indicator 3: Ecological sustainability, calculated as the difference between actual volume growth in trees under varying levels of stress and the reference standard growth. The resulting data are combined with the modeled stress effect on low vegetations, i.e. the percentage of grass cover.

Indicator 4: Financial sustainability, the net revenue of the forest operation. The indicator includes the timber production costs and benefits, and the costs and benefits of recreation, conservation and miscellaneous activities.

Indicator 5: Stock value, calculated by multiplying the standing stock of timber per species with the timber price (corrected for height) per species and then summing totals per species for the whole forest.

8.5. MODEL TESTS

The behaviour of the forest model has been examined and tested with respect to similarity to the structure and behaviour of the case study forest and to Dutch forests on poor sandy soils in general. The model is robust with respect to the model parameters and initial conditions, and sensitive to the scenario parameters. It generates logical results under a considerable range of parameter values. Fluctuations of indicator values through time and sign switches have been explained in terms of the non-linearities in the model structure or distributions in the initial conditions. The model is a plausible representation of the case study forest.

Results of model applications have been compared with independent data and simulation results of other models. The dynamics of the trees in the case study model are shown to be quite close to local values and reasonably close to national average values. The differences can be explained by differences in parameter settings, initialisations and mathematical specifications. With respect to the tree dynamics under normal circumstances, it can be concluded that the case study model produces reliable predictions. Simulated development under stress has not been tested as independent datasets are not available. The model produces a measure which indicates a difference with the unstressed standard situation of 30 to 40% after maximum multiple stress over a period of 60 years. For comparison: forest vitality surveys of the State Forestry Service indicate differences of 30 to more than 50% with the standard values in the past decade, varying with the region and the species (see SBB, 1984-1991).

8.6. SCENARIO ANALYSIS BY SIMULATION

Six scenarios are distinguished:
(1) The *reference* scenario produces the baseline results with which simulation results of other scenarios are compared. It represents continuation of present policies and present forest structure.
(2) The *national forest development plan (nfdp)* scenario represents the interpretation of national forest policy objectives to the case study forest in terms of the 2050 species area distribution.
(3) The *timber* scenario forces the forest towards a monoculture plantation. All available area is allocated to a single highly productive and valuable timber species, Japanese larch, and rotations maximise production and net income.
(4) The *recreation* scenario maximises the numerical value of the recreation indicator. Species area allocation, medium-long rotations and facilities are the tools to realise a maximum number of visitors at the highest recreational attraction value.
(5) The *conservation* scenario explores the hypothetical future of the multiple use forest area as a reserve. The conservation goal is represented by the maximum naturalness. This implies a policy in which exotic species are removed, as fast as technically possible, and natural succession takes over all cleared sites and gaps.
(6) The *multiple use* scenario takes the lessons learned from developing the previous three single use scenarios and aims to improve on the *nfdp* scenario by abandoning the goal species distribution of the *nfdp* scenario and instead search for maximum value of a multiple use forest defined by the indicators.

Scenarios are compared using the major indicators (see Figures 8.3 and 8.4). The *timber* scenario produces the highest harvest indicator end value, but it is clearly unattractive for recreationists and conservationists. Recreational attractiveness is highest in the *recreation* scenario. The *nfdp* scenario produces intermediate values except for the diversity indicator, where the scenario ends a close second after the *recreation* scenario. For the multiple use component indicators, the *reference* scenario, the *nfdp* scenario and the *multiple use* scenario produce rather stable development patterns. The *conservation* scenario's high score for the naturalness indicator is clearly paid for by a very negative net income and initial drop of the capital stock value. Without external subsidies this type of management cannot be sustained.

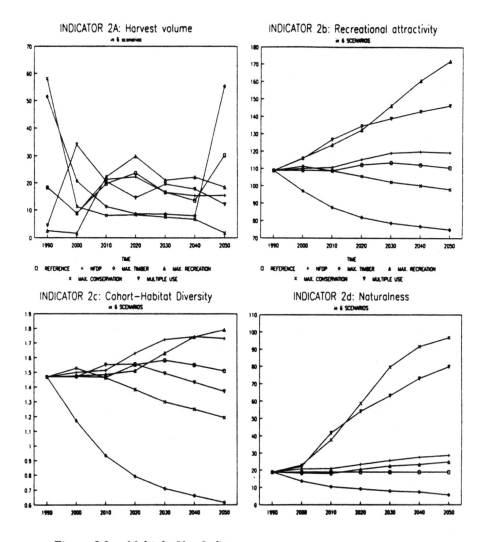

Figure 8.3.   Multiple Use Indicators.

The *nfdp* scenario performs slightly worse than the *reference* scenario with respect to net income of the forest business and the long term development of a valuable capital stock. The *multiple use* scenario also suffers financially from the achievement of higher naturalness scores. None of the scenarios produces an average positive financial result, the *reference* and the *timber* scenarios produce positive results in 2050.

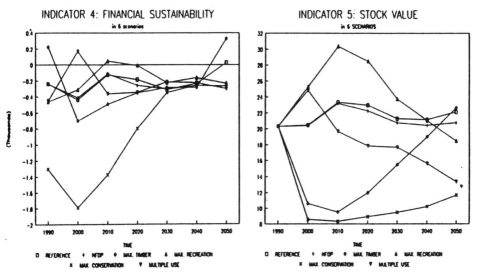

Figure 8.4. Financial Sustainability Indicators.

In addition to the results in a hypothetical, unstressed environment, the impacts of stress are explored (see Table 8.1). The *Reference—Stress* scenario represents an optimistic view of the future. The consequences of this optimistic scenario for the forest development patterns and indicator values include that ecological sustainability decreases with an average of 11% over 60 years. Two alternative stress scenarios are considered for comparison. The scenario called *Reference—Stress 2* assumes that current deposition rates of potential acid and nitrogen compounds will continue through 2050. Soilwater availability is assumed to follow the *Reference—Stress* values.

The result is that the ecological sustainability indicator decreases from 92% in 1990 to 68% in 2050. In the scenario *Reference—stress 3*, with soil water availability class 4 from 2010 through 2050, the same indicator goes down to 61%. The simulation data show a serious impact of stress shows in the area of forest finances. The harvest decreases to a

Table 8.1. Stress Indicators for Multiple Use Forest Type.

SCENARIO	Reference							Stress 2							Reference							Stress 3						
YEAR	1990	2000	2010	2020	2030	2040	2050	1990	2000	2010	2020	2030	2040	2050	1990	2000	2010	2020	2030	2040	2050	1990	2000	2010	2020	2030	2040	2050
INDICATORS																												
1. Evenness	82	82	82	82	82	82	82	82	82	82	82	82	82	82	82	82	82	82	82	82	82	82	82	82	82	82	82	82
2. Sustainable Multiple Use	0.0	0.0	0.0	0.0	0.0	0.0	0.0	0.0	0.0	0.0	0.0	0.0	0.0	0.0	0.0	0.0	0.0	0.0	0.0	0.0	0.0	0.0	0.0	0.0	0.0	0.0	0.0	0.0
2a. Harvest m³/yr	17320	7756	17186	18535	11997	9864	18972	17320	7756	17186	18399	11684	9481	16834	17320	7756	17186	18535	11997	9864	18972	17320	7756	17186	18399	11684	9481	16834
2b. Recreational Attractiveness	109	109	109	112	114	112	111	109	109	109	113	114	112	111	109	109	109	112	114	112	111	109	109	109	113	114	112	111
2c. Cohort-Habitat Diversity	1.48	1.49	1.48	1.56	1.59	1.55	1.51	1.48	1.49	1.48	1.56	1.59	1.56	1.52	1.48	1.49	1.48	1.56	1.59	1.55	1.51	1.48	1.49	1.48	1.56	1.59	1.56	1.52
2d. Naturalness	19	17	16	16	15	15	15	19	17	16	16	15	15	15	19	17	16	16	15	15	15	19	17	16	16	15	15	15
3. Ecological Sustainability	92	87	81	76	72	70	68	92	87	81	75	69	65	61	92	87	81	76	72	70	68	92	87	81	75	69	65	61
4. Financial Sustainability	-254	-452	-162	-259	-381	-295	-150	-254	-452	-162	-261	-386	-301	-182	-254	-452	-162	-259	-381	-295	-150	-254	-452	-162	-261	-386	-301	-182
4a. Timber kfl/yr	37	-162	129	32	-91	-4	141	37	-162	129	30	-95	-10	108	37	-162	129	32	-91	-4	141	37	-162	129	30	-95	-10	108
4b. Recreation kfl/yr	-111	-111	-111	-111	-111	-111	-111	-111	-111	-111	-111	-111	-111	-111	-111	-111	-111	-111	-111	-111	-111	-111	-111	-111	-111	-111	-111	-111
4c. Conservation kfl/yr	-71	-71	-71	-71	-71	-71	-71	-71	-71	-71	-71	-71	-71	-71	-71	-71	-71	-71	-71	-71	-71	-71	-71	-71	-71	-71	-71	-71
4d. Other kfl/yr	-109	-109	-109	-109	-109	-109	-109	-109	-109	-109	-109	-109	-109	-109	-109	-109	-109	-109	-109	-109	-109	-109	-109	-109	-109	-109	-109	-109
4e. Stock value kfl	18854	17548	18539	16852	14784	14338	14693	18854	17548	18539	16650	14208	13182	12881	18854	17548	18539	16852	14784	14338	14693	18854	17548	18539	16650	14208	13182	12881
STRESS FACTOR LEVELS																												
Deposition H+ (1100)	4800	4800	4800	4800	4800	4800	4800	4800	4800	4800	4800	4800	4800	4800	4800	4800	4800	4800	4800	4800	4800	4800	4800	4800	4800	4800	4800	4800
Deposition N (700)	3700	3700	3700	3700	3700	3700	3700	3700	3700	3700	3700	3700	3700	3700	3700	3700	3700	3700	3700	3700	3700	3700	3700	3700	3700	3700	3700	3700
Soilwater availability	2	3	4	3	2	1	1	2	3	4	3	2	1	1	2	3	4	3	2	1	1	2	3	4	4	4	4	4

little over 50 % of the no-stress situation, which is low compared with the decrease of ecological sustainability to 61 %. The net income from timber drops to about a third of the no-stress situation.

8.7. MULTICRITERIA AND COST-BENEFIT EVALUATION

Two evaluation methods are discussed: multicriteria analysis in which weights are assigned to the forest performance and user value indicators, cost-benefit analysis in which the indicators are priced, with market prices and proxy (or shadow) prices. The *Definite* model (see Janssen, 1992) has been used for the multicriteria evaluation such as required for multiple use management. A simple Cost Benefit Analysis model has been implemented in Lotus 123^(TM) based on the theory and specifications described in Janssen (1991). It generates Net Present Value of a scenario, after the user specifies shadow prices for units of naturalness, diversity and recreational attractiveness.

The multiple use set of weights applied to the 1990-2050 averages lead to a number 1 position for the *multiple use* scenario (see Table 8.2). For multiple use management the actions embodied in the timber and conservation scenarios turn out not to be effective. If the 2050 situation is considered most important, and the values during the period from now to the goal situation are taken as they come, the approach represented by the *recreation* scenario should be followed. On the other hand, if the interests of the generations of recreational, conservation and timber users between now and 2050 are considered equally important, then the strategy included in the *multiple use* scenario should be adopted. Interestingly, the *nfdp* scenario takes a third place in both situations, which suggests a rather stable development scenario that could be improved but does take care of both the next few generations and the long term goals.

A cost-benefit analysis which ignores benefits to the public of the recreational and natural aspects of the forest, would reveal the *recreation* scenario as the most lucrative at low discount rates, and the *timber* scenario at high discount rates (see Table 8.3). Pricing the non-marketed values of the forest, leads to a very similar type of evaluation procedure as described in the previous section when weights were assigned to the indicators. The outcome, a strong case for the *multiple use* scenario if all features are considered with approximately similar attention, is very similar too.

Table 8.2. Multicriteria Results.

Indicator Weighting	Weights	Scenario	2050 values		average values	
			rank	score	rank	score
(i) Equal Weights						
1. Evenness	1	*reference*	2	60	4	67
2a. Harvest	1	*nfdp*	3	53	3	68
2b. Recreational		*timber*	5	43	6	33
Attractiveness	1	*recreation*	1	61	1	78
2c. Diversity	1					
2d. Naturalness	1	*conservation*	6	33	5	37
4. Income (relative)	1	*multiple use*	4	45	2	73
5. Capital Stock	1					
(ii) Conservation						
1. Evenness	1	*reference*	5	52	5	59
2a. Harvest	1	*nfdp*	3	57	3	66
2b. Recreational		*timber*	6	20	6	15
Attractiveness	1	*recreation*	1	61	2	68
2c. Diversity	5					
2d. Naturalness	5	*conservation*	4	55	4	61
4. Income (relative)	1	*multiple use*	2	60	1	78
5. Capital Stock	1					
(iii) Monetary						
1. Evenness	1	*reference*	2	62	2	71
2a. Harvest	4	*nfdp*	4	45	4	67
2b. Recreational		*timber*	1	70	5	53
Attractiveness	3	*recreation*	3	51	1	81
2c. Diversity	1					
2d. Naturalness	1	*conservation*	6	15	6	17
4. Income (relative)	5	*multiple use*	5	29	3	70
5. Capital Stock	5					
(iv) Multiple Use						
1. Evenness	1	*reference*	2	53	4	60
2a. Harvest	4	*nfdp*	3	50	3	61
2b. Recreational		*timber*	5	38	6	32
Attractiveness	4	*recreation*	1	60	2	70
2c. Diversity	4					
2d. Naturalness	4	*conservation*	6	36	5	41
4. Income (relative)	2	*multiple use*	4	49	1	73
5. Capital Stock	2					

8.8.   CONCLUSIONS

The model provides aggregate indicator values as well as data about the component variables of these indicators. A Multiple Use indicator has been constructed in such a way that after the decision on minimum acceptable levels for each of the user value indicators the achievement of multiple use is immediately visible as well as the degree of dominance of any particular form of use.

Table 8.3. Cost—Benefit Analysis Results: Best Ranked Scenarios on Net Present Value with Different Discount Rates and Different Proxy Prices for Recreation Attractivity, Naturalness and Diversity.

Discount rate (%)	Prices								
	P_R	0	1	5	10	1	1	1	1
	P_N	0	10	10	10	10	10	20	50
	P_D	0	100	100	100	200	500	100	100
0		recreation	multiple use	...	...	...	...	...	conservation
1		recreation	multiple use	...	...	...	...	...	conservation
5		timber	multiple use	...	...	...	...	...	conservation
10		timber	timber	...	...	...	...	...	multiple use

Notes:
P_R denotes the price for recreation attractivity;
P_N denotes the price for naturalness;
P_D denotes the price for diversity;
'...' denotes that the outcome is the same as in the previous column.

The tests of the model warrant the conclusion that it is an adequate and effective representation of the case study forest. The generality of the descriptions of structure and dynamics make it a useful basis for refinement and application to other forests. The evaluation model provides easily interpretable results which enable the managers to interactively compare the consequences of alternative management objectives and relative biases. The weight distributions and proxy prices used in the case study have illustrative meaning only.

Multiple use is hard to achieve, and even harder to sustain. The numerical values at which the minimum acceptable levels for the three major forest users were set in the case study were not very extreme. The timber harvest scores fluctuates but in many scenarios the minimum level is achieved. The diversity score and related recreational attractiveness level are also rather easily achieved. The level of 40 (out of 100) for naturalness turned out to be rather high. Only rather extreme management strategies will lead to higher scores but in most of those strategies the timber output and the cohort—habitat diversity suffer. Through trial and learn simulations the *multiple use* scenario has been developed which does achieve and sustain multiple use in the sense of the definition. The *reference−stress* scenario demonstrates the fragility of the sustainable multiple use strategy clearly.

The case study results indicate that outdoor recreation, timber production and economic sustainability go together very well, but high naturalness does not go together well with any other type of use in the long run. In the short run (20 years) accelerated harvesting of exotics provide a large harvest, but keeping the exotics out requires a large effort. A natural forest does not go well together with a timber production forest, nor with a forest attractive to recreation. The latter conclusion must be put in the perspective that the visitors with a preference for an indigenous forest over a highly diverse forest are not included in the analysis.

If the stress factors do indeed affect the performance of the forest in the way it has been modeled, then forest values will be affected as timber yields drop and naturalness of the system decreases. Recreational values are not affected noticeably.

The concept of ecological sustainability as used in this study, does not imply that if the score is below 100, the forest will die. It does indicate that the forest values for a variety of users are affected and at risk. In this study the ecological sustainability has concentrated on trees and low vegetation types. The impacts of the stress factors on rare species, soils and fauna are not included, but are nonetheless noteworthy. Trees have a relatively extensive buffer capacity against fluctuations in site conditions and primary production. Smaller individual plants will suffer more quickly of drought and changes in acidity and nutrient balances. The focus on trees is therefore misleading in an attempt to describe the extent and seriousness of the stress effects for the forest ecosystem. On the other hand, if the trees start showing symptoms of injury, then it is likely that we are not facing a short term natural fluctuation in site conditions. The uncertainty regarding the stress response relationships is still very great. A reliable assessment of the impacts of the national and regional environmental stress control policies can therefore not be given here.

In the long run, the sustainability of a management strategy is determined as much by the financial results of the operation as it is by the health state of the forest, at least when subsidies are not considered external factors. It is however not necessary that all the forests generate a monetary profit, as society may choose to subsidise in order to obtain non-monetised recreational and nature benefits which imply higher costs and less timber revenues. With current high planting and harvesting costs and low timber prices, the results of the long rotation scenarios indicate that it is wiser in all respects to leave the trees as long as possible on the sites. As long as the world market timber prices are low, timber should be imported and harvests should be delayed. In other words, the *nfdp* objective of increased self-sufficiency in timber production of the Netherlands to 25% by 2050 should be changed to increased capital stock value!

Value is represented by individual indicator scores in the simulations, and by aggregate scores, weights, and prices in the evaluation exercises. The relativity of the values in a multiple use situation is demonstrated in the multicriteria and cost-benefit valuation exercises. These indicate that the aggregated value of a particular scenario, either in 2050 or averaged over the period 1990−2050, is quite dependent on the weights (and proxy prices respectively) assigned to each of the forest value indicators. The case study results illustrate that the weights are important, but that in the medium range of weight-scores a convergence on the *multiple use* scenario is achieved.

The conclusion from the exercises is that the best ranking sustainable development policy, which maximises value over user groups over the entire period consists of moderate investment in recreational facilities and gradual development of a diverse (in age structure) and natural (in species composition) forest.

Appendix. Symbols of the Energy Language Used to Represent Systems

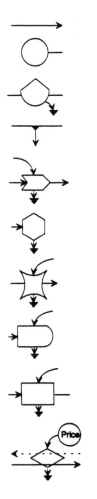

Energy circuit. A pathway whose flow is proportional to the quantity in the storage or source upstream.

Source. Outside source of energy delivering forces according to a program controlled from outside; a forcing function.

Tank. A compartment of energy storage within the system storing a quantity as the balance of inflows and outflows; a state variable.

Heat sink. Dispersion of potential energy into heat that accompanies all real transformation processes and storages; loss of potential energy from further use by the system.

Interaction. Interactive intersection of two pathways coupled to produce an outflow in proportion to a function of both; control action of one flow on another; limiting factor action; work gate.

Consumer. Unit that transforms energy quality, stores it, and feeds it back autocatalytically to improve inflow.

Switching action. A symbol that indicates one or more switching actions.

Producer. Unit that collects and transforms low-quality energy under control interactions of high-quality flows.

Box. Miscellaneous symbol to use for whatever unit or function is labeled.

Transaction. A unit that indicates a sale of goods or services (solid line) in exchange for payment of money (dashed line). Price is shown as an external source.

Source: Odum, 1971 and 1983.

9. A Dynamic Model of Conflicts between Nature and Agriculture in a Dutch Region

9.1. INTRODUCTION[1]

This chapter presents the results of a case study for the Peel region, an area in the Netherlands, where presently agriculture causes considerable damage to groundwater, forests, and protected fen areas due to intensive cattle farming, irrigation and drainage. Several relevant development scenarios for regional sustainable development (RSD) planning are indicated, and the model analyses for each of them are reviewed from the viewpoint of regional sustainable development.

The use of models for sustainable development in a regional context requires integration of economic and ecologal processes, and their interactions. Furthermore, it means that socio-economic and ecological indicators are contained in the policy evaluation. The model considered here is dynamic in order to deal with the mentioned processes. Scenario and simulation models are most appropriate on a regional level, as here the level of detail in describing the economics and ecology can be fairly balanced.

9.2. A CASE STUDY: THE PEEL REGION IN THE NETHERLANDS

The Peel area in the south-east of the Netherlands has been selected as a test case for RSD modelling because of its problematic interactions between the natural resource base and economic activities (see van den Bergh et al., 1988). Two natural fen areas (de Groote Peel and Maria Peel) are situated in an area in which intensive cattle farming and mixed agriculture are the

---

[1] A previously published version of this chapter appeared as van den Bergh and Nijkamp (1994a), which also includes a full set of equations of the simulation model.

dominant users of the land. The study focuses on the use of forests, natural areas and groundwater. Drainage of the land has been instrumental to the historical development of the region. Extensive drainage still occurs each spring, lowering the water level so that machines can work on the land. During summer, potential (as well as actual) shortfalls in soil moisture are circumvented by irrigation sprinklers; water is derived from groundwater reserves. Recharge of groundwater reserves may be constrained by spring drainage, yet the reserves are used intensively during the summer. There are hence various questions and conflicting issues regarding the 'sustainability' of such practices. Economic activities which are directly dependent on the groundwater resource include agriculture and municipal water supply. Other activities in the region are timber production, recreation and nature conservation. Especially agriculture is at the present significantly contributing to regional income. Conflicts between recreation, economy and the environment have increasingly emerged in this area, and therefore it may serve as an interesting pilot study for an RSD analysis.

The natural resources in the region are the starting points of our analysis (see Section 9.3). Economic activities are taken into account insofar as they influence (or are influenced by) these resources. Consequently, the regional boundaries were primarily determined by ecological and geographical criteria, based on the groundwater basin around the Peel-fen reserves (so-called ecohydrological districts).

The renewable natural resources central in our analysis are groundwater, forests and natural vegetation. The issues associated with these may be summarised as follows:

1. High water table, sandy soil and nutrient-poor conditions have led to the development of unique ecological communities;
2. widespread drainage of the land and multiple use of the groundwater resource (for irrigation as well as municipal supply) has lowered the water tables;
3. agricultural activities, with intensive use of fertilizer and with increasing manure production, are causing nitrate enrichment of the groundwater, with impacts on the remnant vegetation as well as decreasing suitability for human consumption;
4. air pollution is also causing acidification of soils, with impacts on the natural vegetation as well as on forests.

For some production activities a further subdivision is useful. For example, timber production is based on two tree species − pines and Douglas fir, both of which are produced in plantations. Agriculture comprises the rearing of livestock (cattle, pigs and poultry), and crop cultivation (for livestock and human consumption); livestock rearing can be either intensive (e.g., bioindustry for meat and egg products) or extensive (e.g., dairy and meat).

The spatial distribution of activities in the region also affects their interactions and relationships with resources. For example, groundwater extraction for agriculture is shallow and widespread, whereas that for municipal supply occurs at a small number of sites and involves deeper extraction. The main regional cross-boundary flows which affect regional processes are visitors of the natural areas, inflow and outflow of air pollution, and export of agricultural and forestry products.

The central focus of this study is the use of the region's natural resource base by the region's economic activities. Multiple use is a prominent feature and a source of conflict, since allocation of a scarce resource among users involves trade-offs. For example, economic activities are not the only users of groundwater, while groundwater is also crucial for the regeneration of wetland communities.

The use of the Peel's natural resources as economic goods includes: extraction of groundwater for drinking water; groundwater for irrigation by agriculture; timber in forestry; and soil for growing crops. The use of the Peel's natural resources as services includes: natural areas for recreation and nature conservation; land for disposal of surplus manure; and air, soil and groundwater as deposits of ammonia and nitrate from manure.

9.3. AN INTEGRATED DYNAMIC MODEL

The description of regional system interactions in this area has resulted in a dynamic simulation model programmed in *Stella* (Richmond *et al.*, 1987). The model is exploratory in nature. It takes a long-term viewpoint via long-term scenarios and policies. It includes descriptions of interactions between the economic activities and the relevant environmental processes.

The main structure (i.e., the modular design) of the RSD model for the Peel region is given in Figure 9.1. The sub-modules describe groundwater, nitrates, forestry and natural vegetation, agriculture (manure), and regional economic activities. The submodule which describes the economic activity accounts profits over time for each sector, on the basis of developments of quantities, costs, prices and technology. The time paths for quantities (number of products actually sold, or services actually delivered, measured in relevant units for each respective sector) is for most sectors based on changes in production capacity, except for recreation, where demand for recreational activity determines the quantity. The development of the economic system is to a large extent determined by exogenous variables, for which time paths were chosen in each development scenario. Models that

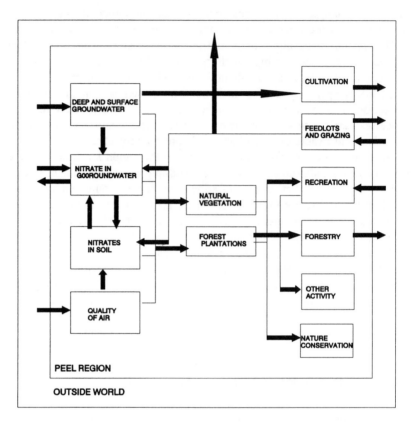

Figure 9.1.   Structure of the economic—ecological model for the Peel region.

include many interactions between sectors (e.g., interindustry supply, or competition on factor and final markets) usually have an economy-wide rather than a regional orientation.

The interrelationships between the modules are listed in Figure 9.1 (see for a more detailed description van den Bergh *et al.*, 1988). A condensed mathematical formulation of the model can be found in the appendix of van den Bergh and Nijkamp (1994a).

9.4.   PERFORMANCE INDICATORS

The indicator variables chosen for the assessment of RSD are listed in Table 9.1. The indicator for nature conservation value is based on areas of vegetation. Recreational attractiveness is based on economic facilities, natural amenities, and disservices (arising from economic activities). In the table, stock variables are chosen to serve as dynamic indicators. This means that they indicate in what direction the dynamic path of the resource base is moving. These stock variables may be replaced by their associated rates of change in the stock variables. But if complete dynamic patterns (i.e., for the whole period under consideration) are shown, the stock variables provide all information about the rates of change in their levels and in addition provide information on actual levels at each point in time as well.

Table 9.1. Regional Sustainable Development Indicators

RSD INDICATORS		Indicator	Measurement units	Graph
physical	1.	Concentration of nitrates in deep groundwater	kg/ML	a
	2.	The total ammonia release from manure	kg	a
	3.	The soil pH	index $(0-12)$	a
	4.	The volume of surface groundwater	ML	a
	5.	The volume of deep groundwater	ML	c
	6.	The air quality	index	c
vegetational	7.	Stock of Alders	m3	b
	8.	Stock of Douglas Pines	m3	b
	9.	Stock of Wet Heathland	m3	b
	10.	Stock of Grass	m3	b
economic	11.	The nature conservation value	index	c
	12.	The total value added	Dutch Guilders	c

9.5. SCENARIO ANALYSIS

For the evaluation of long-run effects we will use policy scenario experiments in combination with simulation modelling. The choice of these scenarios is to a large extent based on current environmental, agricultural and regional policy issues in the Netherlands, following the discussion on sustainable development after the publication of the Brundtland report.

Each scenario that is used for a simulation run has effects that will be evaluated regarding their RSD via the indicators listed in Table 9.1. The last column shows which curves in which graphs represent these indicators. Effects may be compared to standards, and then lead to inferences about acceptation or rejection of the relevance of the scenario used for RSD. The scenarios are determined by choices for both exogenous and management (or control) variables. To limit the number of scenarios some plausible developments consisting of a set of related changes in variables have been identified. The time horizon of the scenarios is 50 years with base year 1980/81, while the time resolution is given in years. The model has been run for a set of 4 different − partly contrasting, partly complementary − scenarios mentioned hereafter. Each scenario description is followed by a concise evaluation of the time paths of indicators.

9.5.1.   Present Development

The assumptions concerning future developments are as follows. The stock of grazing cattle declines from 1980 to 1985 and remains constant during the rest of the simulation period. The stock of feedlot cattle will increase with 10% each period of twenty years. Population will increase with 9,000 per decade. Imported nitrogen and sulphuroxides emissions decline. NOx emissions decrease with 30% and SO2 emissions with 45% after 15 years. The results in Figures 9.2.a−c indicate that, very slowly initially, value added decreases, as the net result of decreasing benefits of grazing cattle, cultivated land and recreational revenues, and increasing benefits from intensive cattle breeding.

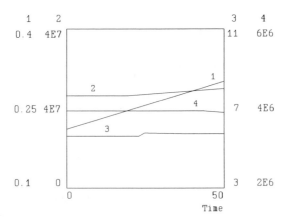

Figure 9.2.a. Present development: Physical indicators.

Agricultural land is less productive as a result of decreasing surface groundwater levels. There is a trend of grassification of heathland. Ammonia and nitrate emissions increase slowly and the concentration of nitrates in deep groundwater stocks is slowly rising.

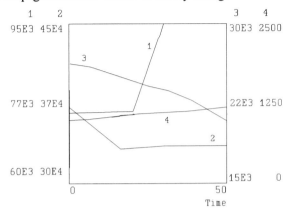

Figure 9.2.b. Present development: Vegetational indicators.

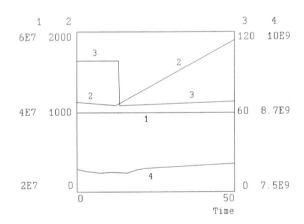

Figure 9.2.c. Present development: Remaining indicators.

Notes
Graphs a: 1=concentration of nitrates in deep groundwater; 2=the total ammonia release from manure; 3=the soil pH; 4=the volume of surface groundwater;
Graphs b: 1=stock of Alders; 2=stock of Douglas Pines; 3=stock of Wet Heathland; 4=stock of Grass.
Graphs c: 1=the volume of deep groundwater; 2=the nature conservation value; 3=the air quality; 4=the total value added.

9.5.2. No Import of SO2 and NOx

This scenario is based on the same assumptions as the first scenario except for import of SO2 and NOx. It is now assumed that their emissions start to decrease after 15 years as a result of foreign policies, and reach a zero level after 50 years. The results in Figures 9.3a−c show that − compared to the first scenario − pH and air quality improve drastically, so that the openness in an ecological sense of this region is very sensitive. The trend of grassification of heathland is reversed. Forest benefits from improvements in Douglas and Alders cause value added for the region as a whole to increase.

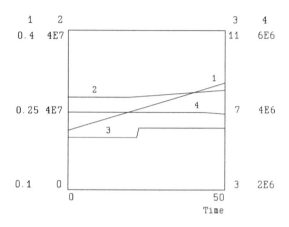

Figure 9.3.a. No import of SO2 and NOx: Physical indicators.

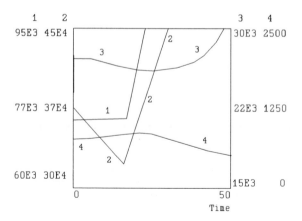

Figure 9.3.b. No import of SO2 and NOx: Vegetational indicators.

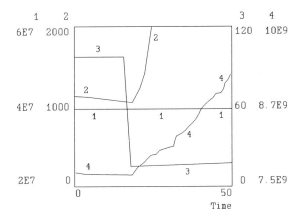

Figure 9.3.c. No import of SO2 and NOx: Remaining indicators.

9.5.3. Environmental policy

Based on the first scenario, the third scenario takes for granted the present government policy to control the utilisation of manure on land, and the intended policy to have all feedlot stables provided with biofiltration equipment after 15 years. The utilisation of manure on land is restricted by 10 % of the total amount of manure generated by the agricultural sector. The downward trend under the first scenario in both Alders and wet heathland is reversed, as can be seen in Figures 9.4a−c.

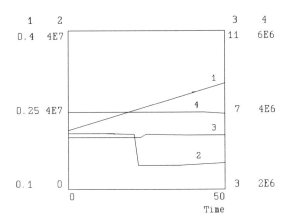

Figure 9.4.a. Environmental policy: Physical indicators.

Costs of environmental policy cause the increase in value added —
compared to the second scenario — to be lower. The total regional value
added does not alter much in size, but in composition it does: costs of
biofiltration are counterbalanced by the increase in recreational demand and
timber production.

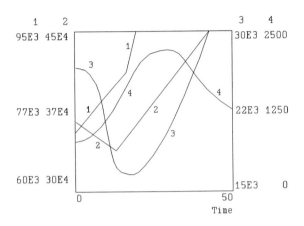

Figure 9.4.b. Environmental policy: Vegetational indicators.

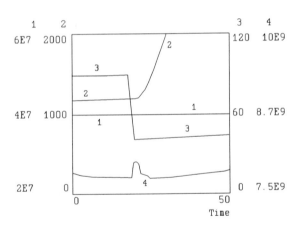

Figure 9.4.c. Environmental policy: Remaining indicators.

9.5.4.   Land use shifts

This is based on the first scenario, but now the area allocated to arable land is reduced with 50% compared to 1980. The area of land allocated to forestry and natural vegetation increases with approximately 125%, with the exception of grassland area, the size of which is constant. The volumes of natural vegetation are significantly higher than under the first scenario (see Figures 9.5a−c). Also due to less crop irrigation the stock of surface groundwater is higher, which has a positive effect on natural vegetation.

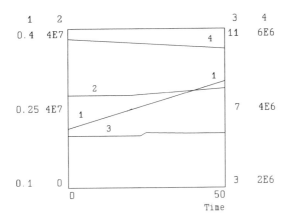

Figure 9.5.a. Land use shifts: Physical indicators.

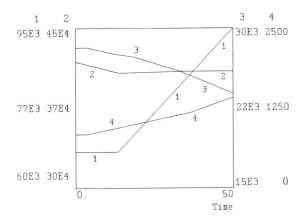

Figure 9.5.b. Land use shifts: Vegetational indicators.

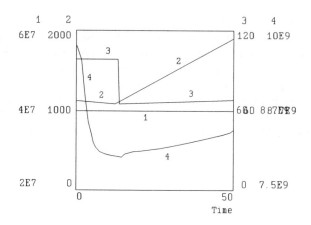

Figure 9.5.c. Land use shifts: Remaining indicators.

We summarise the results as follows:

(a) The region is very sensitive to actions outside its boundaries, namely those causing SO2 and NOx to cross the boundaries; so supraregional agreements will be a prerequisite for a desirable development of this region;

(b) some of the regional activities show opposite effects to changes in the natural environment (agriculture against recreation and forestry), that sometimes may counterbalance one another (in terms of monetary economic benefits); however, the reactions of these activities may have different dynamic characteristics (slow − fast), so that the economic outcomes may vary significantly over longer periods of time.

The above model is clearly only a pilot model for RSD analysis, and further research is required to improve the empirical robustness of the model. Some equations require more reliable data to enable a realistic specification (e.g., recreational amenity, output from crops as a function of fertiliser and groundwater use). The model might also be validated by means of a historical run as a 'backcasting' exercise. Other scenarios may be studied as well with extended versions of the model, such as changes in land use. Therefore, it is clear that the above results are for the time being mainly illustrative for RSD planning. Nevertheless, they have clearly demonstrated the validity of RSD modelling for policy analysis.

9.6. CONCLUSIONS

This chapter has focused attention on sustainable development in a regional context. Conceptualising and analysing sustainable development is clearly not only important at a global level, but certainly also for a regional level of analysis and policy-making. Various advantages of a regional approach have been spelt out, in relation to regional causes and effects of environmental problems, the global character of economic processes, interregional interactions and the possibility of operationalising SD on a regional scale. The use of models for studying sustainable development in a regional context was motivated while specific characteristics of such models were mentioned. Finally, a case study was presented in which some of the general discussions were illustrated, indicators for RSD were specified, and a descriptive systems model was developed. A set of scenarios was studied in which policies or developments were included that impact upon the region's economic−ecological interactions. The conclusions from these experiences are straightforward: modelling RSD in an operational way may substantially contribute to a better understanding of underlying conflicts in a regional development policy analysis.

10. Multicriteria Evaluation for Sustainable Use of Australian Forests[1]

10.1. INTRODUCTION

Australia has at present 43 million hectares of forested land, covering 5% of the total land area. This equals 65% of the area of forested land that existed at the time of European settlement. Another 92 million hectares of woodland cover a further 14% of the country (see Figure 10.1). Regrowth from past logging covers about 60% of the forest area. The remaining 40% is either not logged or has been lightly logged. About 6 million hectares of this relatively undisturbed area is in designated nature reserves.

Recent years have shown economic–environmental conflicts related to the use of Australia's forest and timber resources, and especially that of native forests. Most conservation groups, as well as large sections of the community, oppose the logging of native forests, arguing that values related to various ecological functions are insufficiently taken into account by logging activities and objectives. The forest management agencies generally maintain that logging is compatible with conservation and ecological goals, provided adequate areas of forest are placed in conservation reserves and appropriate measures are taken with regard to production forests to mitigate the negative ecological effects of logging. Against this background the Australian government requested an inquiry to identify and evaluate options for the use of Australia's forest and timber resources (RAC 1992). This chapter presents results of a multicriteria analysis conducted to support this inquiry.

[1] This chapter is written by Ron Janssen. The chapter is based on a multicriteria analysis conducted for the Forest and Timber Inquiry of Australia. The author wishes to thank David James and Charles Zammit of the Forest and Timber Inquiry for their contribution to the multicriteria analysis.

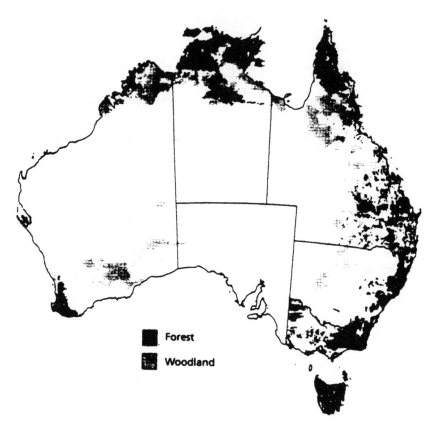

Figure 10.1. Forest and woodland in Australia, 1990.

Forest

Woodland

Source: RAC (1992).

The Inquiry specified six alternatives and used a computer model[2] to predict the effects of these alternatives.

(i) *Alternative CT*

The 'current trends' alternative which adopts existing assumptions for future forest and timber resource use as described by the forest

---

[2] The model used is the INFORM model, which was specially developed for the Inquiry. A full description can be found in RAC (1992), Appendix S. Input to the model are data on the current status of Australian forests and scenario variables linked to policy and management options. Output of the model are economic, social and environmental effects in ten year intervals for the years 1990-2090.

management agencies. It provides the baseline for comparison of the other alternatives.

(ii) *Alternative HII*

The 'high industry investment' alternative. This alternative allows for the establishment of a significant, intensively managed hardwood and softwood plantation resource, and for intensive management of suitable native forest types. Investment in pulp and paper processing facilities is greater than that projected for the 'current trends' alternative.

(iii) *Alternative MII*

The 'moderate industry investment' alternative. This alternative does not allow for intensive management practices in native forest, and pulp and paper processing facilities lie between those proposed for the 'current trends' alternative and those proposed for alternative HII.

(iv) *Alternative NLM*

This alternative specifies immediate withdrawal of logging in mature and old-growth forest but continued logging in regrowth forests. Hardwood plantations are expanded, the export of hardwood woodchips ceases, and pulp and paper mills are of small to medium scale.

(v) *Alternative NL10*

This alternative specifies immediate withdrawal of logging in mature and old-growth forest and a phase-out of logging in regrowth forests by the year 2000. Other specifications are the same as those for alternative NLM.

(vi) *Alternative NL30*

This alternative specifies immediate withdrawal of logging in mature and old-growth forest and a phase-out of logging in regrowth forests by the year 2020.

The Inquiry chose to apply multi-criteria analysis to the alternatives for two reasons:

• To improve understanding of the relative qualities of the alternatives;
• to evaluate the technique's usefulness for comparing and evaluating alternative uses of natural resources.

The *Definite* program (Janssen and van Herwijnen, 1994) was used to apply multicriteria methods for evaluating alternative uses of Australia's forests. This software package has been successfully used in providing advice to the Netherlands government on a number of resource use and environmental issues. It includes a variety of evaluation methods to support a comparison of alternative scenarios for a given problem: multicriteria methods, cost-benefit analysis and graphical techniques. It also includes methods to structure an evaluation problem and to generate scenarios. Finally, it includes a wide range of methods for sensitivity analysis.

In this application of multicriteria analysis reference years (2000 and 2030) are used to compare the expected state of the forest resource and the associated industry in future years. This approach is in accord with the concept of sustainable development which aims to maintain both economic and environmental quality in the long run. Multicriteria analysis, however, contrasts with most applications of cost-benefit analysis in that, in the latter case, expected benefits and costs resulting from an alternative in all future years are discounted to their net present value.

The application includes four steps:

(i) *Problem definition*

Effects tables are created for the years 2000 and 2030. In these tables six alternatives are evaluated against three economic and three environmental criteria.

(ii) *Problem presentation*

Graphical techniques are used to present the effects table in such a form that alternatives can be compared without applying any formal decision rule.

(iii) *Problem evaluation*

This step involves aggregating the criterion scores from the effects table into two categories: an index of economic quality and an index of environmental quality. This presentation makes explicit the trade-off between economic and environmental qualities.

(iv) *Sensitivity analysis*

This step involves applying sensitivity analysis to determine the effect of changing weights and scores on the evaluation results.

10.2.   PROBLEM DEFINITION

Problem definition is the first and possibly the most important step in multicriteria analysis. It involves identification of the feasible alternatives, identification of the evaluation criteria, and assessment of criterion scores. Alternatives, criteria and criterion scores are included in the effects table.

Three criteria were selected to reflect economic aspects of alternatives:

(1) *Value added* – this criterion is defined as the sum of wages and profits in the forest and forest products industry. It is measured in millions of

dollars and reflects the contribution of the forest and forest products industry to gross domestic product.

(2) *Direct employment* — defined as the number of persons directly employed in the forest and forest products industry and reflects the job creation prospects in the economy.

(3) *Balance of trade* — this criterion is defined as forest product exports minus forest product imports. It is measured in millions of dollars.

The following three criteria represent environmental aspects of the alternatives:

(4) *Old-growth forest unused* — this criterion is expressed in hectares land covered by such forests.

(5) *Unavailable for logging* — this criterion is expressed in hectares and reflects the sum of the areas of each forest group that have been allocated to conservation reserves and the area of each forest group that is unavailable for logging in production forest tenures.

(6) *Soil and water quality* — this criterion is expressed as a qualitative index (plus or minus) and reflects an assessment of the predicted impact of human disturbance on soil and water quality under each of the six alternatives. It is derived subjectively, namely by expert judgement.

Projections were made for a large number of response variables or indicators, such as log yield, intermediate and final products, and production areas, for each decade from 1990 to 2090. For the purpose of the multicriteria analysis the year 2000 is selected to represent the expected short-term qualities of the alternatives, and the year 2030 is chosen to represent the medium term. The lack of reliability of projections of consumption trends does not permit analysis of the long-term qualities of the available alternatives. In this example only the results for the year 2030 are presented.

Table 10.1 illustrates two points. First, multicriteria analysis permits the use of criteria having different units of measurement. In this analysis units range from measured variables such as dollar values, employment statistics and forest areas to qualitative indices that are expressed as plus or minus signs. Second, the absolute differences for many of the criteria are small across the alternatives and for some criteria do not vary between subsets of alternatives. This is a consequence of the alternative specifications. It is clear that the criterion values represented here will also be influenced to some extent by other sectors of the Australian economy and by the activities of other countries.

Table 10.1.   Effects Table Medium Term, Year 2030.

Effects in 2030	CT	HII	MII	NLM	NL10	NL30
1. Value Added, mln AUS $/yr	4819	5688	5524	4733	4473	4490
2. Direct Employment, in 100 persons	382	448	442	377	366	367
3. Balance of Trade, mln AUS $/yr	-1427	-208	-528	-1524	-1700	-1655
4. Old Growth Unused, in 1000 hectare	2728	2728	2728	3062	3062	3062
5. Unavailable for logging, in 1000 hectare	23471	23471	23471	23893	34443	34443
6. Soil and water quality, − −/++	+	− −	+	+	++	++

10.3.   PROBLEM PRESENTATION

Problem presentation involves the use of graphical techniques to display the effects table in such a form that alternatives can be compared without applying any formal decision rule. In Figure 10.2 the effects table is presented as a series of histograms. To produce Figure 10.2 the scores for each effect are standardised between zero and one. The standardisation procedure transforms the worst value of a criterion to zero and the best value to one. Intermediate scores are transformed proportionally to their differences with the worst and best value. For each effect, the highest bar in Figure 10.2 indicates the most preferred alternative and an empty box shows the least preferred alternative.

The figure shows that the different economic criteria follow similar patterns: an alternative with a high score for value added also shows a high score for direct employment and balance of trade. Alternatives NL10 and NL30 have the same scores for the environmental criteria.

The alternatives can be ranked by placing the criterion rows in descending priority followed by an exchange of the alternatives in such a way that the shaded area in the upper-left hand corner of the graph is maximised. This is presented for the year 2030 in Figure 10.3. First the rows with environmental criteria are moved to the top. Second the alternatives NL10, NL30 and NLM are moved to the left.

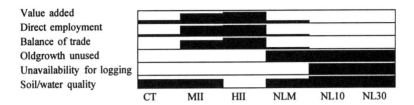

Figure 10.2. Graphic presentation of the effects table, as a series of histograms; to produce this figure the scores for each effect are standardised between zero and one.

Figure 10.3 shows the clear trade-off between economic and environmental criteria for the alternatives examined: a high economic quality is paid for by a low environmental quality and vice versa. Figure 10.3 also shows that changing the order of the criteria within either the environmental quality group or the economic quality group will have little influence on the ranking: exchanging, for example, the value added and balance of trade criteria will not alter the ranking of the alternatives.

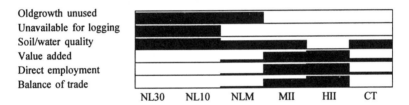

Figure 10.3. Graphical ranking of the effects table, priority given to environmental criteria.

10.4. PROBLEM EVALUATION

Problem evaluation is the third step in this multicriteria analysis. In this section the three economic criteria − value added, direct employment, and balance of trade − are combined into a single index of economic quality. In the same way the three environmental criteria − old-growth forest unused, area unavailable for logging, and soil and water quality − are combined into a single index of environmental quality. With these indices, the trade-off between environmental and economic aspects of the alternatives can be examined.

The criterion scores are transformed into an economic quality index and an environmental quality index in two steps. First, all scores are standardised between zero and 100. Next, the indices are calculated as the weighted sums of these standardised scores. The weights represent the relative importance of the criteria within the index. This is a crucial part of multicriteria analysis because the weightings assigned to criteria can have a significant impact on the final alternative rankings. For this reason it is usually desirable to obtain assessments of the weights assigned to criteria using either expert opinion, or community interest group opinion.

Figures 10.2 and 10.3 in the previous section show high correlation between the three economic criteria and also high correlation between the three environmental criteria. This implies that the ranking will not be sensitive to changes within these two groups. Therefore within these two groups equal weights were given to the criteria. After standardisation the economic and environmental quality indices are as shown in Figure 10.4. To combine scores measured in different measurement units or measurement scales, these scores need to be standardised before they can be aggregated. Figure 10.4 shows again the sharp trade-off between economic and environmental quality.

Figure 10.4. Indices of economic and environmental quality: short term, year 2000

Next a diagram is used to further explore the trade-off between economic and environmental quality. Figure 10.5 shows the economic and environmental quality of the alternatives in the year 2030, as calculated in the appraisal table. The horizontal axis represents the economic quality; the vertical axis represents the environmental quality. The ideal option would combine maximum economic quality with maximum environmental quality. This ideal option would have scored 100 for both economic and environmental quality and would therefore be found in the top right-hand corner of the diagram. The alternatives are ranked on the base of the distance from the ideal option. This multicriteria method is known as the 'Ideal Point' method (see Sections 5.2.2 and 5.2.3).

Various measures are available to determine the distance of the alternatives from the ideal point. In this application, the distance is measured as the sum of the distances along the horizontal and vertical axes. The diagonal in Figure 10.5 intersects the economic and environmental quality axes at equal distance from the ideal point. The slope of the line indicates that equal weight is given to economic and environmental quality.

Since all points on the line share the same distance from the ideal point they all have the same position in the ranking.

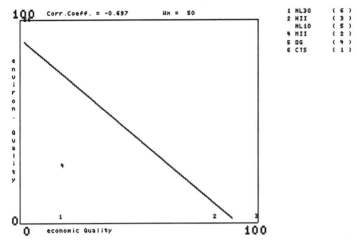

Figure 10.5. Graphical ranking of the alternatives, equal weight.

The alternatives can now be ranked visually by moving the line from top right to bottom left. The first alternative to cross the line, and therefore the most preferred alternative, is alternative NL30, immediately followed by alternatives MII and HII.

The ranking of the alternatives is shown at the right hand side of the diagram. Alternative MII is the most preferred alternative, closely followed by alternative NL30. Alternatives HII and NL10 share the third position. Figure 10.5 shows that the differences in distance to the ideal point between these four alternatives are minimal.

The correlation coefficient listed at the top of the diagram indicates the extent to which it is necessary to trade off economic and environmental quality. A value close to one indicates a minimal need to trade off both qualities because alternatives with high economic quality also have high environmental quality. A value close to minus one shows an extreme need to trade off the qualities: alternatives with a high economic quality have a low environmental quality and vice versa. The correlation coefficient value of -0.817 indicates a substantial level of trade-off between economic and environmental quality. The ranking of the alternatives will therefore be highly sensitive to changes in the priorities (weights) assigned to these.

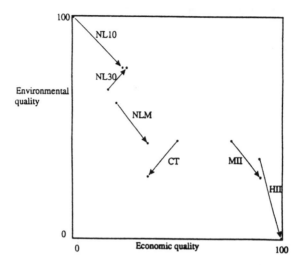

Figure 10.6. Changes in economic and environmental
quality: years 2000 and 2030.

Although it is obviously not possible to trade off an alternative in the
year 2000 against an alternative in the year 2030, it is interesting to analyse
changes in the relative positions of the six alternatives over the years.
Figure 10.6 shows all alternatives for both the short and medium term. The
arrows connect the years 2000 and 2030 for each alternative. All
alternatives are scaled relative to each other and to the minimum and
maximum values within the scores of both years. Alternative NL10 in the
year 2000 sets both the maximum value on environmental quality and the
minimum value on economic quality. Alternative HII in the year 2030 sets
the maximum for economic and the minimum for environmental quality.
Note that because of the change in scale Figure 10.6 can not be compared
with Figure 10.5. Also because this figure combines results from two
periods only relative changes can be observed. Figure 10.6 shows that the
Current trends alternative moves away from the ideal point, showing a loss
in both environmental and economic quality. Both industry alternatives (MII
and HII) and alternatives NLM and NL10 show a relative reduction in
environmental quality and an improvement in economic quality. Alternative
NL30 is the only alternative that shows an improvement in both economic
and environmental quality.

10.5. SENSITIVITY ANALYSIS

For each set of weights problem evaluation results in a ranking of the alternatives. Figure 10.5 showed, for example, that if economic and environmental quality are given equal priority MII is the most preferred alternative and CT the least preferred alternative. If the criterion scores and the criterion weights were completely certain, this conclusion would also be completely certain and sensitivity analysis would not be necessary. Since projections always have a margin of error, and since weights usually represent a range rather than a precise value, the rankings are not completely certain.

The sensitivity of alternatives to overall uncertainty in criterion scores can be analysed using a Monte Carlo approach (Janssen, 1992). An estimate must be provided of the extent (as a percentage) to which actual values may differ from values included in the effects table. A random generator is used to translate this information into a large number of effects tables around the original effects table. Rankings are then determined for all these effects tables. Variations in these rankings are used to determine the sensitivity of the original ranking to uncertainties in effect scores. In this application the scores were varied between plus and minus 25 percent of the scores presented in the effects table.

Table 10.2 shows which part of the rankings (indicated by >) remains valid when the estimated chance of the criterion scores changing by plus or minus 25%. The '?' between two alternatives indicates that the rank order of two alternatives is not certain enough.

Table 10.2. Results of Effects Uncertainty (+/− 25%).

Year 2000						
Equal priority	MII	? HII	? NL10	> NL30	> NLM	? CT
Economic quality	HII	? MII	> CT	> NLM	? NL30	> NL10
Environmental quality	NL10	> NL30	> NLM	> MII	> CT	? HII

Year 2030						
Equal priority	MII	? NL30	? HII	? NL10	> NLM?	> CT
Economic quality	HII	? MII	> NL30	? NLM	? NL10	> CT
Environmental quality	NL30	? NL10	> NLM	> MII	> HII	? CT

10.6.   CONCLUSIONS

Multicriteria analysis can be used to select the best option from a set of alternatives, to rank all alternatives from the most preferred to the least preferred, and to improve understanding of the characteristics of an evaluation problem. In the Inquiry's application, the last function proved to be of greater importance than the first two functions. Determining the most preferred alternative, or the ranking between alternatives in this analysis depended critically on how economic or environmental quality was weighted.

The multicriteria analysis increased the understanding of the usefulness of performance criteria for a comparison of the alternatives. But most of all it improved the insight into the characteristics of the total set of available alternatives in the short and medium term.

11. Integrated Dynamic and Spatial Modelling and Multicriteria Evaluation for a Greek Island Region[1]

11.1. INTRODUCTION

This chapter presents the results of integrated modelling and multicriteria evaluation, performed to study regional sustainable development of an island region, the Sporades, in Greece. A potential conflict exists here between environmental conservation, local interests and rapid growth in tourism. A dynamic model is used to depict the development of the economies of three main islands and their interactions with the terrestrial and marine environment. The presentation of the case study model is followed by a discussion of scenarios, indicators, simulation results, multicriteria evaluation and spatial evaluation.

11.2. REGION AND PROBLEM DESCRIPTION

The Northern Sporades are a complex of islands located in the Aegean Sea close to central Greece (see Figure 11.1). They constitute an area where socio-economic objectives conflict with environmental conservation objectives. This area embraces the inhabited islands Skiathos, Skopelos and Allonisos, and some uninhabited islands. For the purpose of the present study a nearby, low-developed area on the mainland, Pillion, has been included in the analysis as well, because of spill-over effects that may result from quick economic development induced by tourism on the islands. The

[1] This chapter is jointly authored by Jeroen van den Bergh, Ron Janssen, Marjan van Herwijnen and Peter Nijkamp. Support by Vassilios Despotakis, Maria Frantzi and Maria Giaoutzi is greatly acknowledged. For more details, see Giaoutzi and Nijkamp (1993).

population levels in 1985 of Skiathos, Skopelos, Allonisos and Pillion are 5064, 4226, 1621 and 600, respectively. Table 11.1 shows land cover data for the three main islands.

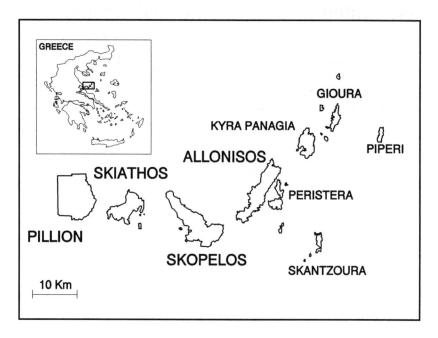

Figure 11.1. The Sporades Region in Greece.

There exists a rich vegetation on the islands, including Pine forests and different types of Mediterranean scrubland (indicated by the French names Maquis and Garrigne). Both flora and fauna include many interesting, and some unique, species. There is a natural process of exchange between different types of vegetation like forest and scrubland. Maquis is naturally transformed into forest vegetation. Occasionally, the rate at which the process in the other direction occurs – from forest vegetation to Maquis, and from Maquis to Garrigne – is increased by fires. These are more likely when many tourists are staying in the natural areas. Bare land constitutes an important part of the natural area, because of natural conditions such as high elevation levels and/or dry or rocky soils. The land use patterns of agriculture (grazing of goats and cultivation for crop and fruit production), urban areas and road development dominate the changes in available land for natural vegetation. Expansion of agricultural land has mainly transformed areas with low-growing scrubs or bare land. Urban land is expanding around the villages, usually into former cultivated or agricultural

Table 11.1. Land Cover Data for the Three Main
Islands (1985)

x ha	Skiathos	Skopelos	Allonisos
natural vegetation	1740	4580	72060
pasture	1580	2630	5660
cultivation	1408	2048	1920
urban-infrastructure	340	390	2250
total area	5068	9648	81890

Source: Frantzi and Despotakis (1991).

Notes: Beaches not included.

area. Degradation of the natural vegetation as a result of agricultural and urban expansion, tourism and natural processes induces soil erosion by wind and water. This makes natural recovery of transformed areas rather unlikely. Disturbance of quiet by tourists is another element that may harm especially the fauna.

The marine environment is rich in species, such as corals, different types of fish, dolphins and the Mediterranean Monk Seal (Monachus monachus). This latter species is very valuable from a conservation point of view: it is unique, rare and highly valued by tourists (laymen) and biologists (experts)[2]. In addition, the Monk Seal is a critical part of the marine ecosystem, in which it is situated at the top of the foodchain. The existence of this species is however threatened by sea water pollution, fishing and tourism in the area. The number of seals has gone down and stabilised in recent years to a present level of approximately 40. Below, the attention is focused on three types of fish and a lobster species, located at one and the same level in the foodchain. The threefold classification of fish is related to their economic value: the first class includes fish like red mullet; the second class includes sword fish and melanuria; and the third class includes gopes and tuna. They are distinguished for economic reasons. The first type

---

[2] The Monk Seal was once found along all shores of the Mediterranean Sea (and a few other places around the world). The World Wide Fund for Nature (WWF) ranks it among the ten most endangered species in the world, with only 400 to 600 individual animals presently surviving. The greatest number is found along Greek and Turkish coasts, and among the Aegean Islands. They are the largest of seals, weigh about 250 kg, measure 2.5 to 3 metres in length, and have an average life span of 10 years. They prefer coastal areas. The main threats to their existence are habitat destruction, marine pollution, competition with fishery for food, and hunting (see, e.g., The World Bank/The European Investment Bank, 1990).

of fish and lobster are the most expensive. Catch of fish types two and three is however much higher, and in effect all of them may be regarded as equally important for realising economic objectives in the fishery sector.

A marine park was established in September 1986 to protect the marine system.[3] The implications are that visits of tourists are limited to certain parts of the marine area. In addition, fishing is being controlled by rules, fishing zones, fishing periods and type of nets. Besides tourism and fishing, a third type of negative impact of human activity on the marine system is occurring, namely through flows of pollution and waste generated by the island population, tourists and economic activities. The model will concentrate on nitrogen and phosphorus derived from tourist and population numbers, and certain economic activities. Additional derived indicators for the consequences on living conditions and organic materials in the marine environment are BOD (Biological Oxygen Demand) and chlorophyll.

The natural environment provides several services and goods to the socio-economic system. Both the terrestrial and marine ecosystems, in particular the existence of seals and dolphins, add to the attractiveness of the areas for tourists. Besides these ecological characteristics, the area provides many nice beaches and watersports facilities. The terrestrial system supplies firewood and resin (for Greek wine), while goats, providing meat and milk (used for making cheese), are herded on the scrub and rock land. And, as mentioned already, the marine system provides fish for fisheries catch.

The past directions of development of the three main islands Skiathos, Skopelos and Allonisos has been greatly influenced by the pattern of tourism. However, the development stages of the three islands differ significantly. Skiathos has a long history as a holiday resort for Greek citizens, mainly those coming from the two largest Greek cities Athens and Thessaloniki. Though originally characterised by a reputation for richness and exclusiveness, it is currently functioning as an attractor for various categories of Greek and foreign tourists. On Skopelos tourism has developed somewhat later, and it is known to be more peaceful. It may be considered at a stage in between those characterising Skiathos and Allonisos. This latter island is especially quiet, due to a relatively large natural area and a late development of commercial tourism activities in only recent years (since 1980). In the model special attention is devoted to the consequences of tourism for Allonisos. This means more detailed attention for its economic activities and endogenous development mechanisms in tourism activities and concern for their interactions with the terrestrial

---

[3] This was part of recovery plans in line with a resolution on the protection of the Monk seal which passed the European Parliament in 1984.

system. Table 11.2 gives relevant tourism data for the three islands. From these data and the respective population levels and land areas we can derive indicators of tourism pressure. Skiathos has then the highest density of tourist-nights per capita (± 23.7) as well as per square metres land (± 2.4). Allonisos comes second with regard to the first of these two pressure indicators (± 12.3), but last in terms of the other (± 0.24) (for Skopelos these indicators have values of 9.5 and 0.42, respectively). More details on the economic structure will be given in the presentation of the model.

*Table 11.2.   Estimated Tourist Data for the
Three Main Islands (1985)*

Indicator	Skiathos	Skopelos	Allonisos
Accommodation (number of beds)	1921	1006	535
Tourists-nights	120,000	40,000	20,000
Employment (people)	325	117	65
Relative price level of services in tourism	131	115	100

Source: Data from questionnaires, and Frantzi and Despotakis (1991).

Notes: Employment in man years; price level of tourism
related to Allonisos.

The island economies are rather small-sized. The following economic sectors can be distinguished: local services, fishery, agriculture, public sector, construction and two tourism based sectors (accommodation and services). Trade and transport are arranged by mainland firms, leaving no special benefits for the local population otherwise than via the local services. This sectoral disaggregation is based on a combination of considerations: labour market operation, interdependencies between activities, and economic – environmental relationships.

In Table 11.3 we list estimated figures of value added per sector and island. Especially the labour market is crucial for the operation of the economy, since it provides the opportunities and constraints for specific sectoral developments. The labour market shows competition for labour within certain categories of activities, e.g. agriculture and fishery. These two latter activities are determined to a large extent by labour remaining after other types of jobs have been fulfilled. A strong pull force is generated by especially the tourism activities. More information will be given in our discussion of specific modules in the next section.

Table 11.3. Estimated Sectoral Value Added
Figures per Island (1985)

x million Greek Drachme	Skiathos	Skopelos	Allonisos
Accommodation	392	115	62.5
Tourism services	3760	987	400
Construction	84	42	131.5
local services	287	240	92
agriculture	3.1	3.6	57
fishery	8.8	10.5	83
Total	4534.9	1397.1	1026

Source: Frantzi and Despotakis (1991).

The Northern Sporades provide an interesting case for testing integrated economic−ecological modelling on a regional scale, and for performing scenario analysis of tourism and economic development. The possible conflict between an (one-sided) economic development focused on tourism can give rise to undesirable long term outcomes both in terms of natural and economic consequences, especially in view of the nature conservation directed at both land and marine ecosystems.

11.3.   MODEL STRUCTURE

Here we will explain the structure of the model that was designed to obtain insight into the long term development of tourism, the island economies and the natural environment. The model is descriptive, formulated as a set of differential and auxiliary equations, and used for dynamic simulation based on well-chosen development and/or policy scenarios. The dynamic structure is based on (dynamic) stock-flow relationships. The stock variables are described in balance equations: they are increased by ingoing flows and decreased by outgoing flows. All but the stock variables are either exogenous or based on other stock and flow variables. This means that the model is to some extent set up according to causal mechanisms. Especially from the dynamic and development point of view this is attractive. For the present model the base year is 1985, the time horizon is 20 years, and the time resolution is years. The dynamic simulation package *Stella* (Richmond *et al.*, 1987) was used to solve the model over time as a set of differential equations. For further details the reader is referred to van den Bergh (1991) and van den Bergh and Nijkamp (1994d). The model's endogenous variables will be discussed hereafter. The exogenous variables are given in the Appendix of van den Bergh (1991, Chapter 9). The variables linking islands among each other, as well as those linking the region with the outside world, will also be discussed below. A less detailed and generalised theoretical analogue of the present environmental – economic development model is contained in van den Bergh and Nijkamp (1991b).

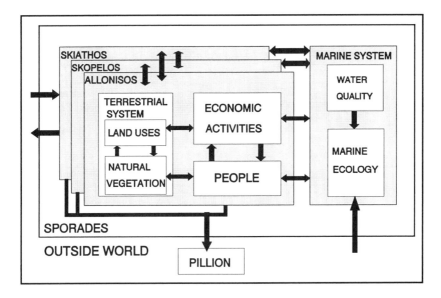

Figure 11.2. Structure of the economic-environmental model.

In Figure 11.2 the overall structure of the model is shown, which is designed according to interactive modular components. On this highest modular level descriptions are given of the three main island economies, the socio-economic relationships with the outside world, the influence on the nearby area Pillion, and the impact of the mainland on the Marine system. The three main islands in the region are separately treated for three reasons. First, their development levels differ. Second, only the Allonisos module includes a terrestrial submodule with a description of land use and natural vegetation cover. And finally, Allonisos receives special attention in the study from the policy perspective. The economy and people modules are set up for each of the islands.

In the 'economic activities' module the economic sectoral classification is adapted to sector – environment interactions. The sectoral structure,

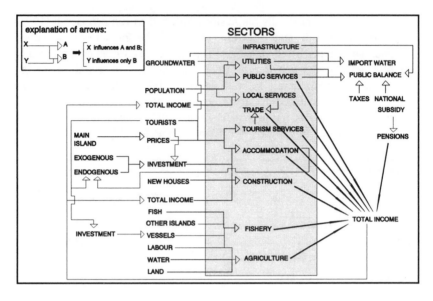

Figure 11.3. Sectoral structure of the economic module.

income composition, and important determinants of sectoral development and production are set up in a similar way for each island, although in somewhat more detail for Allonisos (as shown in Figure 11.3). The following sectors are distinguished: an accommodation sector including hotels, bungalows and pensions; a tourist service sector including restaurants, bars, rental services and souvenir shops; a private service sector; a construction sector for investments in private and public activities; two resource-based sectors – agriculture and fisheries; public services such as education, health care, administration, and police; and utilities – focused on water pumping – and infrastructure.

The operation of the labour market is an important driver to the economic system. Figure 11.4 shows how the labour market is modelled. Labour use in 6 sectors, shown in the block 'activities', is assumed to be purely determined by employment in the respective sectors. The variable 'remaining labour' is determined as a difference between labour supply and the labour used in the 6 activities. This remainder is allocated to agriculture and fishery, based on an agricultural incentive policy and an exogenous competitive element for fishery by a mainland fishery. Labour supply is determined by population size (indirectly including effects of migration and seasonal commuting) and exogenous trends in participation rates as well as a combination of productivity and working hours.

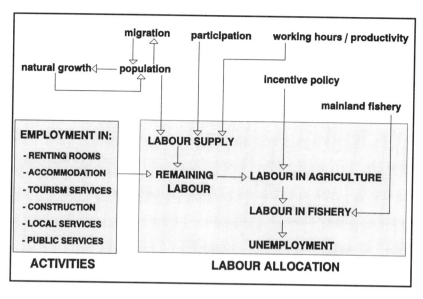

Figure 11.4. Sub-module of labour market in economic module.

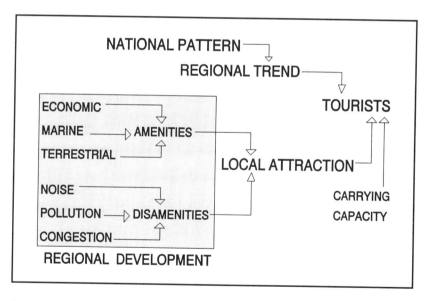

Figure 11.5. Sub-module for development of tourist demand.

The main driving force behind economic development is tourism. The development module of tourism in the region is based on the scheme in

Figure 11.5. The number of tourists is determined by a regional trend, which is to some extent, following a national pattern and a local attraction mechanism, based on economic and environmental amenities and several disamenities. In this way feedback is realised from economic and environmental conditions to touristic growth. This may have a curbing effect on initially high growth in the number of tourists.

One of the structural, long term economic−environmental interactions is taking place by way of land transformation. This is represented in a terrestrial module which describes land use and natural vegetation cover. This was explained in the previous section. Land use and vegetational cover is based on expansion of cultivation, grazing by cattle (encouraging, e.g., the transformation of Maquis in low Maquis), and urban growth.

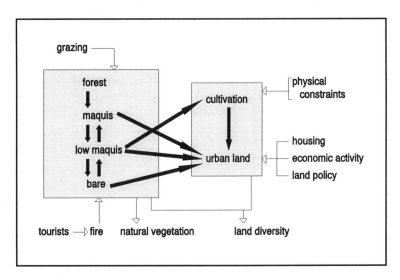

Figure 11.6. Sub-module land-use and vegetational cover.

Note: Fat arrows denote transformation of land from one category to another; thin
            arrows indicate influences.

Figure 11.6 shows which processes and exogenous factors affect the composition of natural area (4 categories) and the two main land uses. A physical constraint based on data about altitudes and ground structure sets limits to changes in land uses. A land diversity index is generated to serve as an input to the tourism module.

A second important economic−environmental interaction occurs through the fisheries (Figure 11.7). Vessels from three islands and the mainland generate a certain amount of fishing effort, which is one determinant of total fish catch. There are two other determinants. One is the sum of the sizes of the four stocks of fish and lobster species being subjected to fishing. The other is the constraint on catch to realise sustainable fishing patterns, operationalised by restrictions on fishing nets, periods, and zones.

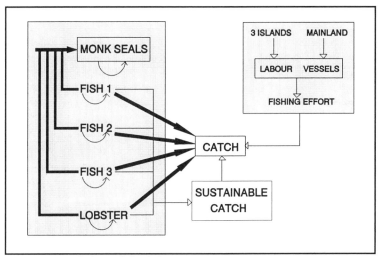

Figure 11.7. Sub-module fisheries

Note: fat arrows denote flows of fish in the ecological system or to the economy.

11.4. SCENARIO ANALYSIS

11.4.1. Scenarios and Control Variables

Two possibly conflicting objectives which have to be resolved for the Sporades region are regional economic development dominated by tourism, and environmental protection of the terrestrial and marine ecosystems, especially conservation of the Monk Seal colony. A constraint to the first objective could be the economy's high dependency on one sector, namely tourism. Therefore, anything with an adverse impact on tourism provides a threat to future income. Economic and human activities cause a range of environmental impacts: water pollution, loss of landscape values, loss of traditional values (culture), transformation of old village, congestion (litter, noise, recreational values), and overfishing. These effects could adversely impact future tourism and threaten economic development. They are also directly contradictory to the second objective. A constraint to the second objective is partly overlapping with that to the first one: growth of certain activities and the size of human impacts may not be sustainable from a nature conservation point of view.

Scenarios are designed by focusing on policies and exogenous patterns or events. Several types of policy actions can be taken: environmental, conservation, economic, infrastructural, and social programs and even changes in institutional arrangements. Three types of exogenous patterns or events can be distinguished, namely internal socio-economic, external economic, and natural events. The future development of the Sporades islands may range from an extrapolation of present trends to strong sectoral deviations of these trends due to environmental or economic opportunities, constraints and policies. The following eight − feasible though not all desirable − scenarios are used to deal with the most obvious and important policy and development options for the Sporades islands:

1. *Steady growth:* a steady growth development path, based on extrapolation of present trends without any specific policy constraints on land or marine use. Tourist numbers continue to rise and tourists are allowed to visit the marine park area in the Sporades. This alternative may act as a zero or reference alternative.

2. *Steady growth and marine park policy:* a steady growth development path like alternative 1, but now with a strict control on the tourist flows to the marine park. The fishing activity is held at a safe (sustainable) level, the waste management and sewage treatment activities are maximised, and tourism in the marine park area is restricted.

3. *Strong growth:* a steady growth development path with a controlled tourist flow to the marine park like in alternative 2, but with a higher potential growth rate of tourism.

4. *Limiting tourism growth:* a steady growth development path with a controlled tourism to the marine park (as alternative 2), and in addition with a strict limit on the growth of tourism on the islands.

5. *Sustainable fishing:* a steady growth development path with a controlled tourism flow to the marine park like in alternative 2. The fishing in this alternative is limited to such levels that the stocks of fish are not reduced.

6. *Tourist limits and sustainable fishing:* a combination of alternatives 4 and 5.

7. *Agricultural incentive:* a steady growth development path with controlled tourism flows to the marine park like in alternative 2. Employment in agriculture, especially cultivation of land, is strongly stimulated.

8. *Very strong growth:* as alternative 2, but with tourist numbers growing at a very high rate.

Table 11.4 shows the control variables in the model and their values in each scenario. The numbers in the table correspond to those of the scenarios.

Table 11.4. Values of Control Variables for the Various Scenarios

	investment in accommodation	investment in local fishery	tourist control in marine park area	catch fishing	change in number of tourists	agricultural employment policy
1.	growth tourism ≤5%	growth tourism ≥2%	1	effort and stock	national and local	none
2.	growth tourism ≤5%	growth tourism ≥2%	0	effort and stock	national and local	none
3.	growth tourism ≤5%	growth tourism ≥2%	1	effort and stock	3% + national and local	none
4.	0	2%	0	effort and stock	0	none
5.	growth tourism ≤5%	growth tourism ≥2%	1	≤ regeneration rate	national and local	none
6.	0	2%	0	≤ regeneration rate	0	none
7.	growth tourism ≤5%	growth tourism ≥2%	1	effort and stock	national and local	supply increase 45 – 145 over 20 years
8.	growth tourism ≤10%	growth tourism ≥2%	1	effort and stock	6% + national and local	none

Note: Scenarios are listed vertically and control variables horizontally.

Performance indicators generated by the 'economic activities' module will be used to test for economic efficiency, equity, and conservation. Value added and unemployment can be used to test for efficiency, on a sectoral, island or regional level. The testing for equity may pertain to equity between sectors or islands.

As indicators related to regional development of tourism may serve the number of tourist-nights spent ('people' module), the land use of accommodation industry ('economic activities' module), the percentage of drinking water that is imported ('economic activities' module). This import of water depends on the extraction in the region, and the demand based on tourists and local people. The natural and economic aspects related to tourism are summarised in indices for amenities and disamenities based on a set of natural, economic and congestion variables (as explained in Figure 11.5). These latter indices can be regarded as attractiveness indicators for tourism.

As indicators for terrestrial disturbance and pollution we use a congestion index that is based on total number of tourists and local people, generated within the 'people module', waste particles generated within the 'economic activities' module, dependent on certain activity levels such as in construction, and sewage, determined by population and tourist levels.

For *land vegetation conservation* two indicators have been selected: the total area of forest and Maquis, and an index for land diversity. These are determined on the basis of the land areas under human control or with different vegetation types, given by stock variables in the 'terrestrial system' module.

Finally, three indicators, generated in the 'marine system' module, were chosen for *marine conservation*, namely adult seals, the total stock of fish, and the quality of marine water. The latter is based on the concentration of nitrogen, phosphorus, and on BOD and chlorophyll.

In the remainder of this section we will discuss results of scenario analysis based on the model described in the previous section, the 8 scenarios mentioned above, and a choice out of the possible indicators mentioned. The performance of economic and tourism indicators for Allonisos will be compared with those for the other islands. The performance of the attractiveness and environmental indicators for tourism on Allonisos will be discussed separately from the environmental indicators for the marine system.

11.4.2. Tourism and Economic Development on Allonisos and the Other Islands

In Figure 11.8 the island patterns of total value added are shown: for Allonisos under four scenarios, namely 1, 6, 7 and 9 (see above); and, for the other two islands under steady growth. The slow down observed on some curves is explained by tourism development under stationary growth (see Figure 11.10). Both the national pattern and the environmental feedback through amities and disamenities are responsible for this. Under strong growth, the size of the economy on Allonisos will approach that of Skopelos, while both will approach that of Skiathos. Scenario 6, reflecting the most strict environmental conservation measures, leads to the slowest pace of growth. The agricultural incentive (scenario 7) gives rise to a higher growth rate than under stationary growth. This growth is a net effect of sectoral growth under the respective scenario, capturing inter-sectoral effects.

Figure 11.9 shows the unemployment rates for Allonisos under the various scenarios, which shows trends consistent with those in Figure 11.8. It is clear that the environmental scenario 6 generates the highest and an increasing unemployment level over the entire period. Unemployment is also increasing under the stationary growth scenario, especially because supply of labour increases faster than demand, as a

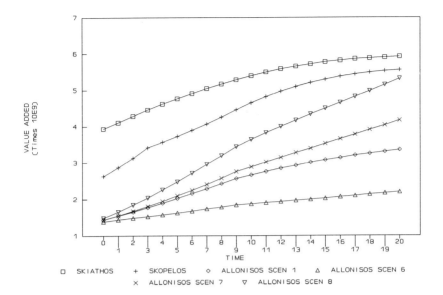

Figure 11.8. Allonisos economy compared with other islands.

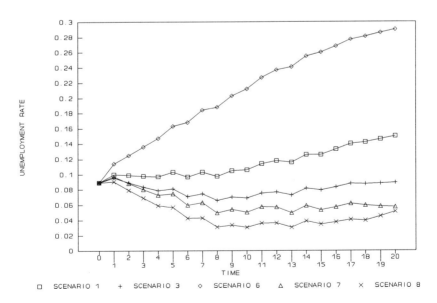

Figure 11.9. Comparison of unemployment rate on Allonisos under 6 scenarios.

result of increased participation – stimulated by clean work in tourism for which little education is necessary – population growth and migration and seasonal commuting. The agricultural incentive and high growth scenarios 7 and 8 lead to the best performance from the viewpoint of employment. Although growth in production per capita is higher under growth scenario 3 than under agricultural incentive scenario 7, unemployment over time is always higher. This can be explained by noticing that the growth under scenario 3 is dominated by the tourism sectors, where receipts per unit of labour input are higher than in agriculture.

Tourist numbers (indicated by total nights spent per year) are shown for Allonisos and Skopelos in Figure 11.10. Under most scenarios the pattern of growth in the number of tourists is curbed as a result of feedback from attractiveness indicators and changes in national trends. The number of tourists is not allowed to increase under the strict conservation scenario 6.

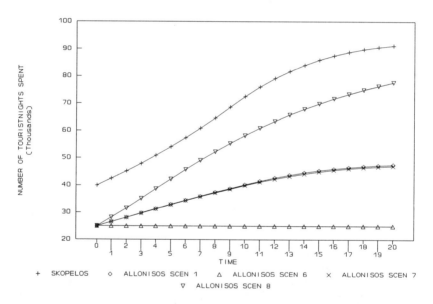

Figure 11.10. Tourist numbers under different scenarios of Allonisos, compared with Skopelos.

11.4.3. Environmental and Attractiveness Indicators: Allonisos

A complete characterisation of the regional situation at a given time includes, in addition to this economic performance levels of the islands, information on the state of the environment, summarised in the amenities and disamenities, a land diversity index, and the marine ecosystem species. This is even so, when only impacts upon economic performance are regarded, especially on tourism development as mentioned before, and on fisheries. Initially, amenities for Allonisos are decreasing under all scenarios, as indicated by an index over time in Figures 11.11 and 11.12. After some time, under scenarios 3, 4, 5, 7, and especially 8, amenities are increasing. The reason is that economic amenities are included in the index, and they are generated by economic growth in the tourism sectors. This is not the case under scenario 7.

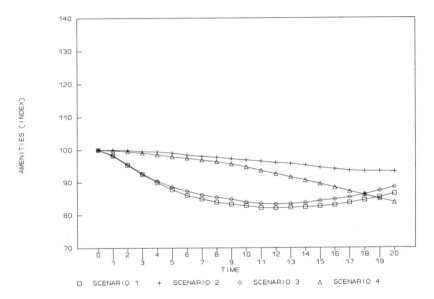

Figure 11.11.   Amenities index under scenarios 1 to 4.

Only for scenarios 2, 4 and 6, that have some form of tourism regulation in common, the trend keeps being negative. This is explained by the direct negative attraction effect of the environmental protection measures on tourism, and as a derived effect by the negative impact upon economic amenities (e.g., less hotels, less shops, less services).

The patterns of a disamenities index, that summarises congestion indicators, are not shown. All these patterns have positive trends, though very modest ones under the environmental conservation scenarios 4 and 6. The growth scenarios 3 and 8 show the strongest increases. This means that

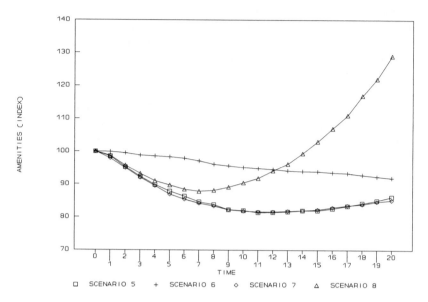

Figure 11.12.   Amenities index over time under scenarios 5 to 8.

the positive final parts of the curves denoting amenities for these scenarios are counterbalanced by increasing levels of disamenities. The ultimate combined effect is reflected by the trends in tourists demand. Essentially, this can be regarded as conflicting development patterns: positive trends of economic amenities, negative trends of natural and congestion amenities and positive trends of natural disamenities. The final levels of can be judged on their capacity for positive versus negative impacts on further economic development and/or nature conservation.

Land diversity indicator patterns over time for Allonisos are all following a downward trend. The strong growth scenario 8 gives rise to the steepest fall of this indicator. Only under scenarios 4 and 6 are stabilised levels attained, namely by restricting negative impacts of tourists, tourism activities, and derived activities (e.g., construction).

11.4.4. Environmental Indicators for the Marine System
The patterns of Monk Seals are given in Figures 11.13 and 11.14. Scenarios 2, 4 and 6 perform best, though only under scenario 6 the level of Monk Seals is stable over time. This means that the negative effect of fishery and tourists has to be minimised, i.e. restricting tourist entrance in certain marine areas and keeping fish catches below sustainable yield. Fish stocks

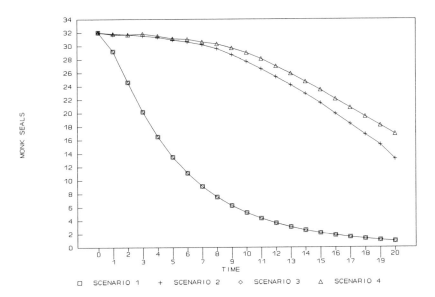

Figure 11.13.   Monk seal population over time under scenarios 1 to 4.

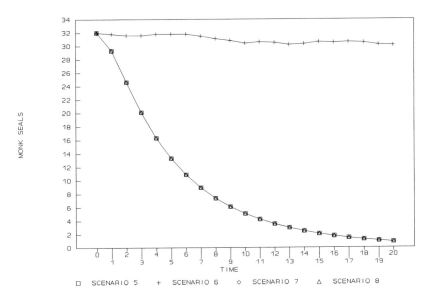

Figure 11.14.   Monk seal population over time under scenarios 5 to 8.

are depleted in most cases (not shown), except under the scenarios 5 and 6, i.e. when sustainable fishing is applied. Scenario 2, which includes the marine park policy of restricting tourist visits to a sensitive marine area, gives better results than the steady growth scenario. Scenario 4, which also limits tourist growth, leads to a decrease in the depletion rate of fish stocks via a derived effect on the fisheries industry, and consequently to a slow down of the decrease in the population of Monk Seals.

11.5. MULTICRITERIA EVALUATION

This and the next section report of the use of multicriteria analysis and geographic information systems (GIS) models as a decision support system (DSS) for sustainable development (SD) planning of the Greek Sporades Islands. One of the most intriguing and difficult dilemmas facing policy--makers is the often mentioned incompatibility between economic efficiency goals, socio-economic equity goals, and ecological sustainability goals. The focus here will be on investigating options for one of the Sporades islands, namely Allonisos. The operational decision support system, *Definite*, was used to evaluate six development options for this area (see for further details on the system and computer software, see van Herwijnen and Janssen 1989; Janssen 1992; Janssen and van Herwijnen 1994). In this evaluation the attention will be focused on development alternatives. Then the rankings of alternatives are determined for these six choice options on the basis of different sets of priorities for these developments by using multi-criteria methods. Finally, the various results are investigated with regard to their sensitivity regarding shifts in policy priorities and in the initial impact scores on the various policy or performance indicators. Later, also the geographic information system SPANS (SPatial ANalysis System 1990) will be used as an illustration of the application of spatial evaluation of different land use alternatives for these development options. The resulting maps of this spatial evaluation are used as input into *Definite* for a compound evaluation of these different land use alternatives in order to offer a comprehensive decision support system.

In our GIS-SD framework, six out of the eight development alternatives defined in Section 11.4 will be evaluated: steady growth (D_1), marine park (D_2), strong growth (D_3), limited tourism growth (D_4), sustainable fishing (D_5), and agricultural incentive (D_6).

A basic notion in any evaluation analysis is the effect table, which comprises for all development alternatives the foreseeable effects on a set of relevant policy criteria. As we have seen, the development alternatives have effects on the socio-economic and ecological development of

Allonisos. These multiple effects can be grouped into various categories. The classification of effects in socio-economic and ecological classes is shown in Table 11.5 and Figures 11.15 and 11.16 The scores of the effects for each of the six development alternatives are presented here in a visually attractive manner by means of computer graphics in the form of histograms (see Janssen and van Herwijnen 1994).

Table 11.5. Compound Development Indicators

Socio-economic Development			
Economic welfare		40%	
GIP	25%		
IncGrowth	25%		
Unemployment	50%		
	100%		
Import water		20%	
Import water	100%		
	100%		
Tourism		40%	
Tourists	50%		
Amenities	25%		
Disamenities	25%		
	100%		
		100%	
Ecological Development			
Emissions		20%	
Dust	20%		
Congestion	20%		
Sewage	60%		
	100%		
Land use		20%	
Land use	60%		
Land diversity	20%		
Nat. vegetation	20%		
	100%		
Marine environment		60%	
Monk Seals	60%		
Fish	20%		
Quality sea	20%		
	100%		
		100%	

The six alternatives in the histograms are ranked in order of preference based on the ranking of the effects, where the most important effect is placed in the first row, the second best in the second row, and so on. In the histogram in Figure 11.15 the socio-economic development effects have been assumed to have a higher priority than the ecological development effects. In Figure 11.16 this order is just reversed. This way of graphically presenting and analysing the effect table is very useful to get a first comprehensive overview of the weak and strong points of the various development alternatives. In the histograms presented in Figures 11.15 and 11.16 the highest bar for each effect indicates the best alternative. The first overall impression of this histogram is that a number of effects have a similar pattern. These effects concern import of water, disamenities sewage, congestion, dust, land use and quality of sea water. The patterns of land use diversity and of natural vegetation are also very similar.

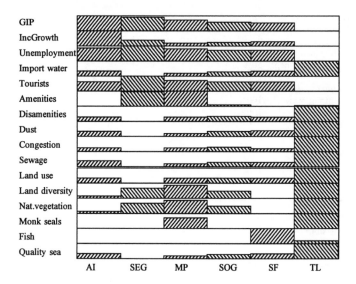

Figure 11.15. *Histogram of Effect Table with Socio-Economic Development Effects More Important than Ecological Development Effects*

Notes: AI = Agricultural Incentive;   SEG = Steady Growth;
MP = Marine Park;   SOG = Strong Growth;
SF = Sustainable Fishing;   TL = Tourist Limits

From the histograms one can observe that the development alternative 'limited tourism', for example, scores on the whole very good for all ecological development effects, but relatively poor for the socio-economic ones. The alternative of 'strong growth', on the other hand, scores poor for all ecological effects, but rather favourably for socio-economic effects. Therefore it can be easily deduced that the alternatives 'strong growth' and 'limited tourism' are essentially contrasting development options.

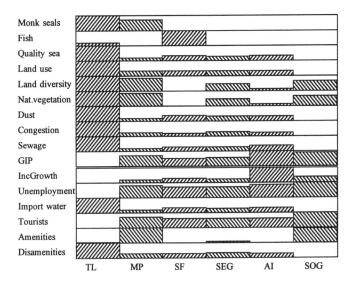

Figure 11.16. Histogram of an Effect Table with Ecological Development Effects More Important than Socio-Economic Effects

Note: See for explanation the notes to Figure 11.15.

The effects which have a favourable score for the alternative marine park are related to both the ecological and the socio-economic development effects. The scores on the effects in the 'land use' category and the 'marine environment' category rank second after, of course, the 'tourism limit' option. Only fish is an exception, which of course scores best for the alternative 'sustainable fishing'. The emission effects for the marine park score about the same as those for 'agricultural incentive', 'steady growth' and 'sustainable fishing'. From these results it can be concluded that the marine park is a very good alternative if socio-economic development is regarded equally important as ecological development.

The use of weights
It is clear that the ordering of alternatives is dependent on policy weights for the successive criteria. By grouping the disaggregate effects (e.g., GIP, IncGrowth etc) into major categories (e.g., economic welfare, import of water etc.) and next the categories into main developments (e.g., socio-economic development), compound indices can be created (Janssen and Hafkamp 1986). The compound indices for development alternatives are thus composed of indices of the various categories which are made up

themselves by the scores on the individual effects. The degree of influence of the effects on each corresponding category is expressed by using percentages attached to the effects within that category. The degree of influence of the categories on their major development options is expressed in the same way. For example, from Table 11.5 we can derive that the influence of unemployment on economic welfare is 50%, while next the impact of economic welfare on socio-economic developments is 40%. The percentages which indicate the degree of influence of the effects on their corresponding category and of the categories on the two major development criteria are given in Table 11.5.

By using the percentages given in Table 11.5 and the original scores of the effect table, a compound development table can be created. This table is presented in the form of a histogram in Figure 11.17.

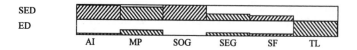

Figure 11.17. Histogram of Compound Development Criteria

Notes: SED   = Socio-economic development
            ED   = Ecological development
See also the notes to Figure 11.15.

In this histogram the alternatives are ranked, based on the assumption that socio-economic development is more important than ecological objectives. This histogram shows that the alternative marine park will always be better ranked than the alternatives 'sustainable fishing' and 'steady growth', whatever priority is given to the two compound development criteria. A look at the alternatives 'strong growth' and 'limited tourism' shows the contrast between these two alternatives with regard to the compound socio-economic and ecological development criteria.

Having discussed these main ideas, we will now deal with rankings of development alternatives in greater detail. The compound socio-economic and ecological development indicators discussed above can be compared for each of the six development alternatives by means of multicriteria analysis (see also Janssen 1992; Carver 1991; Nijkamp *et al.*, 1990b; Voogd 1983).

Application of the well-known summation method (see Nijkamp *et al.*, 1990b) gives a ranking of the alternatives in the same way. Results of a sensitivity analysis for three different weight vectors are shown in Table 11.6. The priorities of the compound developments are given by direct numerical weight values adding up to 1.

Table 11.6. **Weighted Summation Results Derived by Direct Numerical Weights**

WEIGHTS		WEIGHTS		WEIGHTS	
1: ecological dev.	0.80	1: socio-econ. dev.	0.50	1: socio-econ. dev.	0.80
2: socio-econ. dev.	0.20	ecological. dev.	0.50	2: ecological. dev.	0.20
RANKING		**RANKING**		**RANKING**	
1: limited tourism	0.80	1: marine park	0.66	1: strong growth	0.80
2: marine park	0.54	2: agriculture	0.54	2: marine park	0.78
3: agriculture	0.30	3: strong growth	0.50	3: agriculture	0.78
4: sustainable fishing	0.29	4: limited tourism	0.50	4: steady growth	0.44
5: steady growth	0.23	5: sustainable fishing	0.36	5: sustainable fishing	0.42
6: strong growth	0.28	6: steady growth	0.34	6: limited tourism	0.20

A visual method can be used for obtaining insight into the sensitivity of evaluation results; sensitivity of results regarding uncertainty in the weights used can best be shown graphically. In Figure 11.18 the results of the three different weight vectors of Table 11.6 are plotted. Here a weighted summation method (with cardinal weights) is used, so that the vertical axis ranges from 0 (low value) to 1 (high value). This graph clearly shows the turning points (break-even points) where a ranking of two alternatives suddenly changes. The alternative 'limited tourism', for example, will shift from the first to the second position in point X, in which the weight for the ecological development is about 0.6.

Next, the sensitivity of the scores can also be investigated. This is done using a Monte Carlo approach (Nijkamp 1979b). Then the maximum percentage that the actual values can differ from the values included in the effect table has to be estimated. In this case all effects are given a maximum difference percentage of say 25%. By using a random generator this information is translated into a large number of effect tables around the original effect table. Rankings are then determined for all effect tables. The probability table of the results of the weighted summation technique in the first column of Table 11.6 is given in Table 11.7. This table shows that the probability that the alternative 'limited tourism' is selected as the best alternative equals 100%.

Next, the probability for the results from the third column of Table 11.6 is found in Table 11.8. While the probability that the best alternative in Table 11.7 (i.e. limited tourism) ranks first appears to be 100%, the

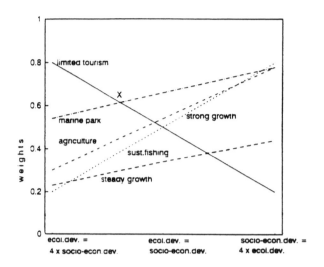

Figure 11.18.　Weight Uncertainty Related to Table 11.6

probability that 'strong growth' is the best alternative in Table 11.8 is only 35%. The alternatives marine park and in particular 'agriculture' also score high on the first three places. The main conclusion which can be drawn from this probability table is that no best alternative can be selected − with sufficient reliability − for the given priorities and uncertainty percentage assumed here. The final comprehensive rankings from the results in Table 11.6 with a given score uncertainty of 25% are shown in Table 11.9.

It is clear from the above results that an overall evaluation of the six development alternatives for the Sporades can be carried out in several ways by means of the multi- criteria evaluation methods, as included in the *Definite* software package. With the help of a graphical presentation a first insight into and a better understanding of the choice and policy problems at hand can be obtained. By grouping the effects into categories and next the categories in turn into compound developments, the problem is easier to handle. The influence of priorities for the socio-economic and ecological development options on the ranking of the alternatives becomes easier to analyse, if the influence of the different effects on their categories is held fixed. The different priorities appear to have a large effect on the ranking of the alternatives 'limited tourism' and 'strong growth'. These two alternatives appear to change position from best through middle to inferior. The alternative 'marine park', on the other hand, always ranks on the first two places, while the alternative 'agriculture' always ranks one position below 'marine park'.

Table 11.7. Probability Table of Results from the First Column of Table 11.6 with a Score Uncertainty of 25%

Probabilities	first	second	third	fourth	fifth	sixth
limited tourism	1.00					
marine park		0.94	0.04		0.02	
agriculture		0.01	0.26	0.31	0.18	0.24
sustainable fishing		0.05	0.56	0.24	0.11	0.04
steady growth		0.08	0.36	0.34	0.22	
strong growth		0.06	0.09	0.35	0.50	

Table 11.8. Probability Table of Results from the First Column of Table 11.6 with a Score Uncertainty of 25%

Probabilities	first	second	third	fourth	fifth	sixth
strong growth	0.35	0.20	0.28	0.14	0.05	
marine park	0.21	0.30	0.24	0.11	0.14	0.01
agriculture	0.37	0.37	0.15	0.09	0.03	
steady growth	0.03	0.07	0.16	0.31	0.30	0.13
sustainable fishing	0.05	0.08	0.18	0.29	0.29	0.12
limited tourism				0.07	0.20	0.74

Summarising all results – given also the sensitivity analysis on the results – it seems plausible that the alternative marine park is the best alternative, except when the ecological development is deemed far more important for the Sporades Islands than the socio-economic development. In that case the alternative 'limited tourism' appears to be the best alternative.

Table 11.9.   Conclusive Ranking with a Score Uncertainty of 25%

WEIGHTS	WEIGHTS	WEIGHTS
1: ecological dev. 0.800 2: socio-econ. dev. 0.200	1: socio-econ. dev. 0.500 2: ecological dev. 0.500	1: socio-econ. dev. 0.800 2: ecological dev. 0.200
RANKING	**RANKING**	**RANKING**
1: limited tourism	1: marine park	1: strong growth
2: marine park	2: agriculture	marine park
3: agriculture	strong growth	agriculture
sustainable fishing	limited tourism	4: steady growth
5: steady growth	5: sustainable fishing	sustainable fishing
6: strong growth	6: steady growth	6: limited tourism

11.6.   SPATIAL EVALUATION

11.6.1. Spatial Scenarios

The six development alternatives described in the previous section did not (or hardly) discriminate in a geographical sense. A detailed spatial evaluation of these alternatives is therefore not possible. Nevertheless, it is clear that various development options may be judged in a different way if their geographical pattern differs significantly. To evaluate these alternatives from a geographical perspective, five spatially different policies (called land use alternatives) are here assumed and developed focusing on the growth of urban areas on the island of Allonisos (see for details also Despotakis 1991). These distinct five policies can be combined with the above mentioned individual six development alternatives, which leads altogether to 30 different combined alternatives. For the sake of illustration but without loss of generality, in this section the development alternative 'marine park', D_2, is selected for further spatial evaluation. The method used here applies equally well to the other development alternatives.

The five different policies to control urban growth differ with respect to the place on the island where growth of the urban areas is encouraged. In the policies analysed here, urbanisation on Allonisos is assumed to be encouraged in certain areas and discouraged in other areas. The five land use policies distinguished here and denoted by LU are:

LU_1: encourage urbanisation within 200m of the sea;
LU_2: encourage urbanisation in the central part of the island;
LU_3: encourage urbanisation in the south half of the island;
LU_4: encourage urbanisation in the east half of the island;
LU_5: encourage urbanisation in the city.

The five different policy scenarios are sketched in Figure 11.19. The symbols X indicate the places where urbanisation is encouraged.

It goes without saying that the previous sketches can also be represented in more professional GIS maps by making more specific assumptions regarding these policy alternatives. In order to offer a multi-dimensional evaluation, the following assumptions are made for each successive scenario:

Scenario LU_1: the first spatial scenario encourages urban growth within 200m of the sea. The beaches themselves fall then in the influence sphere of urban areas. This scenario is to be interpreted as a 'sea-shore' development scenario, where the sea is considered as the major attraction force for tourism. Hotels, shops, public services, etc. are clustering in a zone between 0 and 200m from the sea.

Scenario LU_2: the second spatial scenario encourages urban growth in the central part of the island. The beaches and a zone of 500m from the sea may not be changed into urban areas. This scenario is to be interpreted as an 'inner-land' development scenario. The old Allonisos village and transportation in the centre of the island are the primary attraction poles for tourism. Sea plays a secondary role for tourism and, consequently, for urban activities. Beaches are fully protected.

Scenario LU_3: the third spatial scenario allows the urban area to expand only at the southern half of the island. Beaches are allowed to change into urban-dominated areas in the southern half of the island only. The north half of the island remains 'untouched'. This scenario is to be interpreted as a marine park laboratory protection scenario. The marine park laboratory resides at the northern gulf of the island and, under this scenario, no one is authorised to approach it.

Scenario LU_3: the fourth spatial scenario allows urban activities to expand only in the eastern half of the island. Beach areas are allowed to change to urban in the eastern part of the island only. The western part of the island remains 'untouched'. This scenario is to be interpreted as an encouragement for exploiting the island Peristera for urban activities and tourism. In this way the main western part of Allonisos island is relieved from any distortion by human activities.

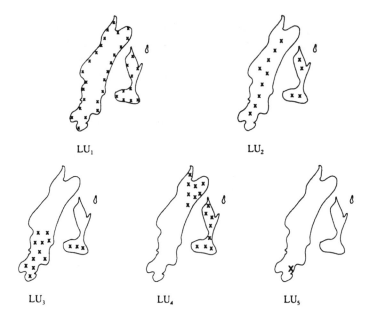

Figure 11.19. Land use alternatives for Allonisos.

Scenario LU₅: the fifth spatial scenario allows urban land to expand only within the existing urban areas of the islands. This means that any type of urban growth in a horizontal direction is strictly prohibited, so that only urban growth in a vertical direction is allowed. That is, any type of urban growth is to be accommodated by constructing more floors on the already existing buildings. This scenario is to be interpreted as a policy scenario which aims at maintaining the existing land use in terms of areal totals. In this case the urban area remains constant, but the urban density increases within the existing urban areas.

Now the allocation of urban areas on Allonisos can be depicted using the above GIS model. This model uses a basic land use map and generates as a result of the above spatial development options a number of new land use maps in which urban area is spatially allocated (unfortunately the maps were coloured and cannot be reprinted here; they are available in Despotakis, 1991; see also van Herwijnen *et al.*, 1993). A resulting land use map of one specific urban allocation, for example LU_2, in relation to a given development alternative D_2 is named here D_2LU_2. The land use allocation maps represent the policy alternatives in a spatial evaluation context. For each of the basic land uses, D_2, and the five allocation patterns, D_2LU_1 to D_2LU_5, the maps show the places where urbanisation will take place. The change of land use can be further investigated by comparing the basic map with the successive five urbanisation maps. The size of the land use classes in the basic land use map of development alternative D_2 and in the five land use allocation maps is shown in Table 11.10.

Clearly, the land use size from the basic map and the urban allocation maps D_2LU_1, D_2LU_5 should be the same. Table 11.10 shows that the size of forest area in all allocation maps remains the same. The size of beach area remains the same, except for the allocation map in which the policy aim is to encourage urbanisation within 200 metres of the sea, i.e. D_2LU_1. An important conclusion from this map is that the urban area appears to grow with a factor five to six for all allocation maps, except for the allocation map in which the urbanisation is encouraged in the city. The results have also shown that Maquis and low Maquis are best protected, of course, within the policy to encourage urbanisation in the city (i.e. D_2LU_5). The worst policy for Maquis is to encourage urbanisation in the central parts of the island (i.e. D_2LU_4) and for low Maquis to encourage urbanisation in the eastern part of the island (i.e. D_2LU_4).

Table 11.10. Area Table of the Basic Land Use Map and the Urban Allocation Maps

Class	Legend	D_2	D_2LU_1	D_2LU_2	D_2LU_3	D_2LU_4	D_2LU_5
1	Sea	272.074	269.932	269.932	269.932	269.932	269.932
2	Forest	5.813	6.000	6.000	6.000	6.000	6.000
3	Maquis	32.187	29.141	26.316	28.729	30.680	32.860
4	Low Maquis	29.938	26.872	27.941	25.207	21.470	29.676
5	Valleys	2.180	2.109	1.924	1.951	2.239	2.268
6	Bare rocks	3.285	2.745	3.368	3.042	3.113	3.437
7	Trees	3.352	2.492	2.358	2.142	3.441	3.480
8	Agriculture	1.803	1.654	1.276	1.545	1.622	1.917
9	Urban	2.235	11.558	12.717	13.285	13.355	2.261
10	Beach	1.119	0.483	1.153	1.153	1.153	1.153
Total		352.985	352.985	352.985	352.985	352.985	352.985

11.6.2. Evaluation Criteria

Having identified now five spatial development scenarios in combination with a given base development alternative D_2 (i.e. marine park), we will next use four judgement criteria to evaluate the five alternative land use maps, D_2LU_1 to D_2LU_5, representing the land use options corresponding to the five different ways to allocate urban area on Allonisos, and assuming the marine park development alternative as a given policy option. The relevant criteria to be used here are: tourism (C_1), nature (C_2), landscape (C_3), and transportation (C_4).

These four criteria are measured on a 10-point scale and can of course be mapped separately as extreme policy choices. For each development alternative and each land use option a GIS map was made for each of the four individual criteria. On the basis of four evaluation criteria (i.e. tourism, nature, landscape and transport) and five land use options (LU_1 to LU_5) for a given base development alternative (i.e. 19 marine park), the total number of resulting maps would be 20. By mapping also all six base development alternatives, the total number of combinations would even be 120. In the graphical presentation above we have made a cross-section of all four criteria for a given spatial development option, viz. D_2LU_1 (i.e. the policy to encourage urbanisation within 200m distance from the sea). It is of course also possible to make a different cross-section, viz. a mapping of all five land use options for a given criterion.

The GIS maps can of course also be translated into numerical information. The value areas of all maps will be described, so that the results of all alternatives can be compared for all criteria. To allow a numerical comparison of all alternatives for all criteria, in this subsection the island areas associated with the land use classes of all resulting maps are systematically listed in tables grouped for each of the four criteria. The classes represent the estimated values for each criterion and range from 1 to 10.

Each land use alternative is assessed for each criterion by calculating a weighted sum of the areas of each class. This compound valuation is found in the bottom row of each table. The valuation is carried out by multiplying the area of the worst class by 1, the class 'very bad' by 2 etc., until the 'best' class by 10. After adding up all multiplied values, a correction has to be made for the classified total areas; the total area which is classified from 1 to 10 is not equal for all alternatives, so that a standardisation is needed. By dividing the weighted sum by the total classified area this problem is solved. In this way each weighted sum gives an estimation of the value of each judgement criterion for a given land use alternative. The higher the criterion value, the higher the performance of that land use alternative for that criterion. These estimations can finally be included in an overall effect table which can be evaluated by means of the software program *Definite*, as described before. The various criteria can separately be treated; for the sake of illustration we will only discuss in greater detail the tourism criterion C_1.

The successive land use options related to the performance classes of the tourist criterion in the basic land use map (i.e. D_2) and the five land use alternatives (i.e. D_2LU_1 to D_2LU_5) are listed in Table 11.11.

For criterion 1 (i.e. tourism) each land use alternative is provided with a prefix C,, so that we have six possibilities, viz. C_1D_2 and $C_1D_2LU_1$ to $C_1D_2LU_5$. The tourist criterion values only urban areas. Due to the fact that in alternative S urbanisation is encouraged in the city only, the total urban area is here smaller than in other alternatives. For this reason the unclassified area, which equals the non-urbanised area, is everywhere larger for the fifth land use alternative. The calculation of the weighted estimations listed in the bottom row is corrected for this.

The bottom row of Table 11.11 shows that land use alternative 2 (i.e. $C_1D_2LU_2$), encouraging tourism in the central part of the island, scores worst. The other four alternatives are better and score roughly the same.

Table 11.11. Area Table of Tourism Criterion

Class	Legend	C_1D_2	$C_1D_2LU_1$	$C_1D_2LU_2$	$C_1D_2LU_3$	$C_1D_2LU_4$	$C_1D_2LU_5$
1	Worst		0.159	0.493	0.303	0.024	
2	Very bad		1.171	3.131	1.042	0.874	
3	Bad	0.31	1.025	3.687	0.713	1.160	0.045
4	Rather bad	0.109	0.687	1.950	0.861	0.343	0.092
5	Rather fair	0.334	0.577	0.997	0.712	0.320	0.303
6	Fair	0.539	1.380	1.160	2.199	2.455	0.523
7	Rather good	0.743	3.392	0.729	4.506	4.687	0.729
8	Good						
9	Very good	0.397	3.027	0.537	2.831	3.226	0.537
10	Best	0.083	0.140	0.033	0.118	0.244	0.033
11	Unclassified	84.620	72.141	70.982	70.415	70.364	81.438
12	Sea	266.129	269.286	269.286	269.286	269.286	269.286

11.6.3. An overall evaluation

After the computation of the 20 value maps, the compound effect table can be produced by extracting a single value from each evaluation map. This value is a weighted areal average of the value map. The weighted sums for each of the four criteria to be found in the bottom line of the corresponding criterion Table 11.11 are listed in Table 11.12. At this stage also the transformation from spatial (pixel level) to non-spatial (relative importance of each criterion per alternative) is carried out. These values give an indication of the quality of the criteria for the five land use alternatives. This table is evaluated with *Definite* to find the ranking of the alternatives taking into account the outcomes of the criteria.

The following comments are in order for this effect table.

(1) It appears that scenario LU_2 (urban growth in the middle of the island) has a very low relative score for the 'tourism' criterion, whereas scenario LU_5 (no urban expansion) has the highest score for the same criterion. This results from the fact that the urban distances to the sea − which determine the 'happy tourists' in this scenario − are at a maximum for the case of scenario 2 and minimal for the case of scenario LU_5.

Table 11.12.   *The Effect Table Used for Numerical Application of the GIS-SD-DSS System in the Test Area*

	Alternatives				
Criteria	LU_1	LU_2	LU_3	LU_4	LU_5
tourism	6.219	3.761	6.242	6.543	6.817
nature	4.128	3.841	3.906	3.879	5.516
landscape	4.663	5.742	4.575	4.427	4.353
transportation	6.299	5.635	6.945	5.168	8.691

(2) The 'best' sustainable scenario for the criterion 'nature', determined by the related land use changes, is scenario LU_5. This is due to the fact that for this scenario the natural area for the year 2005 remains almost equal to the natural area for the year 1985. The 'worst' scenario from the point of view of natural sustainability in this case is scenario LU_2; in this case the scarce natural areas in the central part of the island are destroyed and changed into urban areas. We also observe here that the

scenario LU_3 (urban expansion in the southern half of the island) puts more environmental stress than the scenario LU_4 (urban expansion in the eastern half of the island). This is so because the existing urban area for the year 1985 is already located at the southern half of the island; therefore, a scenario according to which additional urban expansion at the eastern half of the island takes place, will place a heavier burden on the natural areas than on the southern (already congested) areas.

(3) Scenario LU_2 is the 'best' in terms of preserving the original landscape of the island: the urban expansion takes place in the middle of the island and therefore the urban areas are not visible from either the sea or other parts of the island (notably beaches). This non-visibility results in high scores for the landscape criterion.

(4) Scenario LU_5 is the 'best' in terms of road transportation; in other words, this scenario results in the minimum load of road transportation required for local people or tourists to move on the island. The 'worst' scenario in terms of road transportation load is scenario LU_4 (urban expansion only in the eastern half of the island). This is due to the fact that the distances from the harbour, located at the southern part of the island, are maximised and this is, in turn, taken into account for the computation of the road transportation burden.

A compound effect table was produced and imported into *Definite* (van Herwijnen and Janssen, 1989; and Janssen and van Herwijnen, 1994) in order to obtain a final ranking of alternatives. The choice of weights here was such that all criteria were considered equally important. The ranking results based on the four selected criteria are given in Table 11.13.

Table 11.13. The Ranking Results for the Five Spatial (Land Use) Alternatives on Allonisos

Alternative	LU_1	LU_2	LU_3	LU_4	LU_5
Rank	3	5	2	4	1

We thus conclude that, based on the above assumptions and ranking methods, scenario LU_5 is to be selected as a stronger 'sustainable' scenario than the others. The term 'sustainable' here refers to a development (until the year 2005) which focuses simultaneously on four sustainability criteria selected: (1) touristic sector activities are favoured and enhanced; (2) natural areas are preserved as much as possible and/or changed into urban areas as little as possible; (3) landscape values are preserved; and (4) the road transport annoyance becomes minimal. However, such a conclusion is expected from development scenarios of the type of scenario LU_5: if the urban areas are to be restricted to their original locations, then this is the 'best' sustainable scenario, at least in an eco-centric sense. Since often such 'no expansion' policies tend to be unrealistic (and much more difficult to implement and control), we might, alternatively select scenario LU_3, i.e. the scenario which was ranked as the second best. According to this scenario, urban growth is encouraged in the southern part of the island, notably in areas surrounding the existing village of the island. This may also be interpreted as a 'marine park preservation' scenario, since the marine park laboratory is located in the northern part of the island. This scenario minimises the road transportation load, but it is not a strong sustainable scenario for the natural ecosystem (like e.g. scenario LU_1). However, it may be easier and more realistically implemented in practice than scenario LU_5.

The next less strong sustainable scenario is scenario LU_1. This scenario however, seems to have a fair chance of actually being implemented, because: (1) urban expansion is allowed without too many restrictions and (2) the beach areas are exploited for the creation of touristic services. The only barriers to urban activities are natural conditions or existing policy regulations (high slopes, forest area restrictions, etc.). Therefore, it may happen that scenario LU_3 is fairly realistic, even though from a normative sustainable viewpoint it is less favourable.

Scenario LU_4 is the next 'worst' scenario. This is plausible since, according to this scenario, we force the population to move away from the existing urban areas toward the eastern half of the island. This in turn requires heavy road transport, destroys the natural areas and does not favour tourism.

The 'worst' scenario, according to our ranking results, is scenario LU_2. This was also expected, since (1) we 'move' the local population and tourists to the central part of the island and thus the access to the beaches is very difficult; this in turn creates 'unhappy tourists'; (2) although the landscape is best preserved, transportation needs to be increased; (3) the natural ecosystem is mainly negatively affected, since urban activities destroy natural areas and disturb wild life.

11.7.   CONCLUSIONS

The case study clearly illustrates the risk of environmental unsustainability of regional development. This is partly due to the open character of the region. External forces related to tourism push the regional economy beyond certain environmental carrying capacity limits. It is shown that formal dynamic models can give us insight into the operation of long term processes of tourism and economic development, and economic–environmental interactions on a regional scale. Our model indicates that if the Monk Seal is to be protected, policy measures should be directed at restricting both negative environmental impacts of tourism and fishery. Even strict limits on tourism growth may by required, e.g., via spatial (land use) or admittance policies. High unemployment is however likely to result from such policy measures. In order to evade this, tourism growth may be allowed but should go along with a set of very restrictive measures to prevent negative impacts on fisheries and Monk Seals. Further formal modelling work might give more attention to endogenous growth and development processes, labour market processes, and seasonal patterns.

The adoption of new information technology results depends on their scientific merits and political willingness. In the case study described above the most desirable development direction was very clear: much emphasis on protection of the marine environment and on restricting the negative externalities of tourism. In a geographical setting this would mean a concentrated land use pattern rather than a dispersion of tourist activities all over the island. It is at the same time clear however, that any policy choice will affect the interest of various actors involved (e.g., fishermen, land owners, hotel owners, environmentalists etc.). The way the results were presented here, viz. in a conditional 'what ... if' scenario form, makes the range of policy strategies and of citizen's interests more transparent. Whether or not policy recommendations will be accepted, depends on attitudes and perceptions of people. The methodology developed here is able to generate various best compromise solutions, but in case of rigid extreme interests by actors involved it may be difficult to pave the road to a sustainability-oriented future. At best one may claim that decision support based on tools of dynamic modeling, multicriteria analysis and geographical information, as presented above, may increase awareness of current frictions and future incompatibilities in economic development, environmental sustainability and land use shifts.

References

Note: When more than one article from an edited book is included, the book is separately mentioned by the name of the (first) editor.

Ackoff, R.L., 1981. 'The art and science of mess management'. *TIMS Interfaces*, Vol. 11: 20–26.

Ahearn, C.S., J.L.D. Smith and C. Wee, 1990. 'Framework for a geographically referenced conservation database: Case Study Nepal'. *Photogrammetric Engineering and Remote Sensing*, Vol. 56: 1477–81.

Ahmad, Y.J., S. El Serafy and E. Lutz (eds.), 1989. *Environmental Accounting for Sustainable Development*. The World Bank, Washington, D.C.

Alcamo, J., R. Shaw and L. Hordijk (eds.), 1990. *The Rains Model of Acidification: Science and Strategies in Europe*. Kluwer Academic Publishers, Dordrecht.

Allen, P.M., 1988. 'Evolution, innovation and economics'. In: G. Dosi *et al.* (eds.),

Amir, S., 1994. 'The role of thermodynamics in the study of economic and ecological systems'. *Ecological Economics*, Vol. 10: 125–142.

Ancot, J.P., 1988. *Micro-Qualiflex; An Interactive Software Package for the Determination and Analysis of the Optimal Solution to Decision Problems*. Kluwer Academic Publishers, Dordrecht.

Ancot, J.P. and J.H.P. Paelinck, 1982. 'Recent experiences with the Qualiflex multicriteria method'. In: J.H.P. Paelinck (ed.), *Qualitative and Quantitative Mathematical Economics*. Martinus Nijhoff, The Hague: 217–266.

Anderson, D.R., D.J. Sweeney and T.A. Williams, 1988. *An Introduction to Management Science. Quantitative Approaches to Decision Making*. Wes Publishing Co., St. Paul.

Anderson, J.M., 1981. *Ecology for Environmental Sciences: Biosphere, Ecosystems and Man*. Edward Arnold, London.

Anderson, K. and R. Blackhurst (eds.), 1992. *The Greening of World Trade Issues*. Harvester Wheatsheaf, New York.

Archibugi, F. and P. Nijkamp (eds.), 1989. *Economy and Ecology: Towards Sustainable Development*. Kluwer Academic Publishers, Dordrecht.

Ariav, G. and M.J. Ginzberg, 1985. 'DSS design: A systematic view of decision support'. *Communications of the ACM*, Vol. 28: 1045–52.

Arntzen, J., 1989. *Environmental Pressure and Adaptation in Rural Botswana*. Ph.D. Dissertation, Free University, Amsterdam.

Arntzen, J. and L.C. Braat, 1983. 'An integrated environmental model for regional policy analysis'. In: T.R. Lakshmanan and P. Nijkamp (eds.), *Systems and Models for Energy and Environmental Analysis*. Gower, Aldershot.

Arrow, K.J., 1973a. 'Some ordinalist–utilitarian notes on Rawls's theory of justice'. *Journal of Philosophy*, Vol. 70: 245–263.

Arrow, K.J., 1973b. 'Rawls's principle of just saving'. *Swedish Journal of Economics*, Vol. 75: 323–335.

Ayres, R.U., 1978. *Resources, Environment and Economics: Applications of the Materials/ Energy Balance Principle*. Wiley-Interscience, New York.

Ayres, R.U., 1989. 'Industrial Metabolism'. In: J.H. Ausubel and H.E. Sladovich (eds.), *Technology and Environment*. National Academy Press, Washington D.C.: 23–49.

Ayres, R.U., 1993. 'Cowboys, cornucopians and long-run sustainability'. *Ecological Economics*, Vol. 8: 189–207.

Ayres, R.U. and A.V. Kneese, 1969. 'Production, consumption and externalities'. *American Economic Review*, Vol. 59: 282–97.

Ayres, R.U. and A.V. Kneese, 1989. 'Externalities: Economics and thermodynamics'. In: F. Archibugi and P. Nijkamp (eds.): 89–119.

Barbier, E.B., 1989. *Economics, Natural Resource Scarcity and Development: Conventional and Alternative Views*, Earthscan Pub., London.

Barbier, E.B., 1990. 'Alternative approaches to economic–environmental interactions'. *Ecological Economics*, Vol. 2: 7–26.

Barbier, E.B., 1994. 'Valuing environmental functions: Tropical wetlands'. *Land Economics*, Vol. 70: 155–173.

Barbier, E.B., J.C. Burgess and C. Folke, 1994. *Paradise Lost? The Ecological Economics of Biodiversity*. Earthscan, London.

Barbier, E.B. and M. Rauscher, 1994. 'Trade, tropical deforestation and policy interventions'. *Environmental and Resource Economics*, Vol. 4: 75–94.

Barendregt, A., S.M.E. Stam and M.J. Wassen, 1992. 'Restoration of fen ecosystems in the Vecht River plain: cost–benefit analysis of hydrological alternatives'. In: L. van Liere and R.D. Gulati (eds.), *Restoration and Recovery of Shallow Eutrophic Lake Ecosystems in the Netherlands*. Kluwer Academic Publishers, Dordrecht.

Barney, G.O. (ed.), 1980. *The Global 2000 Report to the President of the U.S., Entering the Twenty-first Century*. 2 volumes, Penguin books, Harmondsworth.

Bartelmus, P., 1986. *Environment and Development*. Allen and Unwin, Boston.

Batabyal, A.A., 1995. 'Leading issues in domestic environmental regulation: A review essay'. *Ecological Economics*, Vol. 12: 23–39.

Baumol W.J. and W.E. Oates, 1988. *The Theory of Environmental Policy*. 2nd edition. Cambridge University Press, New York.

Beach, L.R., 1990. *Image theory: Decision making in personal and organizational contexts*. John Wiley and Sons, Chichester.

Beach, L.R. and T.R. Mitchell, 1987. 'Image theory: principles, goals and plans in decision making'. *Acta Psychologica*, Vol. 66: 201–220.

Beckermann, W., 1976. *In Defence of Economic Growth*. Jonathan Cape, London.

Beckermann, W., 1993. 'The environmental limits to growth: A fresh look'. In: H. Giersch, (ed.), *Economic Progress and Environmental Concerns*. Springer-Verlag, Berlin.

Beers, C. van and J.C.J.M. van den Bergh, 1995. International trade and environment: An overview and comparison of methodological approaches. TRACE Discussion Paper TI 95-56, Tinbergen Institute, Amsterdam-Rotterdam.

Bennett, R.J. and R.J. Chorley, 1978. *Environmental Systems*. Methuen & Co., London.

Bergh, J.C.J.M. van den, 1991. *Dynamic Models for Sustainable Development*. Ph.D. Dissertation. Thesis Publishers, Amsterdam.

Bergh, J.C.J.M. van den, 1992. 'Tourism development and natural environment: a model for the Northern Sporades islands'. In: J. van der Straaten and H. Briassoulis, *Tourism and the Environment: Regional, Economic and Policy Issues*. Kluwer Academic Publishers: 67–82.

Bergh, J.C.J.M. van den, 1993. 'A framework for modelling economy–environment–development relationships based on dynamic carrying capacity and sustainable development feedback'. *Environmental and Resource Economics*, Vol. 3: 395–412.

Bergh, J.C.J.M. van den, L.C. Braat, A.J. Gilbert, D.E. James, G. Klaassen, F.J. Soeteman and I. Steetskamp, 1988. 'Sustainable Use of Natural Resources and Economic Development in the Peel'. Interim SPIDER report, Institute for Environmental Studies and Department of Regional Economics, Free University, Amsterdam.

Bergh, J.C.J.M. van den and R. de Mooij, 1995. 'Economic growth and environmental conservation: A comparison of perspectives'. Research Memorandum FEWEC 1995-15, Faculty of Economics, Free University, Amsterdam (in Dutch).

Bergh, J.C.J.M. van den and P. Nijkamp, 1990. 'Ecologically sustainable economic development: concepts and model implications'. *Studies in Regional Science*, Vol. 20: 1–23.

Bergh, J.C.J.M. van den and P. Nijkamp, 1991a. 'Operationalizing sustainable development: Dynamic ecological economic models'. *Ecological Economics*, Vol: 4: 11–33.

Bergh, J.C.J.M. van den and Nijkamp, P., 1991b. 'Aggregate economic–ecological models for sustainable development'. *Environment and Planning A*, Vol. 23: 187–206.

Bergh, J.C.J.M. van den and P. Nijkamp, 1991c. 'A general dynamic economic–ecological model for regional sustainable development'. *Journal of Environmental Systems*, Vol. 20: 189–214.

Bergh, J.C.J.M. van den and P. Nijkamp, 1994a. 'Modelling ecologically sustainable economic development in a region: A case study in the Netherlands'. *Annals of Regional Science*, Vol. 28: 7–29.

Bergh, J.C.J.M. van den and P. Nijkamp (eds.), 1994b. 'Sustainability, resources and region'. *The Annals of Regional Science*, Vol. 28 (1), special issue.

Bergh, J.C.J.M. van den and P. Nijkamp, 1994c. 'Dynamic macro modelling and materials balance: Economic–environmental integration for sustainable development'. *Economic Modelling*, Vol. 11: 283–307.

Bergh, J.C.J.M. van den and P. Nijkamp, 1994d. 'An Integrated Model for Economic Development and Natural Environment: An Application to the Greek Sporades Islands'. *The Annals of Operations Research*, Vol. 54: 143–174.

Bergh, J.C.J.M. van den and P. Nijkamp, 1995. 'Growth, trade and sustainability in the spatial economy'. TRACE Discussion Paper TI 95-170. Tinbergen Institute, Amsterdam-Rotterdam.

Bergh, J.C.J.M. van den and J. van der Straaten (eds.), 1994a. *Toward Sustainable Development: Concepts, Methods and Policy*, Island Press, Washington D.C..

Bergh, J.C.J.M. van den and J. van der Straaten, 1994b. 'Historical and future models of economic development and natural environment'. In: J.C.J.M. van den Bergh and J. van der Straaten (eds.): 209–234.

Bergman, L., 1991. 'General equilibrium effects of environmental policy: A CGE approach'. *Environmental and Resource Economics*, Vol. 1, 43–61.

Bergström, J.C., J.R. Stoll, J.P. Titre and V.L. Wright, 1990. 'Economic value of wetland-based recreation'. *Ecological Economics*, Vol. 2: 129–147.

Berry, R.S., P. Salamon and G. Heal, 1978. 'On a relation between economic and thermodynamic optima'. *Resources and Energy*, Vol. 1: 125–137.

Beverton, R.J.H. and S.J. Holt, 1957. *On the Dynamics of Exploited Fish Populations*. Ministry of Agriculture, Fisheries and Food, London. Fish. Invest. Ser. 2(19).

Bianciardi, C., E. Tiezzi and S. Ulgiati, 1993a. 'Complete recycling of matter in the frameworks of physics, biology and ecological economics'. *Ecological Economics*, Vol. 8: 1–5.

Bianciardi, C., A. Donati and S. Ulgiati, 1993b. 'On the relationship between the economic process, the Carnot cycle and the entropy law'. *Ecological Economics*, Vol. 8: 7−10.

Biswas, A.K. (ed.), 1976. *Systems Approach to Water Management.* McGraw-Hill, New York.

Biswas, A.K. (ed.), 1981. *Models for Water Quality Management.* McGraw-Hill, New York.

Blamey, R. and M. Common, 1994. 'Sustainability and the limits to pseudo market valuation'. In: J.C.J.M. van den Bergh and J. van der Straaten (eds.): 165−205.

Blaug, M., 1978. *Economic Theory in Retrospect.* Cambridge University Press, Cambridge.

Blaug, M., 1991. *The Methodology of Economics: How Economists Explain.* Cambridge University Press, Cambridge.

Bogardi, I., 1987. 'Water resources models'. In: L.C. Braat and W.F.J. van Lierop (eds.).

Bohm, P. and C.S. Russell, 1985. 'Comparative analysis of alternative policy instruments'. In: A.V. Kneese and J.L. Sweeney (eds.), Vol. 1.

Bojö, J., K.-G. Mäler and L. Unemo, 1989. *Environment and Development: An Economic Approach.* Kluwer Academic Publishers, Dordrecht.

Boo, B de, P. Bosch, C. Gorter and S. Keuning, 1991. 'An environmental module and the complete system of national accounts'. Paper presented at the Special IARIW Conference on Environmental Accounting, Baden, Austria, 27−29 May 1991.

Boskin, M., 1979. *Economics and Human Welfare.* Academic Press, New York.

Boulding, K.E., 1966a. 'Economics and ecology'. In: F.F. Darling and J.P. Milton (eds.). *Future Environments in North America.* Natural History Press, New York: 225−234.

Boulding, K.E., 1966b. 'The economics of the coming spaceship earth'. In: H. Jarret (ed.), *Environmental Quality in a Growing Economy.* Johns Hopkins University Press, Baltimore: 3−14.

Boulding, K.E., 1978. *Ecodynamics: A New Theory of Societal Evolution.* Sage Publications, Beverly Hills.

Bovenberg, A.L. and R.A. de Mooij, 1994a. 'Environmental policy in a small open economy with distortionary labor taxes: A general equilibrium analysis'. In E.C. van Ierland (ed.).

Bovenberg, A.L. and R.A. de Mooij, 1994b. 'Environmental levies and distortionary taxation'. *American Economic Review*, Vol. 94: 1085−1089.

Bowes, M.D. and J.V. Krutilla, 1985. 'Multiple use management of public forestlands'. In: A.V. Kneese and J.L. Sweeney (eds.), Vol. 2.

Braat, L.C., 1991. 'The predictive meaning of sustainability indicators'. In: O. Kuik and H. Verbruggen (eds.): 57−70.

Braat, L.C., 1992. *Sustainable Multiple Use of Forest Ecosystems: An Economic−Ecological Analysis for Forest Management in the Netherlands.* Ph.D. dissertation, Free University, Amsterdam.

Braat, L.C. and W.F.J. van Lierop (eds.), 1987. *Economic−Ecological Modelling.* North-Holland.

Briassoulis, H., 1986. 'Integrated economic−environmental−policy modeling at the regional and multiregional level: methodological characteristics and issues'. *Growth and Change* Vol. 17: 22−34.

Brink, B. ten, 1991. 'The AMOEBE approach as a useful tool for establishing sustainable development'. In: O. Kuik and H. Verbruggen (eds.).

Bromley, D.W., 1990. 'The ideology of efficiency: Searching for a theory of policy analysis'. *Journal of Environmental Economics and Management*, Vol. 19: 86−107.

Brookhaven National Laboratory, 1969. *Diversity and Stability in Ecological Systems.* Brookhaven Symposia in Biology, no. 22, Brookhaven National Laboratory, Associated Universities inc. and U.S. Atomic Energy Commission.

Brouwer, F.M., 1987. *Integrated Environmental Modelling: Design and Tools.* Martinus Nijhoff, Dordrecht.

Brown, B.J., M.E. Hanson, D.M. Liverman and R.W. Meredith jr., 1987. 'Global sustainability: Towards a definition'. *Environmental Management* Vol. 11: 713−719.

Bruyn, S.M. de, J.C.J.M. van den Bergh and J.B. Opschoor, 1994. 'Ecological restructuring in industrial economies: Some empirical evidence on materials consumption'. Research Memorandum FEWEC 1994-54, Faculty of Economics and Econometrics, Vrije Universiteit, Amsterdam.

Burrough, P.A., 1983. *Principles of Geographical Information Systems for Land Resources Assessment.* Monographs on Soil and Resources Survey 12, Clarendon Press, Oxford.

Butter, F.A.G. den, 1992. 'The mirror of cleanliness: On the construction and use of an environmental index'. In: J.J. Krabbe and W.J.M. Heijman (eds.), *National Income and Nature: Externalities, Growth and Steady State.* Kluwer Academic Publishers, Dordrecht.

Butter, F.A.G. den and H. Verbruggen, 1994. 'Measuring the trade-off between economic growth and a clean environment'. *Environmental and Resource Economics*, Vol. 4: 187−208.

Carver, S., 1991. 'Integrating multi-criteria evaluation with geographical information systems'. *International Journal of Geographical Information Systems*, Vol. 5: 312−339.

CBS, 1992. *Kwartaalbericht Milieustatistieken.* Central Bureau for Statistics, 1992, Nr.1.

Chankong, V. and Y.Y. Haimes, 1983. *Multiobjective Decision Making: Theory and Methodology.* North Holland, Amsterdam.

Charnes, A. and W.W. Cooper, 1977. 'Goal programming and multiple objective optimization'. *European Journal of Operations Research*, Vol. 1: 39−54.

Chaudhuri, P., 1989. *The Economic Theory of Growth.* Harvester Wheatsheaf, London.

Christensen, P.P., 1989. 'Historical roots for ecological economics: Biophysical versus allocative approaches'. *Ecological Economics*, Vol. 1: 17−36.

Ciriacy-Wantrup, S.V., 1952. *Resource Conservation: Economics and Policies.* Division of Agricultural Sciences, Univ. of California, Berkeley.

Claessen F.A.M., F. Klijn, J.P.M. Witte and J.G. Nienhuis, 1994. 'Ecosystems Classification and Hydro−ecological Modelling for National Water Management'. In: F. Klijn (ed.), *Ecosystem Classification for Environmental Management.* Kluwer Academic Publishers, Dordrecht.

Clark, C.W., 1976. *Mathematical Bioeconomics: The Optimal Management of Renewable Resources.* Wiley-Interscience, New York.

Clark, C.W., 1985. *Bioeconomic Modelling and Fisheries Management.* Wiley-Interscience, New York.

Clark, W.C. and R.E. Munn (eds.), 1986. *Sustainable Development of the Biosphere.* Cambridge University Press, Cambridge.

CLTM, 1990. *The Environment: Ideas for the 21st Century.* Commissie Lange Termijn Milieubeleid, Kerckebosch, Zeist (in Dutch).

CLTM, 1994. *The Environment: Towards a Sustainable Future.* Dutch Committee for Long-term Environmental Policy. Kluwer Academic Publishers, Dordrecht (in English).

Coase, R.H., 1960. 'The problem of social cost'. *Journal of Law and Economics*, Vol. 3: 1−44.

Cohon, J.L., 1978. *Multiobjective Programming and Planning.* Academic Press, New York.

Collard, D., D.W. Pearce and D. Ulph (eds.), 1988. *Economics, Growth and Sustainable Environments.* St. Martin's Press, New York.

Common, M., 1988. 'Poverty and progress revisited'. In: D. Collard, D.W. Pearce and D. Ulph (eds.): 15−39.

Common, M. and C. Perrings, 1992. 'Towards an ecological economics of sustainability'. *Ecological Economics*, Vol. 6: 7–34.

Common, M.S. and T.W. Norton, 1994. 'Biodiversity, natural resource accounting and ecological monitoring'. *Environmental and Resource Economics*, Vol. 4: 29–53.

Conrad, K. and M. Schröder, 1991. 'The control of CO2-emissions and its economic impact'. *Environmental and Resource Economics*, Vol. 1: 289–312.

Consumentengids Nederland (Consumerguide Netherlands), 1990 and 1992 (in Dutch).

Copius Peereboom, J.W. and J.H.J. Copius Peereboom-Stegeman, 1981. 'Exposure and health effects of cadmium. Part 2: Toxic effects of cadmium to animals and man'. *Toxicological and Environmental Chemistry Reviews*, Vol. 4: 67–178.

Costanza, R., 1981a. 'Embodied energy, energy analysis and economics'. In: H.E. Daly and A.F. Umaña (eds.): 119–145.

Costanza, R., 1981b. 'Reply: An embodied energy theory of value'. In: H.E. Daly and A.F. Umaña (eds.): 187–192.

Costanza, R. (ed.), 1991. *Ecological Economics: The Science and Management of Sustainability*. Columbia University Press, New York.

Costanza, R., 1994. 'Three general policies to achieve sustainability'. In: AM. Jansson *et al.* (eds.).

Costanza, R., H.E. Daly and J.A. Bartholomew, 1991. 'Goals, agenda and policy recommendations for ecological economics'. In: Costanza, R. (ed.).

Costanza, R., C.S. Farber and J. Maxwell, 1989. 'Valuation and management of wetland ecosystems'. *Ecological Economics*, Vol. 1: 335–361.

Costanza, R., B.G. Norton and B.D. Haskell (eds.), 1992. *Ecosystem Health: New Goals for Environmental Management*. Island Press, Washington D.C.

Costanza, R. and C. Perrings, 1990. 'A flexible assurance bonding system for improved environmental management'. *Ecological Economics*, Vol. 2: 57–76.

Costanza, R., L. Wainger, C. Folke and K.-G. Mäler, 1993. 'Modeling complex ecological economic systems'. *BioScience*, Vol. 43: 545–555.

Crocker, T.D., 1995. 'Ecosystem functions, economics and the ability to function'. In: J.W. Milon and J.F. Shogren (eds.), *Integrating Economic and Ecological Indicators: Practical Methods for Environmental Policy Analysis*. Praeger, Westport, Connecticut.

Crocker, T.D. and J. Tschirhart, 1992. 'Ecosystems, externalities and economics'. *Environmental and Resource Economics*, Vol. 2: 551–567.

Cropper, M.L. and W.E. Oates, 1992. 'Environmental economics: A survey'. *Journal of Economic Literature*, Vol. 30: 675–640.

Cumberland, J.H, 1966. 'A regional inter-industry model for analysis of development objectives'. *Papers of the Regional Science Association*, Vol. 17: 65–95.

Cumberland, J.H., 1994. 'Ecology, economic incentives and public policy in the design of a transdisciplinary pollution control'. In: J.C.J.M. van den Bergh and J. van der Straaten (eds.): 265–278.

Dales, 1968. *Pollution, Property and Prices*. University of Toronto Press, Toronto.

Daly, H.E., 1968. 'On economics as a life science'. *Journal of Political Economy*, Vol. 76: 392–406.

Daly, H.E., 1977. *Steady-State Economics*. Freeman, San Francisco.

Daly, H.E., (ed.), 1980. *Economics, Ecology and Ethics: Essays Toward a Steady-State Economy*. Freeman & Co., San Francisco.

Daly, H.E., 1981. 'Postscript: Unresolved problems and issues for further research'. In: H.E. Daly and A.F. Umaña (eds.): 165–185.

Daly, H.E., 1989a. 'Sustainable development of regions'. Unpublished mimeo.

Daly, H.E., 1989b. 'Steady-state and growth concepts for the next century'. In: F. Archibugi and P. Nijkamp (eds.): 73–87.

Daly, H.E., 1989c. 'Toward a measure of sustainable social net national product'. In: Y.J. Ahmad, S. El Serafy and E. Lutz (eds.).

Daly, H.E., 1990. 'Toward some operational principles of sustainable development'. *Ecological Economics*, Vol. 2: 1−6.

Daly, H.E., 1992. 'Is the entropy law relevant to the economics of natural resource scarcity? − Yes, of course it is!'. *Journal of Environmental Economics and Management*, Vol. 23: 91−95.

Daly, H.E. and W. Cobb, 1989. *For the Common Good: Redirecting the Economy Toward Community, the Environment and a Sustainable Future*. Beacon Press, Boston.

Daly, H.E. and A.F. Umaña (eds.), 1981. *Energy, Economics and the Environment*. AAAS Selected Symposia Series, Westview Press, Boulder, Col.

Dangermond, J., 1990. 'How to cope with geographical information systems in your organization'. In: H.J. Scholten and J.C.H. Stillwell. *Geographical Information Systems for Urban and Regional Planning*. Kluwer Academic Publishers, Dordrecht.

Dasgupta, A.K. and D.W. Pearce, 1972. *Cost-Benefit Analysis: Theory and Practice*. MacMillan, London.

Dasgupta, P.S., 1974. 'On some alternative criteria for justice between generations'. *Journal of Public Economics*, Vol. 3: 405−423.

Dasgupta, P.S. and G.M. Heal, 1979. *Economic Theory and Exhaustible Resources*. Cambridge University Press, Cambridge.

Despotakis, V.K., 1991. *Sustainable Development Planning Using Geographical Information Systems*. Ph.D. dissertation, Free University, Amsterdam.

Devall, B. and G. Sessions, 1984. *Deep Ecology*. Peregrine Smith, Layton, Utah.

DHV Raadgevend Ingenieursbureau BV, 1990. 'Environmental Impact Statement − processing/storage of jarosite' (in Dutch). Report Budelco\svnwl commissioned by Budelco BV, Budel. April 1990.

Dietz F.J. and W.J.M. Heijman (eds.), 1988. *Environmental Policy in a Market Economy*. PUDOC, Wageningen.

Dietz, F.J., U. Simonis and J. van der Straaten (eds.), 1992. *Sustainability and Environmental Policy*. Sigma Verlag, Berlin.

Dietz, F.J. and J. van der Straaten, 1992. 'Rethinking environmental economics: Missing links between economic theory and economic environmental policy'. *Journal of Economic Issues*, Vol. 26: 27−51.

Dosi, G., C. Freeman, R. Nelson, G. Silverberg and L. Soete, 1988 (eds.), *Technical Change and Economic Theory*. Pinter Publishers, London.

Dovers, S.R., 1995. 'A framework for scaling and framing policy problems in sustainability'. *Ecological Economics*, Vol. 12: 93−106.

Duncan, O.D., 1959. 'Human ecology and population studies'. In: P.M. Hauser and O.D. Duncan (eds.), *The Study of Population: An Inventory and Analysis*. University Press of Chicago.

Ecological Economics, Special issue: 'Trade and the Environment'. Vol. 9(1), January 1994.

Edwards, W., I. Kiss, G. Majone and M. Toda, 1984. 'What constitutes a good decision?'. *Acta Psychologica*, Vol. 56: 5−27.

Ekins, P., 1994. 'The environmental sustainability of economic processes: A framework for analysis'. In: J.C.J.M. van den Bergh and J. van der Straaten (eds.): 25−55.

El Serafy, S., 1981. 'Absorptive capacity, the demand for revenue and the supply of petroleum'. *Journal of Energy and Development*, Vol. 7: 73−88.

El Serafy, S., 1989. 'The proper calculation of income from depletable natural resources'. In: Y.J. Ahmad, S. El Serafy and E. Lutz (eds.).

El Serafy, S., 1991. 'The environment as capital'. In: R. Costanza (ed.): 168−175.

El Serafy, S. and E. Lutz., 1989a. 'Environmental and resource accounting: An overview'. In: Y.J. Ahmad, S. El Serafy and E. Lutz (eds.).

El Serafy, S. and E. Lutz, 1989b. 'Environmental and natural resource accounting'. In: G. Schramm and J.J. Warford (eds.).

Erdman, G., 1993. 'Evolutionary economics as an approach to environmental problems'. In: H. Giersch, (ed.), *Economic Progress and Environmental Concerns*. Springer-Verlag, Berlin.

Faber, M., H. Niemes and G. Stephan, 1987. *Entropy, Environment and Resources: An Essay in Physico-Economics*. Springer-Verlag, Heidelberg.

Faber, M. and J.L.R. Proops, 1990. *Evolution, Time, Production and the Environment*. Springer-Verlag, Heidelberg.

Faber, M. and J.L.R. Proops, 1993. 'Natural Resource Rents, Economic Dynamics and Structural Change: A Capital Theoretic Approach'. *Ecological Economics*, Vol. 8: 17–44.

Faber, M., R. Manstetten, J.L.R. Proops, 1995. 'On the conceptual foundations of ecological economics: A teleological approach'. *Ecological Economics*, Vol. 12: 41–54.

Faludi, A. and H. Voogd (eds.), 1985. *Evaluation of Complex Policy Problems*. Delftse Uitgeversmaatschappij, Delft.

Faludi, A., 1971. *Planning theory*. Pergamon Press, Oxford.

Fedra, K. 1991. 'A computer-based approach to environmental impact assessment'. In : A.G. Colombo and G. Premazzi (eds.), *Proceedings of the workshop on indicators and indices for environmental impact assessment and risk analysis*. International Institute for Applied Systems Analysis, Laxenburg, Austria: 11–40.

Fedra, K. and R.F. Reitsma, 1990. 'Decision support and geographical information systems'. In: H.J. Scholten and J.C.H. Stillwell. *Geographical Information Systems for Urban and Regional Planning*. Kluwer Academic Publishers, Dordrecht.

Feenstra, J.F. 1975. 'Use and dispersion of Cadmium in the Netherlands' (in Dutch). IVM-VU, Amsterdam, rapport nr. C6.

Fischer, M.M. and P. Nijkamp, 1992. *Geographic Information Systems and Spatial Modelling*. Springer-Verlag, Berlin.

Flaaten, O., 1988. *The Economics of Multispecies Harvesting: Theory and Application to the Barents Sea Fisheries*. Springer-Verlag, Berlin.

Folke, C., 1991a. 'The societal value of wetland life-support'. In: C. Folke and T. Kåberger (eds.).

Folke, C. and T. Kåberger, 1991b. 'Recent trends in linking the natural environment and the economy'. In: C. Folke and T. Kåberger (eds.).

Folke, C. and T. Kåberger (eds.), 1991. *Linking the Natural Environment and the Economy: Essays from the Eco-Eco Group*. Kluwer Academic Publishers, Dordrecht.

Forrester, J.W., 1971. *World Dynamics*. Wright-Allen Press, Cambridge, Mass.

Foy, G.E., 1991. 'Accounting for non-renewable natural resources in Louisiana's gross state product'. *Ecological Economics*, Vol. 3: 25–41.

Frantzi M. and V.K. Despotakis, 1991. 'The Sporades Database Management System: Design and Structure'. Interim report. National Technical University of Athens, Athens.

Freeman III, A.M., 1993. *The Measurement of Environmental and Resource Values: Theory and Methods*. Resources for the Future, Baltimore.

French, S., 1988. *Decision Theory: An Introduction to the Mathematics of Rationality*. Ellis Horwood, Chichester.

Friend, A.M., 1991. 'Pluralism in national accounting'. Paper presented at the Special IARIW Conference of Environmental Accounting, Baden, Austria, May 27–29, 1991.

Gagné, R.M., 1984. *The Conditions of Learning and Theory of Instruction*. Holt, Rinehart and Winston, New York.

Georgescu-Roegen, N., 1971a. *The Entropy Law and the Economic Process.* Harvard University Press, Cambridge, MA.

Georgescu-Roegen, N., 1971b. Process analysis and the neoclassical theory of production. In: N. Georgescu-Roegen (1976): 37−52.

Georgescu-Roegen, N., 1972. Energy and economic myths. Chapter 1 in N. Georgescu-Roegen (1976): 3−36.

Georgescu-Roegen, N., 1976. *Energy and Economic Myths.* Pergamon, New York.

Gershon, M., L. Duckstein and R. McAniff, 1982. 'Multiobjective river basin planning with qualitative criteria'. *Water Resources Research,* Vol. 18: 193−202.

Giaoutzi, M. and P. Nijkamp, 1993. *Decisions Support Models for Regional Sustainable Development.* Avebury, Aldershot.

Gijsbers, D. and P. Nijkamp, 1988. 'Non-uniform social rates of discount in natural resource models: An overview of arguments and consequences'. *Journal of Environmental Systems,* Vol. 17: 221−236.

Gilbert, A.J., 1996. *Environmental Accounting and Sustainable Development.* Ph.D. dissertation, forthcoming.

Gilbert, A.J. and L.C. Braat (eds.), 1991. *Modelling for Population and Sustainable Development,* Routledge, London.

Gilbert, A.J. and J.F. Feenstra, 1991. 'Sustainability from the materials flows approach'. In: J. de Greef and B. de Vries (eds.), *Sustainable Development as a framework for environmental policy.* RIVM Report 481501001, May 1991 (in Dutch).

Gilbert, A.J. and J.F. Feenstra, 1992. 'A Sustainability Indicator for the Netherlands − Diffusion of Cadmium'. Report No. R-92/06, Instituut voor Milieuvraagstukken, Vrije Universiteit, Amsterdam.

Gilbert, A.J. and J.F. Feenstra, 1994. 'A sustainability indicator for the Dutch environmental policy theme "Diffusion"': Cadmium accumulation in soil'. *Ecological Economics,* Vol. 9: 253−265.

Gilbert, A.J., O. Kuik and J. Arntzen, 1990. 'Natural resource accounting: Issues related to classification and valuation of environmental assets'. Paper prepared for the United Nations Environmental Programme. IvM Report E-90/1. Institute for Environmental Studies, Free University, Amsterdam.

Ginzberg, M.J. and E.A. Stohr, 1982. 'Decision support systems: Issues and perspective'. In: Ginzberg, M.J. et al. (eds.), *Decision Support Systems.* North Holland, Amsterdam: 9−32.

Glantz, M.H. and J.D. Thompson (eds.), 1981. *Resource Management and Environmental Uncertainty: Lessons from Coastal Upwelling Fisheries.* Wiley, New York.

Glasser, H., 1995. 'Naess's Deep Ecology Approach and Environmental Policy'. Mimeo, February, 1995, 37 pp, forthcoming in special issue of *Inquiry.*

Goldsmith, E. (ed.), 1973. *Blueprint for Survival.* Ecologist 1972, Penguin, Harmondsworth.

Goodland, R., 1995. 'Environmental sustainability: Universal and rigorous'. World Bank Environment Working Paper, ENVLW, World Bank, Washington D.C. 71 pp.

Goodland, R. and G. Ledec, 1987. 'Neoclassical economics and principles of sustainable development'. *Ecological Modelling,* Vol. 38: 19−46.

Gordon, H.S., 1954. 'Economic theory of a common-property resource: The fishery'. *Journal of Political Economy,* Vol. 62: 124−142.

Gowdy, J., 1994. *Coevolutionary Economics: The Economy, Society and the Environment.* Kluwer Academic Publishers, Dordrecht.

Gradus, R. and S. Smulders, 1993. 'The trade-off between environmental care and long-term growth: Pollution in three proto-type growth models'. *Journal of Economics,* Vol. 58: 25−52.

Gren, I.-G., C. Folke, K. Turner and I. Batemen, 1994. 'Primary and secondary values of wetland ecosystems'. *Environmental and Resource Economics*, Vol.4: 55−74.

Groot, R. de, 1992. *Functions of Nature*. Wolters-Noordhoff, Groningen.

Gross, L.S. and E.C.H. Veendorp, 1990. 'Growth with exhaustible resources and a materials-balance production function'. *Natural Resource Modeling*, Vol. 4: 77−94.

Günther, F. and C. Folke, 1993. 'Characteristics of nested living systems'. *Journal of Biological Systems*, Vol. 1: 257−274.

Gupta, T.R. and Foster, J.H., 1975. 'Problems and solutions in estimating the demand for and value of rural outdoor recreation'. *American Journal of Agricultural Economics*, Vol. 57: 558−566.

Hafkamp, W.A., 1984. *Triple Layer Model: A National-Regional Economic-Environmental Model for the Netherlands*. North-Holland, Amsterdam.

Hagishima, S., K. Mitsuyoshi and S. Kurose, 1987. 'Estimation of pedestrian shopping trips in a neighbourhood by using a spatial interaction model'. *Environment and Planning A*, Vol. 19: 1139−52.

Hamies, Y.Y., 1977. *Hierarchical Analysis of Water Resources Systems*. McGraw-Hill, New York.

Hamilton, K., 1993. Sustainable development, the Harwick rule and optimal growth. CSERGE Working Paper GEC 93-23, Centre for Social and Economic Research on the Global Environment, University of East Anglia, Norwich, and University College London.

Hanley, N. and S. Craig, 1991. 'The economic value of wilderness areas: An application of the Krutilla−Fisher model to Scotland's Flow Country'. In: F. Dietz, F. van der Ploeg and J. van der Straaten. *Environmental Policy and the Economy*. North-Holland, Amsterdam.

Hanley, N. and C.L. Spash, 1993. *Cost−Benefit Analysis and the Environment*. Edward Elgar Publishers, Aldershot.

Hannon, B., 1973. 'The structure of ecosystems'. *Journal of Theoretical Biology*, Vol. 41: 535−46.

Hannon, B., 1976. 'Marginal product pricing in the ecosystem'. *Journal of Theoretical Biology*, Vol. 56: 253−267.

Hannon, B., 1986. 'Ecosystem control theory'. *Journal of Theoretical Biology*, Vol. 121: 417−437.

Hannon, B., 1991. 'Accounting in ecological systems'. In: R. Costanza (ed.).

Hannon, B. and M. Ruth, 1994. *Dynamic Modeling*. Springer-Verlag, Berlin.

Hardin, G., 1963. 'The cybernetics of competition: A biologist's view of society'. *Perspectives in Biology and Medicine*, Vol 7: 58−84.

Hardin, G., 1968. 'The tragedy of the commons'. *Science*, Vol. 162: 1243−1248.

Hardin, G., 1985. 'Human ecology: The subversive, conservative science'. *Amer. Zool.*, Vol. 25: 469−476.

Hardin, G., 1991. 'Paramount positions in ecological economics'. In: R. Costanza (ed.).

Harnos, Z., 1987. 'Agricultural models'. In: L.C. Braat and W.F.J. van Lierop (eds.).

Hartog, H. den and R.J.M. Maas, 1990. 'A sustainable economic development: Macro-economic aspects of a priority for the environment'. In: P. Nijkamp and H. Verbruggen (eds.), *The Dutch Environment in the European Space*. Stenfert Kroese, Leiden.

Hartwick, J.M., 1977. 'Intergenerational equity and the investing of rents from exhaustible resources'. *American Economic Review*, Vol. 67: 972−974.

Haynes, K. and A. Stewart, 1988. 'Gravity and spatial interaction models'. In: G.I. Thrall (ed.), *Scientific Geographic Series, Vol. 2*. Sage Publishing Co., Beverly Hills.

Hedrick, P.W., 1984. *Population Biology: The Evolution and Ecology of Populations*. Jones and Bartlett Pub., Boston.

Herwijnen, M. van and R. Janssen, 1989. 'DEFINITE: A System to Support Decision on a Finite Set of Alternatives'. Institute for Environmental Studies, Free University, Amsterdam, 1989.

Herwijnen, M. van, P.C. Koppert and A. Olsthoorn, 1989. 'Lange termijn milieubelasting gebruik afvalstoffen'. Rijkswaterstaat, D.W.W. Nr. MI-OW-89-38. Delft 1989.

Herwijnen, M. van, R. Janssen and P. Nijkamp, 1993. 'A multi-criteria decision support model and geographic information system for sustainable development planning of the Greek Islands'. *Project Appraisal*, Vol. 8: 9−22.

Heuvelink, G.B.M., P.A. Burrough and A. Stein, 1989. 'Propagation of errors in spatial modelling with GIS'. *Int. Journal of Geographical Information Systems*, Vol. 3: 303−22.

Hicks, J.R., 1946. *Value and Capital, 2nd. ed.* Oxford University Press, Oxford.

Hilhorst, M.T., 1987. *Responsible for Future Generations: A Social−Ethical Contemplation of Population Size, Nuclear Energy, Natural Resources and Genetics.* Ph.D. disseration. Kok, Kampen (in Dutch).

Hinloopen, E. and P. Nijkamp, 1990. 'Qualitative multiple criteria choice analysis, the dominant regime method'. *Quality and Quantity*, Vol. 24: 37−56.

Hinterberger, F., 1993. 'A note on sociobiology: Schumpeter, Georgescu-Roegen and beyond'. In: J.C. Dragan, E.K. Seifert and M.C. Demetrescu (eds.), *Entropy and Bioeconomics*. Nagard, Milano.

Hinterberger, F., 1994. 'Biological, cultural and economic evolution and the economy−ecology−relationship'. In: J.C.J.M. van den Bergh and J. van der Straaten (eds.): 57−81.

Hirsch, F., 1977. *Social Limits to Growth.* Routledge, London.

Hodgson, G.M., W.J. Samuels and M.R. Tool (eds.), 1994. *The Elgar Companion to Institutional and Evolutionary Economics.* Edward Elgar Publishers, Aldershot.

Hodgson, G.M. (ed.), 1995. *Economics and Biology.* The International Library of Critical Writings in Economics Series. Edward Elgar Publishers, Aldershot.

Hoevenagel, R., 1994. *The Contingent Valuation Method: Scope and Validity.* Ph.D. dissertation, Vrije Universiteit, Amsterdam.

Holling, C.S. (ed.), 1978. *Adaptive Environmental Assessment and Management.* Wiley, International Series on Applied Systems Analysis, Vol. 3, New York.

Holling, C.S., 1986. 'The resilience of terrestrial ecosystems: Local surprise and global change'. Ch. 16 In: W.C. Clark and R.E. Munn (eds.).

Holling, C.S., 1994. 'New science and new investments for a sustainable biosphere'. In: AM. Jansson *et al.* (eds.).

Holling, C.S., L. Guderson and G. Peterson, 1993. 'Comparing ecological and social systems'. Beijer Discussion Papers 93-36, The Beijer International Institute of Ecological Economics, Stockholm.

Hotelling, H., 1931. 'The economics of exhaustible resources'. *Journal of Political Economy*, Vol. 39, 137−175.

Howe, C.W., 1979. *Natural Resource Economics: Issues, Analysis and Policy.* Wiley, New York.

Huber, G.P., 1983. 'Cognitive style as a basis for MIS and DSS designs: Much ado about nothing'. *Management Science*, Vol. 29: 567−579.

Hueting, R., 1980. *New scarcity and economic growth: More welfare through less production?* North-Holland, Amsterdam (Translated and updated from Dutch, 1974).

Hueting, R., 1990. 'The Brundtland report: A matter of conflicting goals'. *Ecological Economics*, Vol. 2: 109−117.

Hueting, R., P. Bosch and B. de Boer, 1992. 'Methodology for the calculation of sustainable national income'. Publication M44, Central Bureau for Statistics, Voorburg (in English).

Hwang, C.L. and A.S.M. Masud, 1979. *Multiple Objective Decision Making*. Methods and Applications. Springer, Berlin.

Idenburg, A.M., 1993. *Gearing Production Models to Ecological–Economic Analysis: A Case Study within the Input–Output Framework of Fuels for Road Transport*. Ph.D. dissertation. Faculty of Management Science, University of Twente, Enschede, Netherlands.

Ierland, E.C. van, 1993. *Macroeconomic Analysis of Environmental Policy*. Elsevier Science Publishers, Amsterdam.

Ierland, E.C. van (ed.), 1994. *International Environmental Economics: Theories, Models and Applications to Global Warming, International Trade and Acidification*. Elsevier Science Publishers, Amsterdam.

Ierland E.C van and N.Y.H. de Man, 1993. *Sustainability of Ecosystems: Economic Analysis*. RMNO Internal Report, 1993.

IIASA/FEMA, 1990. 'Chemical time bombs'. Report of a European Workshop, Netherlands, 21–23 June, 1990. Cooperative Project of the International Institute of Applied Systems Analysis (IIASA) and the Foundation for Ecodevelopment 'Mondiaal Alternatief' (FEMA).

Ikeda, S., 1987. 'Economic–ecological models in regional total systems'. In: L.C. Braat and W.F.J. van Lierop (eds.).

Isard, W., 1969. 'Some notes on the linkage of ecologic and economic systems'. *Papers of the Regional Science Association*, Vol. 22: 85–96.

Isard, W., 1972. *Ecologic–Economic Analysis for Regional Development*. The Free Press, New York.

Jacquet-Lagrèze, E., 1990. 'Interactive assessment of preferences using holistic judgements: the PREFCALC system'. In: C.A. Bana e Costa (ed.), *Readings in multiple criteria decision aid*. Springer-Verlag, BerlIn: 335–350.

James, D.E., 1985. 'Environmental economic, industrial process models, and regional–residuals management models'. In: A.V. Kneese and J.L. Sweeney (eds.), Vol. 1.

James, D.E., H.M.A. Jansen and J.B. Opschoor, 1978. *Economic Approaches to Environmental Problems*. Elseviers Scientific Publishers, Amsterdam.

James, D.E., P. Nijkamp and J.B. Opschoor, 1989. 'Ecological sustainability and economic development'. In: F. Archibugi and P. Nijkamp (eds.): 27–48.

Janssen, R., 1992. *Multiobjective Decision Support for Environmental Management*. Kluwer Academic Publishers, Dordrecht.

Janssen, R. and W. Hafkamp, 1986. 'A decision support system for conflict analysis'. *The Annals of Regional Science*, Vol. 20: 67-85.

Janssen, R. and M. van Herwijnen, 1994. *DEFINITE: A System to Support Decisions on a Finite Set of Alternatives*. Kluwer Academic Publishers, Dordrecht.

Janssen, R., P. Nijkamp and P. Rietveld, 1990. 'Qualitative multicriteria methods in the Netherlands'. In: C.A. Bana e Costa (ed.), *Readings in Multiple Criteria Decision Aid*. Springer, BerlIn: 383–409.

Janssen, R. and P. Rietveld, 1990. 'Multicriteria analysis and GIS; An application to agricultural land use in the Netherlands'. In: H.J. Scholten and J.C.H. Stillwell (eds.), *Geographical Information Systems and Urban and Regional Planning*. Kluwer Academic Publishers, Dordrecht.

Jansson, AM. (ed.), 1984. *Integration of Economy and Ecology*. Proceedings of the Wallenberg Conference on Energy and Economics. Asko Lab., Stockholm.

Jansson, AM., M. Hammer, C. Folke and R. Costanza (eds.), 1994. *Investing in Natural Capital: The Ecological Economics Approach Sustainability*. Island Press, Washington D.C.

Jansson, AM. and J. Zucchetto, 1978. *Energy, Economic and Ecological Relationships for Gotland, Sweden: A Regional Systems Study*. Ecological Bulletins 28. Swedish Natural Science Research Council, Stockholm.

Jantzen, J. and J.W. Velthuijsen, 1991. 'An integrated environment–economy simulation model for the Netherlands'. Paper presented at the 2nd conference of the European Association of Environmental Economists, Stockholm, June 1991.

Johansson, P.-O., 1987. *The Economic Theory and Measurement of Environmental Benefits*. Cambridge University Press, Cambridge.

John, K.H., R.G. Walsh and R.L. Johnson, 1994. 'An integrated model of human-wildlife interdependence'. *Ecological Economics*, Vol. 11: 65–75.

Jørgenson, S.E., 1992. *Integration of Ecosystem Theories: A Pattern*. Kluwer Academic Publishers, Dordrecht.

Kairiukstis, L., A. Buracas and A. Straszak (eds.), 1989. *Ecological Sustainability and Regional Development*. Proceedings of a workshop held in the USSR, June 1987. IIASA and Polish Academy of Sciences, Laxenburg, Austria.

Kamien, M.I. and N.L. Schwartz, 1982. 'The role of common property resources in optimal planning models with exhaustible resources'. In: V.K. Smith and J.V. Krutilla (eds.), *Explorations in Natural Resource Economics*. Johns Hopkins University Press, Baltimore.

Kandelaars, P.P.A.A.H., J.C.J.M. van den Bergh and J.B. Opschoor, 1995. 'Analysis of materials–product chains: Theory and application'. TRACE Discussion Paper TI 95-27, Tinbergen Institute, Amsterdam-Rotterdam.

Kapp, K.W., 1950. *The Social Costs of Private Enterprise*. Harvard Univ. Press, Cambridge, Mass.

Kay, J.J., 1991. 'A non-equilibrium thermodynamic framework for discussing ecosystem integrity'. *Environmental Management*, Vol. 15: 483–495.

Keen, P.G.W. and M.S. Scott Morton, 1978. *Decision Support Systems: An Organizational Perspective*. Addison-Wesley, Reading Mass.

Keeney, R.L., 1982. 'Decision analysis: An overview'. *Operations Research*, Vol. 30: 380–392.

Keeney, R.L., R.H. Möhring, H. Otway, F.J. Radermacher and M.M. Richter, 1988. 'Design aspects of advanced decision support systems'. *Decision Support Systems*, Vol. 4: 381–508.

Keeney, R.L. and H. Raiffa, 1976. *Decisions with Multiple Objectives: Preferences and Value Trade-Offs*. Wiley, New York.

Kendall, M.G., 1970. *Rank Correlation Methods*. Griffin, London.

Kestin, J., 1966. *A Course in Thermodynamics*. Blaisdell.

King, J. and M. Slessor, 1994. 'The natural philosophy of natural capital: Can solar energy substitute?'. In: J.C.J.M. van den Bergh and J. van der Straaten (eds.): 139–163.

Klaassen, G.A.J. and J.B. Opschoor, 1991. 'The economics of sustainability and the sustainability of economics'. *Ecological Economics*, Vol. 4: 93–117.

Klaassen, L.H. and T.H. Botterweg, 1976. 'Project evaluation and intangible effects – a shadow project approach'. In: P. Nijkamp (ed.), *Environmental Economics, Vol. 1: Theories*. Martinus Nijhoff, Leiden.

Knecht, J.A. de, P.L.M. Koevoets, J.A.C. Verkleij and W.H.O. Ernst, 1992. 'Evidence against a role for phytochelatins in naturally selected increased cadmium tolerance in *Silene vulgaris* (Moench) Garcke. *New Phytol*, Vol. 122: 681–688.

Kneese, A.V., R.U. Ayres and R.C. D'Arge, 1970. *Economics and the Environment: A Materials Balance approach*, Johns Hopkins Press, Baltimore.

Kneese, A.V. and B.T. Bower (eds.), 1972. *Environmental Quality Analysis: Theory and Method in the Social Sciences*. Johns Hopkins University Press, Baltimore.

Kneese, A.V. and B.T. Bower, 1979. *Environmental Quality and Residuals Management*. Johns Hopkins University Press, Baltimore.

Kneese, A.V. and W.D. Schulze, 1985. 'Ethics and environmental economics'. In: A.V. Kneese and J.L. Sweeney (eds.), Vol. 1.

Kneese, A.V. and J.L. Sweeney (eds.), 1985/1993. *Handbook of Natural Resource and Energy Economics*, Vol. 1–3. North-Holland, Amsterdam.

Krautkraemer, J.A., 1990. 'Neoclassical Economics and Sustainability'. Mimeo. Department of Economics. Washington State University.

Kruttila, K. 1991. 'Environmental regulation in an open economy'. *Journal of Environmental Economics and Management*, Vol. 20: 127–142.

Krysanova, V. and I. Kaganovich, 1994. 'Modelling of ecological and economic systems at the watershed scale for sustainable development'. In: AM. Jansson *et al.* (eds.): 215–132.

Kuik, O. and H. Verbruggen (eds.), 1991. *In Search of Indicators of Sustainable Development*. Kluwer Academic Publishers, Dordrecht.

Kümmel, R., 1989. 'Energy as a factor of production and entropy as a pollution indicator in macroeconomic modelling'. *Ecological Economics*, Vol. 1: 161–180.

Kümmel, R. and U. Schüssler, 1991. 'Heat equivalents of noxious substances: A pollution indicator for environmental accounting'. *Ecological Economics*, Vol. 3: 139–156.

Larkin, P.A., 1977. 'An epitaph for the concept of Maximum Sustainable Yield'. *Trans. Amer. Fish. Soc.*, Vol. 106: 1–11.

Latour J.B., R. Reiling and J. Wiertz 1994. 'A flexible multiple stress model'. In: F. Klijn (ed.), 1994. *Ecosystem Classification for Environmental Management*. Kluwer Academic Publishers, Dordrecht.

Laurini, R. and D. Thompson, 1991. *Fundamentals of Spatial Information Systems*. Academic Press, London.

Lecomber, R., 1975. *Economic Growth versus the Environment*. MacMillan, London.

Leontief, W.W., 1970. 'Environmental repercussions and the economic structure: An input–output approach'. *Review of Economic Studies*, Vol. 52: 262–271.

Leontief, W.W. and D. Ford, 1972. 'Air pollution and the economic structure: Empirical results of input–output computations'. In: A. Brody and A.P. Carter (eds.), *Input–Output Techniques*. North-Holland, Amsterdam: 9–30.

Lind, R. (ed.), 1982. *Discounting for Time and Risk in Energy Policy*. Johns Hopkins University Press, Baltimore.

Liverman, D.M., M.E. Hanson, B.J. Brown and R.W. Meredith, Jr., 1988. 'Global sustainability: Towards measurement'. *Environmental Management*, Vol. 12(2): 133–143.

Lonergan, S.C., 1981. 'A methodological framework for resolving ecological/economic problems'. *Papers of the Regional Science Association*, Vol. 3: 117–134.

Lotka, A.J., 1925. *Elements of Physical Biology*. Williams and Wilkins, Baltimore.

Lovelock, J.E., 1979. *Gaia: A New Look at Life on Earth*. Oxford University Press, Oxford.

Low, P., 1992. *International Trade and Environment*, World Bank Discussion Papers, 159, World Bank, Washington D.C.

Lutz, E. (ed.), 1993. *Toward Improved Accounting for the Environment*. The World Bank, Washington D.C., 329 p.

Lynne, G.D., P.D. Conroy and F.J. Prochaska, 1981. 'Economic valuation of marsh areas for marine production processes'. *Journal of Environmental Economics and Management*, Vol. 8: 175–186.

Maarel, E. van der and P.L. Dauvellier, 1978. *Global Ecological Model* (In Dutch). SDU, Den Haag.

Maclean, D. and P.G. Brown (eds.), 1983. *Energy and the Future*. Rowman and Littlefield, Totowa, New Jersey.

Mäler, K.-G., 1974. *Environmental Economics: A Theoretical Inquiry*. Johns Hopkins University Press, Baltimore.

Mäler, K.-G., 1992. 'Multiple use of environmental resources: The household-production function approach'. Beijer Discussion Paper Series, No. 4. The Beijer International Institute of Ecological Economics, Stockholm.

Mäler, K.-G., I.-M. Gren and C. Folke, 1994. 'Multiple use of environmental resources: A household production function approach to valuing natural capital'. In: AM. Jansson *et al.* (eds.): 233–249.

Markandya, A. and D.W. Pearce, 1988. 'Natural environments and the social rate of discount'. *Project Appraisal*, Vol. 3: 2–12.

Martinez-Alier, J. 1987. *Ecological economics*. Basil Blackwell, Oxford (with K. Schluepmann).

Martinez-Alier, J., 1991. 'Ecological perception and distributional conflict: A historical view'. In: F.J. Dietz, F. van der Ploeg and J. van der Straaten (eds.), *Environmental Policy and the Economy*. North-Holland Publishers, Amsterdam.

Martinez-Alier, J., 1994. 'Distributional conflicts and international environmental policy on carbon dioxide emissions and agricultural biodiversity'. In: J.C.J.M. van den Bergh and J. van der Straaten (eds.): 235–263.

Maxwell, T. and R. Costanza, 1994. 'Spatial ecosystem modeling in a distributed computational environment'. In: J.C.J.M. van den Bergh and J. van der Straaten (eds.): 111–138.

May, R.M. (ed.), 1976. *Theoretical Ecology: Principles and Applications*, 2nd ed. Basil Blackwell, Oxford.

Maynard Smith, J., 1974. *Models in Ecology*, Cambridge University Press, Cambridge.

Maynard Smith, J., 1982. *Evolution and the Theory of Games*. Cambridge University Press, New York.

McLean, E. and H.G. Sol (eds.), 1986. *Decision Support Systems: A Decade in Perspective*. North Holland, Amsterdam.

Meadows, D.H., D.L. Meadows, J. Randers and W.W. Behrens III, 1972. *The Limits to Growth*. Universe Books, New York.

Meadows, D.H., D.L. Meadows and J. Randers, 1992. *Beyond the Limits: Confronting Global Collapse; Envisioning a Sustainable Future*. Chelsea Green Publishing Co., Post Mills.

Meadows, D.H., J. Richardson and G. Bruckmann, 1982. *Groping in the Dark: The First Decade of Global Modeling*. Wiley, New York.

Méaille, R. and L. Wald, 1990. 'Using geographical information system and satellite imagery within a numerical simulation of regional urban growth'. *Int. J. of Geographical Information Systems*, Vol. 4: 445–56.

Mendoza, G.A., 1988. 'Multi-objective programming framework for integrating timber and wildlife management'. *Environmental Management*, Vol. 12: 163–171.

Minister van Volkshuisvesting, Ruimtelijke Ordening en Milieubeheer, 1991. *Cadmiumbeleid*. 22 197, nr. 1, SDU Uitgeverij, Den Haag.

Mintzberg, H., D. Raisinghani and A. Théorêt, 1976. 'The structure of unstructured decision processes'. *Administrative Science Quarterly*, Vol. 21: 246–275.

Mishan, E.J., 1967. *The Cost of Economic Growth*. Staples Press, London.

Mishan, E.J., 1977. *The Economic Growth Debate: An Assessment*. George Allen & Unwin, London.

Mishan, E.J., 1988. *Cost−benefit Analysis*. George Allen & Unwin, London.

Mitsch, W.J., 1991. Ecological Engineering: 'Approaches to sustainability and biodiversity in the US and China'. In: R. Costanza (ed.).

Mitsch, W.J. and J.G. Gosselink, 1986. *Wetlands*. Van Nostrand Reinhold, New York.

Mitsch, W.J. and S.E. Jørgensen (eds.), 1989. *Ecological Engineering: An Introduction to Ecotechnology*. Wiley, New York.

Morril, R., G.L. Gaile and G.I. Thrall, 1988. 'Spatial diffusion'. In: G.I. Thrall (ed.), *Scientific Geographic Series, Vol. 10*. Sage Publishing Co.

Munda, G., 1993. *Fuzzy information in Multicriteria Environmental Evaluation Models*. Ph.D. dissertation, Free University, Amsterdam.

Munda, G., P. Nijkamp and P. Rietveld. 'Qualitative multicriteria evaluation for environmental management'. *Ecological Economics*, Vol. 10: 97−112.

Naess, A., 1973. 'The shallow and the deep, long-range ecology movement: A summary'. *Inquiry*, Vol. 16: 95−100.

NAVF, 1990. *Sustainable Development, Science and Policy*. Conference report Norwegian Research Council for Science and the Humanities, NAVF, Oslo.

Neher, P.A., 1990. *Natural Resource Economics: Conservation and Exploitation*. Cambridge University Press, New York.

Neisser, V., 1976. *Cognition and Reality: Principles and Implications of Cognitive Psychology*. W.H. Freeman & Co., San Fransisco.

Nelson, R. and S. Winter (1982). *An Evolutionary Theory of Economic Change*. The Belknap Press of Harvard University Press, Cambridge, Mass.

Nijkamp, P., 1979a. *Theory and Application of Environmental Economics*. North-Holland, Amsterdam.

Nijkamp, P., 1979b. *Environmental Policy Analysis*. Wiley, Chichester/New York.

Nijkamp, P. (ed.), 1986. *Handbook of Regional and Urban Economics, Vol. 1*. North Holland, Amsterdam.

Nijkamp, P., J.C.J.M. van den Bergh and F.J. Soeteman, 1990a. 'Regional sustainable development and natural resource use'. *World Bank Economic Review, Proceedings* 1990: 153−188.

Nijkamp, P., P. Rietveld and H. Voogd, 1990b. *Multicriteria Evaluation in Physical Planning*. North-Holland, Amsterdam.

Nijkamp, P. and J. Spronk, 1981. *Multicriteria Analysis: Operational Methods*. Gower, Aldershot.

Nordhaus, W.D., 1973. 'World Dynamics: Measurement without data'. *Economic Journal*, Vol. 83: 1156−1183.

Nordhaus, W.D., 1974. 'Resources as a constraint on growth'. *American Economic Review*, Vol. 64: 22−26.

Nordhaus, W.D., 1982. 'How fast should we graze the global commons?' *American Economic Review*, Vol. 72: 242−246 (AEA papers and proceedings).

Nordhaus, W.D., 1990. 'To slow or not to slow: The economics of the greenhouse effect'. *Economic Journal*, Vol. 101: 920−937.

Nordhaus, W.D., 1992. 'Lethal Model 2: The limits to growth revisited'. *Brooking Papers on Economic Activity*, Vol. 2: 1−59.

Nordhaus, W.D., 1993. 'How much should we invest in preserving our current climate'. In: H. Giersch, (ed.), *Economic Progress and Environmental Concerns*. Springer-Verlag, Berlin.

Nordhaus, W.D. and J. Tobin, 1972. 'Is growth obsolete?'. In: National Bureau of Economic Research, *Economic Growth, Fiftieth Anniversary Colloquium*, Vol. 5, New York.

Norgaard, R.B., 1984. 'Coevolutionary development potential'. *Land Economics*, Vol. 60: 160 – 173.

Norgaard, R.B., 1985. 'Environmental Economics: An Evolutionary Critique and a Plea for Pluralism'. *Journal of Environmental Economics and Management*, 12: 382 – 394.

Norgaard, R.B. 1989. 'The case for methodological pluralism'. *Ecological Economics*, Vol 1: 37 – 57.

Norton, B.G., 1989. 'Intergenerational equity and environmental decisions: A model using Rawls' veil of ignorance'. *Ecological Economics*, Vol. 1: 137 – 159.

O'Connor, M., 1991. 'Entropy, Structure and Organisational Change'. *Ecological Economics*, Vol. 3: 95 – 122.

Odum, E.P., 1976. *Ecology*, 2nd edition. Holt, Rinehart and Winston, New York.

Odum, H.T., 1962. 'Man in the ecosystem'. *Bulletin of Connecticut Agricultural Station*, Vol. 652: 57 – 75.

Odum, H.T., 1971. *Environment, Power and Society*. Wiley, New York.

Odum, H.T., 1973. 'Energy, ecology and economics'. *Ambio*, Vol. 6: 220 – 227.

Odum, H.T., 1983. *Systems Ecology: An Introduction*. Wiley, New York.

Odum, H.T., 1987. 'Models for national, international and global systems policy'. In: L.C. Braat and W.F.J. van Lierop (eds.).

Odum, H.T. and E.C. Odum, 1981. *Energy Basis for Man and Nature*, 2nd. ed. McGraw-Hill, New York.

OECD, 1991. 'Green − A multi-sector, multi-region, dynamic general equilibrium model for quantifying the costs of curbing CO_2 emissions: A technical manual'. Economics and Statistics Department, Organisation for Economic Cooperation and Development, Paris.

Openshaw, S., 1990. 'Spatial analysis and geographical information systems: A review of progress and possibilities'. In: H.J. Scholten and J.C.H. Stillwell. *Geographical Information Systems for Urban and Regional Planning*. Kluwer Academic Publishers, Dordrecht.

Opschoor, J.B. 1974. *Economic Valuation and Environmental Pollution*. Ph.D. dissertation. Van Gorcum, Assen (in Dutch).

Opschoor, J.B., 1987. *Sustainability and Change − On the Ecological Sustainability of Economic Development*. Vrije Universiteit, Free University Press, Amsterdam (in Dutch).

Opschoor, J.B., 1989. *After us the deluge: Conditions for a Sustainable Use of the Environment*. Kok Agora, Kampen (in Dutch).

Opschoor, J.B., 1992. 'Sustainable development, the economic process and economic analysis'. In: J.B. Opschoor (ed.), *Environment, Economy and Sustainable Development*. Wolters-Noordhoff, Groningen.

Opschoor, J.B., 1994. 'Chain management in environmental policy: Analytical and evaluative concepts'. In: J.B. Opschoor and R.K. Turner. *Economic Incentives and Environmental Policies*. Kluwer Academic Publishers, Dordrecht.

Opschoor, J.B. and S.W.F. van der Ploeg, 1990. 'Survival, life and let live: Sustainability and quality as main goals of environmental policy'. In: CLTM (in Dutch).

Opschoor, J.B. and L. Reijnders, 1991. 'Towards Sustainable Development Indicators'. In: O. Kuik and H. Verbruggen (eds.): 7 – 28.

Opschoor, J.B., A.F. de Savornin Lohman and J.B. Vos, 1994. *Managing the Environment: The Role of Economic Instruments*. OECD, Paris.

Opschoor, J.B. and J. van der Straaten, 1993. 'Sustainable development: An institutional approach'. *Ecological Economics*, Vol 7: 203−222.

Opschoor, J.B. and J.B. Vos, 1989. *Economic Instruments for Environmental Protection*. OECD, Paris.

Opschoor, J.B. and R. Weterings, 1994 (eds.). 'Environmental Utilisation Space'. *The Netherlands' Journal of Environmental Science (Milieu)*, Vol. 9, 1994/5, special issue (in English).

Orlob, G.T. (ed.), 1983. *Mathematical Modeling of Water Quality: Streams, Lakes and Reservoirs*. Wiley, New York.

Paelinck, J.H.P., 1974. 'Qualitative multiple criteria analysis, environmental protection and multiregional development'. *Papers of the Regional Science Association*, Vol. 36: 9−74.

Paelinck, J.H.P., 1977. 'Qualitative multiple criteria analysis: An application to airport location'. *Environment and Planning*, Vol. 9: 883−895.

Page, T., 1977. *Conservation and Economic Efficiency*. Johns Hopkins Press, Baltimore.

Patten, B.C. (ed.), 1971. *Systems Analysis and Simulation in Ecology*, Volumes I−IV, Academic Press.

Pearce, D.W., E.B. Barbier and A. Markandya, 1990. *Sustainable Development: Economics and Environment in the Third World*. Edward Elgar Publishers, Aldershot.

Pearce, D.W. and M. Redclift (eds.), 1988. 'Sustainable Development'. *Futures* 20, special issue.

Pearce, D.W. and R.K. Turner, 1990. *Economics of Natural Resources and the Environment*. Harvester Wheatsheaf, New York.

Pearce, D.W. and J.J. Warford, 1993. *World Without End: Economics, Environment and Sustainable Development*. Oxford University Press.

Pelt, M.J.F. van, A. Kuyvenhoven and P. Nijkamp, 1990. 'Project appraisal and sustainability: Methodological challenges'. *Project Appraisal*, Vol. 5: 139−158.

Perrings, C., 1987. *Economy and Environment*. Cambridge University Press, New York.

Perrings, C., 1991. 'Ecological sustainability and environmental control'. *Structural Change and Economic Dynamics*, Vol. 2: 275−295.

Perrings, C., 1994. 'Stress, shock and the sustainability of resource use in semi-arid environments'. *The Annals of Regional Science*, Vol. 28: 31−54.

Perrings, C. and J.B. Opschoor, 1994. 'The loss of biological diversity: Some policy implications'. *Environmental and Resource Economics*, Vol 4: 1−13.

Perrings, C. and D.W. Pearce, 1994. 'Threshold effects and incentives for the conservation of biodiversity'. *Environmental and Resource Economics*, Vol. 4: 13−28.

Peskin, H.M., 1989. 'Environmental and nonmarket accounting in developing countries'. In: Y.J. Ahmad, S. El Serafy and E. Lutz (eds.): 59−64.

Pezzey, J., 1989. *Economic Analysis of Sustainable Growth and Sustainable Development*. Environmental Department Working paper no. 15, Environmental Department, The World Bank.

Pezzey, J., 1993. 'Sustainability: An interdisciplinary guide'. *Environmental Values*, Vol. 1: 321−62.

Phelps, E.S. (ed.), 1969. *The Goal of Economic Growth: An Introduction to a Current Issue of Public Policy*, revised edition. W.W. Norton, New York.

Pigou, A.C., 1932. *The Economics of Welfare*, 4th edition. Macmillan & Co., London.

Ploeg, S.W.F. van der, 1976. 'Economics and Ecology'. In: P. Nijkamp (ed.), *Environmental Economics. Vol I: Theories*, Martinus Nijhoff, Leiden.

Ploeg, S.W.F. van der, 1990. *Multiple Use of Natural Resources*. Ph.D. dissertation, Free University, Amsterdam.

Ponting, C., 1991. *A Green History of the World*. Sinclair-Stevenson, London.

Porter, R., 1982. 'The new approach to wilderness appraisal through cost–benefit analysis'. *Journal of Environmental Economics and Management*, Vol. 11: 59–80.

Portney P.R., ed., 1990. 'Public Policies for Environmental Protection'. Resources for the Future, Washington DC.

Posthuma, L., R.F. Hogervorst and N.M. van Straalen, 1992. 'Adaptation to soil pollution by cadmium excretion in natural population of *Orchesella cincta* (L.) (Collembola)'. *Arch. Environ. Contam. Toxicol*, Vol. 22: 146–156.

Prigogine, I., P.M. Allen and R. Herman, 1977. 'Long term trends and the evolution of complexity'. In: E. Laszlo and J. Bierman (eds.), *Goals in a Global Community, Vol. I.* Pergamon Press, New York: 1–63.

Proops, J.L.R., 1989. 'Ecological economics: Rationale and problem areas'. *Ecological Economics*, Vol. 1: 59–76.

RAC, 1992. *Forest and Timber Inquiry.* Resource Assessment Commission, Final Report. Australian Government Publishing Service, Canberra.

Rawls, J., 1972. *A Theory of Justice.* Harvard University Press, Cambridge, Mass.

Redclift, M., 1987. *Sustainable Development: Exploring the Contradictions.* Methuen, London.

Repetto, R., 1986. *World Enough and Time: Successful Strategies for Resource Management.* Yale University Press, New Haven.

Repetto, R. W. Magrath, M. Wells, C. Beer and F. Rossini. 1989. *Wasting Assets: Natural Resources in the National Income Accounts.* World Resource Institute, Washington.

Richmond, B. et al., 1987. *STELLA Userguide.* Dartmouth College, Lyme, New Hampshire.

Ricker, W.E., 1954. 'Stock and recruitment'. *J. Fish. Res. Board. Can.*, Vol. 11: 559–563.

Rietveld, P., 1980. *Multiple Objective Decision Methods in Regional Planning.* North-Holland, Amsterdam.

Rietveld, P., 1984a. 'Public choice theory and qualitative discrete multicriteria evaluation'. In: G. Bahrenberg (ed.), *Recent Developments in Spatial Data Analysis.* Gower, Aldershot: 409–426.

Rietveld, P., 1984b. 'The use of qualitative information in macro economic policy analysis'. In: M. Despontin, P. Nijkamp and J. Spronk (eds.), *Macro Economic Planning with Conflicting Goals.* Springer-Verlag, Berlin: 263–280.

Rinaldi, S., 1979. *Environmental Systems Analysis and Management.* North-Holland, Amsterdam.

Rostow, W.W., 1990. *Theorists of Economic Growth from David Hume to the Present – With a Perspective on the Next Century.* Cambridge University Press, New York.

Roszak, Th., 1986. *The Cult of Information: The Folklore of Computers and the True Art of Thinking.* Pantheon Books, New York.

Roughgarden, R., R.M. May and S.A. Levin (eds.), 1989. *Perspectives in Ecological theory.* Princeton University Press, Princeton, NJ.

Roy, B., 1985. *Méthodologie multicritère d'Aide à la Décision.* Economica, Paris.

Rozema, J., M.L. Otte, R. Broekman, G. Kamber and H. Punte, 1990. 'The response of Spartina anglica to heavy metal pollution'. In: A.J. Gray and P.E.M. Benham (eds.), *Spartina anglica* – Research Review. HMSO, London, p 63–68.

Ruitenbeek, H.J., 1994. 'Modelling economy–ecology linkages in mangroves: Economic evidence for promoting conservation in Bintuni Bay, Indonesia'. *Ecological Economics*, Vol. 10: 233–247.

Ruth, M., 1993. *Integrating Economics, Ecology and Thermodynamics.* Kluwer Academic Publishers, Dordrecht, Netherlands.

Saaty, T.L., 1980. *The Analytical Hierarchy Process.* McGraw Hill, New York.

Sagoff, M., 1988. *The Economy of the Earth.* Cambridge University Press, Cambridge.

Sahu, N.C. and B. Nayak, 1994. 'Niche diversification in environmental/ecological economics'. *Ecological Economics*, Vol. 11: 9–19.

Sandstrom, E., 1989. 'Challenges for the economists on multiple use of forests'. In: L. Mattson and D.P. Sodal (eds.), *Multiple Use of Forests-Economics and Policy*. Scandinavian Forest Economics No. 30.

SBB 1984–1991. *The Vitality of the Dutch Forests*. Department of Agriculture, Nature Management and Fisheries, The Hague.

Schaefer, M.B., 1954. 'Some aspects of the dynamics of populations important to the management of commercial marine fisheries'. *Bull. Inter-Amer. Trop. Tuna Comm.*, Vol. 1: 25–56.

Schneider, E.D. and J.J. Kay, 1994. 'Complexity and thermodynamics: Towards a new ecology'. *Futures*, Vol. 24: 626–647.

Scholten, H.J. and J.C.H. Stillwell, 1990. *Geographical Information Systems for Urban and Regional Planning*. Kluwer Academic Publishers, Dordrecht.

Schramm, G. and J.J. Warford (eds.), 1989. *Environmental Management and Economic Development*. World Bank and Johns Hopkins University Press, Washington D.C. and Baltimore.

Schumacher, E.F., 1973. *Small is Beautiful: Economics as if People Mattered*. Harper and Row, New York.

Schumpeter, J., 1934. *The Theory of Economic Development*. Harvard University Press, Cambridge, Mass.

Scitovsky, T., 1976. *The Joyless Economy*. Oxford University Press, Oxford.

Scott, A.D, 1955. 'The fishery: The objectives of sole ownership'. *Journal of Political Economy*, Vol. 63: 116–124.

Second Chamber, 1989. *National Environmental Policy Plan – To Choose or to Lose*. Second Chamber of the States General. Letter of the Minister of Housing, Physical Planning and Environment, SDU Publishers, The Hague.

Shogren, J.F. and C. Nowell, 1992. 'Economics and Ecology: A Comparison of Experimental Methodologies and Philosophies'. *Ecological Economics*, Vol. 5: 101–126.

Siebert, H., 1982. 'Nature as a life support system: Renewable resources and environmental disruption'. *Journal of Economics*, Vol. 42: 133-142.

Siebert, H., 1985. 'Spatial aspects of environmental economics'. In: A.V. Kneese and J.L. Sweeney (eds.), Vol. 1.

Siebert, H., 1987. *Economics of the Environment: Theory and Policy*, 2nd ed. Springer-Verlag, Berlin.

Siebert, H., J. Eichberger, R, Gronych and R. Pethig, 1980. *Trade and Environment. A Theoretical Enquiry*, Studies in Environmental Science 6, Elsevier Science Publishers, Amsterdam.

Silverberg, G., 1988. 'Modelling economic dynamics and technical change: Mathematical approaches to self-organisation and evolution'. In: G. Dosi *et al.* (eds.).

Simmons, I.G., 1989. *Changing the Face of the Earth: Culture, Environment, History*. Basil Blackwell, Oxford.

Simon, H.A., 1957. *Models of Man: Social and Rational*. Wiley, New York.

Simon, H.A., 1959. 'Theories of decision making in economics and behavioural sciences'. *American Economic Review*, Vol. 49: 253–283.

Simon, H.A., 1960. *The New Science of Management Decision*. Harper and Row, New York.

Simon, H.A., 1976. *Administrative Behaviour: A Study of Decision-Making Processes in Administrative Organization*. Harper and Row, New York.

Simon, J.L. and H. Kahn, 1984. *The Resourceful Earth*. Basil Blackwell, Oxford.

Simonis, U.E., 1990. *Beyond Growth: Elements of Sustainable Development*. Edition Sigma, Berlin.

Slessor, M., 1975. 'Accounting for energy'. *Nature*, Vol. 254: 170–172.

Smith, J.B. and S. Weber, 1989. 'Contemporaneous externalities: rational expectations and equilibrium production functions in natural resource models'. *Journal of Environmental Economics and Management*, Vol. 17: 155–170.

Smith, S., 1992. 'Taxation and the environment: A survey'. CSERGE Working Paper GEC 92–31. The Centre for Social and Economic Research on the Global Environment, University of East Anglia, Norwich.

Smulders, S., 1994. *Growth, Market Structure and the Environment: Essays on the Theory of Endogenous Economic Growth*. Ph.D. Thesis, Tilburg University (KUB), Tilburg.

Söderbaum, P., 1992. 'Neoclassical and institutional approaches to development and the environment'. *Ecological Economics*, Vol. 5: 127–144.

Solórzano, R., R. de Camino, R. Woodward, J. Tosi, V. Watson, A. Vásquez, C. Villalobos, J. Jiménez, R. Repetto and W. Cruz, 1991. *Accounts Overdue: Natural Resource Depreciation in Costa Rica*. World Resources Institute, Washington, D.C.

Solow, R.M., 1974. 'Intergenerational equity and exhaustible resources'. *Review of Economic Studies*, Vol. 41: 29–45.

Solow, R.M., 1986. 'On the intergenerational allocation of natural resources'. *Scandinavian Journal of Economics*, Vol. 88: 141–149.

SPANS, 1988. 'Spatial Analysis System, User's Manual'. Tydac Technologies Inc., Canada.

Sprague, R.H. and H.J. Watson (eds.), 1986. *Decision Support Systems: Putting Theory into Practice*. Prentice Hall, New Jersey.

Spronk, J., 1981. *Interactive Multiple Goal Programming for Capital Budgeting and Financial Planning*. Martinus Nijhoff, Dordrecht.

Steenkiste, G.C. van, 1981. *Modeling, Identification and Control in Environmental Systems*. North-Holland, Amsterdam.

Steininger, K. 1994. *Trade and Environment: The Regulatory Controversy and a Theoretical and Empirical Assessment of Unilateral Environmental Action*. Physica-Verlag, Heidelberg.

Stephan, G., 1989. *Pollution Control, Economic Adjustment and Long-Run Equilibrium: A Computable Equilibrium Approach to Environmental Economics*, Springer–Verlag, Berlin.

Steuer, R.E., 1986. *Multiple Criteria Optimization: Theory, Computation and Application*. Wiley, New York.

Stoop, J.M. and A.J.M. Rennen, 1990. 'Harmful Substances for Agriculture and Horticulture'. Centrum voor Landbouw en Milieu, Utrecht (in Dutch).

Straaten, J. van der, 1990. *Acid Rain, Economic Theory en Policy in the Netherlands*. Jan van Arkel Publishers, Utrecht (in Dutch).

Svedin, U., 1985. Economic and ecological theory: differences and similarities. In: D.O. Hall, N. Myers and N.S. Margaris (eds.), *Economics of Ecosystems Management*. Dr w. Junk Publishers, Dordrecht.

Swallow, S.K., 1990. 'Depletion of the environmental basis for renewable resources: The economics of interdependent renewable and non-renewable resources'. *Journal of Environmental Economics and Management*, Vol. 19: 281–296.

Tahvonen, O. and J. Kuuluvainen, 1991. 'Optimal growth with renewable resources and pollution'. *European Economic Review*, Vol. 35: 650–661.

Tahvonen, O. and J. Kuuluvainen, 1993. 'Economic growth, pollution and renewable resources'. *Journal of Environmental Economics and Management*, Vol. 24: 101–118.

Taylor, A.M., 1977. 'The historical evolution of mankind's inner and outer dimensions'. In: E. Laszlo and J. Bierman (eds.), *Goals in a Global Community, Vol. I.* Pergamon Press, New York: 65–116a.

Thibodeau, F.R. and B.D. Ostro, 1981. 'An economic analysis of wetland protection'. *Journal of Environmental Management*, Vol. 12: 19–30.

Thomas, R., W.C. van Arkel, H.P. Baars, E.D. van Ierland, K.F. de Boen, E. Buijsman, T.J.H.M. Hutten and R.T. Swart, 1988. 'Emission of SO_2, NO_x, VOC and NH_3 in the Netherlands and Europe in the period 1990–2030'. RIVM, Bilthoven.

Thrall, G.I. (ed.), 1988. *Scientific Geographic Series*, Sage Publishing Co.

Tietenberg T., 1988. *Environmental and Natural Resource Economics*, 3rd edition. Harper Collins, USA.

Tolba, M.K., 1987. *Sustainable Development: Constraints and Opportunities.* Butterworths, London.

Toman, M.A., J. Pezzey and J. Krautkraemer, 1994. 'Neoclassical economic growth theory and "sustainability"'. In: D. Bromley (ed.), *Handbook of Environmental Economics.* Blackwell, Oxford, 1994.

Townsend, K.N., 1992. 'Is the entropy law relevant to the economics of natural resource scarcity? Comment'. *Journal of Environmental Economics and Management*, Vol. 23: 96–100.

Trevor, C.B. and A.G. Munford, 1991. 'A case study employing GIS and spatial interaction models in location planning'. In: J. Haarts, H.F.L. Ottens and H.J. Scholten (eds.), *EGIS '91, Second European conference on GIS.* EGIS Foundation: 55–65.

Turner, R.K., 1988a. 'Wetland conservation: Economics and ethics'. In: D. Collard, D.W. Pearce and D. Ulph (eds.), *Economics, Growth and Sustainable Environments.* Macmillan, London.

Turner, R.K. (ed.), 1988b. *Sustainable Environmental Management: Principles and Practice.* Belhaven Press, London.

Turner, R.K., 1991. 'Economics and wetland management'. *Ambio*, Vol. 20: 59–63.

Turner, R.K. and J. Brooke, 1988. 'Management and valuation of an environmentally sensitive area: the Norfolk Broadland case study'. *Environmental Management*, Vol. 12: 193–207.

Turner, R.K. and T. Jones (eds.), 1991. *Wetlands, Market and Intervention Failures.* Earthscan, London.

Turner, R.K., C. Folke, I.-M. Gren and I.J. Bateman, 1993. 'Wetlands valuation: Three case studies'. Beijer Discussion Papers Series, No 30. The Beijer International Institute of Ecological Economics, Stockholm.

Umaña, A.F., 1981a. 'Introduction'. In: H.E. Daly and A.F. Umaña (eds.): 1–19.

Umaña, A.F., 1981b. 'Toward a biophysical foundation for economics'. In: H.E. Daly and A.F. Umaña (eds.): 1–19.

United Nations, 1993. 'Integrated Environmental and Economic Accounting'. Interim report, Studies in Methods, Series F, No. 61.

Vedeld, P.O., 1994. 'The environment and interdisciplinarity. Ecological and neoclassical economical approaches to the use of natural resources'. *Ecological Economics*, Vol. 10: 1–13.

Verhoef, E.T., 1994. Efficiency and equity in externalities: A partial equilibrium analysis. *Environment and Planning A*, Vol. 26: 361–382.

Verhoef, E.T. and J.C.J.M. van den Bergh, 1995a. 'A Spatial Price Equilibrium Model for Environmental Policy Analysis of Mobile and Immobile Sources of Pollution'. In: J.C.J.M. van den Bergh, P. Nijkamp and P. Rietveld (eds.). *Recent Advances in Spatial Equilibrium Modelling: Methodology and Applications.* Springer-Verlag, forthcoming.

Verhoef, E.T. and J.C.J.M. van den Bergh, 1995b. 'Transport, spatio-economic equilibrium and global sustainability: Markets, technology and policy'. TRACE Discussion Paper TI 95-80, Tinbergen Institute, Amsterdam-Rotterdam.

Victor, P.A., 1972. *Pollution: Economy and Environment*. Allen and Unwin, London.

Victor, P.A., 1991. 'Indicators of sustainable development: Some lessons from capital theory'. *Ecological Economics*, Vol. 4, 191−213.

Vliet, H.P.M. van and J.F. Feenstra, 1982. 'Use of cadmium in the Netherlands'. IVM-VU, Amsterdam, R82/13 (in Dutch).

Voet, E. van der, P.C. Koppert, W.G.H. Van der Naald, G. Huppes and J.F. Feenstra, 1989. 'Flow schemes for substances in the economy and environment of the Netherlands and Zuid-Holland. Deel II: Cadmium'. IVM-VU, CML/RUL, Amsterdam/Leiden (in Dutch).

Volterra, V., 1931. *Lecons sur la Theorie Mathematique de la Lutte pour la Vie*. Gauthier-Villars, Paris.

Voogd, H., 1983. *Multicriteria Evaluation for Urban and Regional Planning*. Pion, London.

Voogt, P. de, B. van Hattum, J.F. Feenstra and J.W. Copius Peereboom, 1980. 'Exposure and health effects of cadmium'. *Toxicological and Environmental Chemistry Reviews*, Vol. 3: 89−109.

Vos, J.B., J.F. Feenstra, J. de Boer, L.C. Braat and J. van Baalen, 1985. 'Indicators for the state of the environment'. Institute for Environmental Studies, Free University of Amsterdam, Report R-85/1.

Vries, H.J.M. de, 1989. *Sustainable Resource Use: An Enquiry into Modelling and Planning*. University Press, Groningen.

Walters, C., 1986. *Adaptive Management of Renewable Resources*. MacMillan, New York.

Watt, K.E.F., 1968. *Ecology and Resource Management: A Quantitative Approach*. McGraw-Hill, New York.

WCED, 1987. *Our Common Future*. World Commission on Environment and Development, Oxford University Press, Oxford/New York.

WCN/IUCN, 1980. *World Conservation Strategy: Living Resource Conservation for Sustainable Development*. World Conservation Strategy/International Union for the Conservation of Nature, Gland, Switzerland.

Werner, C., 1988. 'Spatial Transportation Modelling'. In: G.I. Thrall (ed.), *Scientific Geographic Series, Vol. 4*. Sage Publishing Co., Beverly Hills.

White, B. and R. Wadsworth, 1994. 'A bioeconomic model of heather moorland management and conservation'. *Ecological Economics*, Vol. 9: 167−177.

Wilen, J.E., 1985. 'Bioeconomics of renewable resource use'. In: A.V. Kneese and J.L. Sweeney (eds.), Vol. 1.

Wilkinson, R., 1973. *Poverty and Progress: An Ecological Model of Economic Development*, Methuen & Co., London.

Williams, M. (ed.), 1990. *Wetlands: A Threatened Landscape*. Basil Blackwell, Oxford, UK.

Wilson, E.O., 1975. *Sociobiology: The New Synthesis*. Harvard University Press, Cambridge, Mass.

Winterfeldt, D. van and W. Edwards, 1986. *Decision Analysis and Behavioural Research*. Cambridge University Press, Cambridge.

Wit, A.J.F. de (ed.), 1990. *Sustainable Development: An Inquiry into the Consequences for Science and Research*. RMNO (The Dutch Advisory Council for Research on Nature and Environment), Rijswijk, publication 49 (in Dutch with English summary).

World Bank and The European Investment Bank, 1990. *The Environmental Program for the Mediterranean: Preserving a Shared Heritage and Managing a Common Resource*, World Bank/European Investment Bank, Washington and Luxembourg.

Wright, J.C., 1988. 'Future Generations and the Environment'. Studies in Resource Management No. 6, Centre for Resource Management, Lincoln College. Canterbury, New Zealand.

WRR, 1987. *Capacity for Growth: Opportunities and Threats for the Dutch Economy in the Next Ten Years.* Wetenschappelijke Raad voor het Regeringsbeleid, rapporten aan de regering 1987/29, Staatsuitgeverij, The Hague (in Dutch).

Young, J.T., 1991. 'Is the entropy law relevant to the economics of natural resource scarcity?' *Journal of Environmental Economics and Management*, Vol. 21: 169–179.

Yu, P.L., 1985. *Multi Criteria Decision Making: Concepts, Techniques and Extensions.* Pelenum Press, New York.

Yu, P.L., 1990. *Forming Winning Strategies: An Integrated Theory of Habitual Domains.* Springer, Berlin.

Zeleny, M., 1982. *Multiple Criteria Decision Making.* McGraw Hill, New York.

Zoeteman, K. and F. Langeweg, 1988. 'The organization of integrated environmental research in the Netherlands'. *Environmental management*, Vol. 2: 151–161.

Zuchetto, J. and AM. Jansson, 1985. *Resources and Society: A Systems Ecology Study of the Island of Gotland, Sweden.* Springer-Verlag, New York.

Index

Heterick Memorial Library
Ohio Northern University

	DUE	RETURNED		DUE	RETURNED
1.			13.		
2.			14.		
3.			15.		
4.			16.		
5.			17.		
6.			18.		
7.			19.		
8.			20.		
9.			21.		
10.			22.		
11.			23.		
12.			24.